Nonconformist Theology in the Twentieth Century

The Didsbury Lectures 2006

Nonconformist Theology in the Twentieth Century

Alan P.F. Sell

First published 2006 by Paternoster Press

Paternoster Press is an imprint of Authentic Media
9 Holdom Avenue, Bletchley, Milton Keynes, Bucks,
MK1 1QR, UK
285 Lynnwood Avenue, Tyrone, GA 30290
OM Authentic Media, Medchal Road, Jeedimetla Village,
Secunderabad 500 055, A. P.
www.authenticmedia.co.uk/paternoster
Authentic Media is a division of Send the Light Ltd., a company limited by
guarantee (registered charity no. 270162)

British Library Cataloguing in Publication Data

A catalogue record for this book is available from the
British Library

ISBN-13: 978-1-84227-471-2
ISBN-10: 1-84227-471-6

Design by James Kessell for Scratch the Sky Ltd (www.scratchthesky.com)
Print Management by Adare Carwin
Printed in Great Britain by J.H. Haynes & Co., Sparkford

To Jon

Didsbury Lecturers

1979   Professor F.F. Bruce
1980   The Revd Professor I. Howard Marshall
1981   The Revd Professor James Atkinson
1982   The Very Revd Professor T.F. Torrance
1983   The Revd Professor C.K. Barrett
1984   The Revd Professor A.R.G. Deasley
1985   Dr Donald P Guthrie
1986   Professor A.F. Walls
1987   The Revd Dr A. Skevington Wood
1988   The Revd Professor Morna D. Hooker
1989   The Revd Professor Ronald E. Clements
1990   The Revd Professor Colin E. Gunton
1991   The Revd Professor J.D.G. Dunn
1992   The Revd Professor P.M. Bassett
1993   Professor David J.A. Clines
1994   The Revd Professor James B. Torrance
1995   The Revd Dr R.T. France
1996   Professor Richard Bauckham
1997   Professor H.G.M. Williamson
1998   Professor David Bebbington
1999   Professor L.W. Hurtado
2000   Professor Clark Pinnock
2001   Professor Robert P. Gordon
2002   The Revd Dr Herbert McGonigle
2003   Professor David Wright
2004   The Very Revd Dr Stephen S. Smalley
2005   The Revd Dr N.T. Wright
2006   The Revd Professor Alan P.F. Sell

Contents

Preface

I count it a great honour to join the ranks of those who have given the Didsbury Lectures. I thank the former Principal of the Nazarene College, Manchester, the Revd Dr. Herbert McGonigle and the Revd Dr. Kent Brower for their kind invitation to undertake this enjoyable task. I very much look forward to delivering the lectures in October of this year, and to meeting the present Principal, the Revd Dr. David McCulloch, Dr. Brower, and members of the audience.

I have attempted the subject of these lectures not only because the time is ripe for a review of the theological contributions made by Nonconformists during the twentieth century, but also because the tradition of theological scholarship which they represent is not well known in some quarters either at home or abroad. Nothing but good could accrue from a fresh appreciation of their insights on the part of theologians and ecumenists near and far.

I dedicate this volume to our latest grandson, Jon, who will be raised in an environment far removed from that of English Nonconformity, but who may one day turn to these pages for a glimpse of his father's religious roots.

As ever, Karen has supported me in this venture, which, for me, has been not simply one more piece of scholarly research, but an act of pious remembrance.

Alan P.F. Sell
Milton Keynes
2 March 2006

Lecture 1

Surveying the Landscape

'Vote for the man who promises least; he'll be the least disappointing.' These words of Bernard Baruch have haunted me ever since I agreed to write a paper on 'The theological contribution of Protestant Nonconformists in the Twentieth Century' for the Millennium Conference of the Association of Denominational Historical Societies and Cognate Libraries.[1] The task was to produce some ten thousand words. By the time I had written thirty thousand words, I embarked on a pruning endeavour; I removed twenty thousand words and realistically and modestly added 'Some soundings' to my title as given. The honour of giving these Didsbury Lectures has afforded me the opportunity of expanding my text to more than eighty thousand words (including the original ten thousand), though I shall not be able to utter them all in your hearing. Even with this expansion, I cannot fail to disappoint. Almost certainly I shall omit somebody's favourite theologian, somebody else's pet doctrinal skirmish. Rigorous selection has been the only way of avoiding the creation of a mere bibliographical list.

I intend no disrespect to other Nonconformists in restricting my attention, passing references apart, to those of the Congregational, Baptist, Presbyterian, Unitarian, Methodist and United Reformed traditions. These were theologically active throughout the twentieth century, and they are more than enough to handle. My omission of theologians who have concentrated upon biblical, moral, pastoral, and liturgical theology implies no lack of interest in those fields, but my focus here is upon doctrinal, systematic, constructive and, to a very limited extent, philosophical theology.[2] I recognize that these classifications are not

---

[1] For the papers of this conference see Alan P.F. Sell and Anthony R. Cross, eds., *Protestant Nonconformity in the Twentieth Century*.

[2] See further, Alan P.F. Sell, *The Philosophy of Religion 1875–1980*; and 'Friends and Philosophy', 72–82, 111–122.

unproblematic, for disciplinary boundaries are blurred, and more poly-
mathic (or omniscient) theologians tend to respect them less than others.
I am relieved of the necessity of plunging into the whirlpool of evangelical pamphlets and magazine articles, not a little of it associated with the
polarities represented by devotees of Keswick on the one hand and
Martyn Lloyd-Jones and his acolytes on the other, because Keswick has
found a scholar of sufficient courage and insight in Ian M. Randall,[3]
while John Brencher has run the gauntlet with a fair-minded study of
Lloyd-Jones which, if it does not revel in 'warts and all', at least draws
attention, with good reason, to some disturbingly disfiguring pimples.[4]

Although I am concerned with *Protestant*, not Roman Catholic,
Nonconformity, my preference is to think of myself and of the groups
about whom I shall speak as Free Churchpeople. By this freedom I
understand that liberty under the gospel whereby the saints can order
their worship and practise their polity without state interference. The
problem is, however, that to others 'Free' in 'Free Church' has a different connotation: in Scotland it refers to Presbyterians who, though
apart from the national Church, uphold the principle of a national
church possessing spiritual independence; in the United States it is
used as an umbrella term covering a diversity of groups, but excluding mainline denominations whose sister churches in England are, in
the English sense, Free Churches. Where Wales is concerned both
terms, 'Nonconformist' and 'Free Church', denote those who continue in the non-Anglican Protestant traditions, notwithstanding that the
disestablishment of the Anglican Church in Wales, which took effect
in 1920, gives the terms a somewhat anachronistic flavour.

I am also aware of the fact that some Methodists sit uneasily under
the umbrella term 'Nonconformist'. 'It cannot be said too plainly, or
too often,' declared Rupert Davies, 'that Methodists are not
Dissenters, or even Nonconformists';[5] and certainly it is true that John

---

[3] See Ian M. Randall, *Evangelical Experiences: A Study in the Spirituality of
English Evangelicalism 1918–1939.* To this may be added his *Educating
Evangelicalism: The Origins, Development and Impact of London Bible College,*
which, far from being an alumni brochure, is a careful study showing the
bearing of disparate inner-evangelical tendencies and tensions upon a par-
ticular institution. For a brief account of 'The Keswick tradition' see David
Bebbington's Didsbury Lectures, *Holiness in Nineteenth-Century England,*
Lecture 4.

[4] J. Brencher, *Martyn Lloyd-Jones (1899–1981) and Twentieth-Century
Evangelicalism.*

[5] R.E. Davies, *Methodists and Unity,* 23.

Wesley had no desire to break from the Church of England, the friction some of his actions caused notwithstanding, and that he intended his people to be a society within the established Church. However, Davies proceeds to qualify his assertion by claiming that 'Methodism did more than any other denomination to give meaning to the phrase "the nonconformist conscience"',[6] and he grants that a number of late eighteenth- and nineteenth-century Methodist strands which later flowed into present-day Methodism, 'were much more "nonconformist" and "dissenting" than the Wesleyan Methodist Church ever was.'[7] Dr. Henry Rack goes further with respect to the Wesleyan Church: 'the Wesleyanism of 1900,' he writes, 'was much more obviously a part of the nonconformist world and antagonistic to Anglicanism than it had been in 1800. It was, in short, less Wesleyan.'[8] It would seem, therefore, that in terms of their attitudes, Methodists may be reluctant, or partial, or committed Nonconformists. But there is no denying that they, no less than the Roman Catholics in England, are technically Nonconformists. I therefore judge that it would be more difficult to explain their exclusion from these lectures than to defend their inclusion.

Having completed my work, I am faintly embarrassed to find that so many of my references are to those of the Congregational Way. As one who resumed contact with that tradition out of conviction, I insist that this does not indicate partisanship. Having reviewed as much of the twentieth-century Nonconformist theological *corpus* as possible, it really does appear that the Congregationalists made the largest contribution to the fields with which I am concerned. Statistically, this is not surprising given that for much of the twentieth century they were second only to the totality of Methodists in size, and considerably more numerous than the Unitarians and the English Presbyterians. But it also appears that whereas the Methodists spawned a number of church historians and not a few biblical scholars, and the Baptists all but cornered the market in Old Testament studies in the middle decades of the twentieth century, the Congregationalists, though not lacking biblical scholars and historians, were more prone than other Nonconformists to produce theologians. This may have something to do with the fact that at the beginning of the twentieth century their prominent theological teachers included A.M. Fairbairn and Robert Mackintosh, who received their theological

---

[6] Ibid., 24.

[7] Ibid., 25.

[8] H.D. Rack, 'Wesleyanism and "the world" in the later nineteenth century', 36.

education in Scotland where the tradition of systematic, dogmatic and apologetic theology was strong, and P.T. Forsyth and A.E. Garvie, who read Arts at Aberdeen and Glasgow respectively, and the latter of whom studied under Fairbairn in Oxford. All of these Scots thoroughly identified themselves with the English Nonconformity into which they came and, in turn, they trained a number of English and Welsh Congregational theological college principals and professors including the theologians W.B. Selbie, Robert Franks, Thomas Rees, D. Miall Edwards, J.D. Vernon Lewis, Sydney Cave, H.F. Lovell Cocks, and George Phillips.[9]

While I shall concentrate upon published works, it should not be forgotten that most theologizing has been done in quite other ways. When A.J. Grieve prepared a bibliography of Congregational theology he inserted the following footnote, which applies to other denominations as well:

> While one is naturally expected and obliged to keep to literary contributions, it is imperative to remember that these, so far from exhausting the subject, are probably but a small part of it. The teachers in our Academies and Colleges have not always reduced their instruction to the printed page;[10] our preachers for 350 years have delivered more sermons than they have published; and perhaps as effective contributions

---

[9] There was a long-standing link between Scotland and Old Dissent. Excluded from the universities of Oxford and Cambridge, a number of eighteenth- and nineteenth-century divines received some of their theological education in Scotland. Some of these, together with others – the Independent Philip Doddridge, the Baptist John Gill and the Presbyterian Arian John Taylor among them – were awarded the degree of Doctor of Divinity by Scottish universities. See further, Alan P.F. Sell, *Philosophy, Dissent and Nonconformity 1689–1920*. We should also note that a number of Nonconformist theologians studied abroad, among them Fairbairn, Mackintosh and Garvie; the Baptists Arthur Dakin and Leonard G. Champion in Germany, and W. Morris S. West in Switzerland; the Congregationalist/United Reformed John Heywood-Thomas, and the Welsh Presbyterian Stephen N. Williams in the United States.

[10] In this category should be placed the greatly respected and fondly remembered George Phillips of Lancashire Independent College. A few fugitive articles, from one of which I shall make a point of quoting in due course, may be tracked down by the diligent; but his self-effacing nature and his characteristic mode of expression are epitomized in his reply to my youthful query concerning his literary output. In deep, fruity, tones he cheerfully expostulated: 'Bless my soul, Alan! Who on earth would wish to read anything I might write?'

to theology as any, if theology is a knowledge of God, have been those made one to another by members of the household of faith, the fellowship of the saints, in one generation after another.[11]

To all of which, we shall not be surprised to discover, the Welsh Presbyterian J. Young Evans added hymns: 'Modern Welsh theology is no less the product of Welsh hymnody than of catechisms and sermons . . .'[12]

I

What was the general state of theology in the declining years of the nineteenth century? It is possible to detect a spirit of hopefulness among commentators of the period. With reference to the assimilation of modern biblical criticism, for example, Thomas Lewis, in the year in which he became Principal of Memorial [Congregational] College, Brecon, declared, 'The breeze of Biblical Criticism only blows away the chaff. The grain remains.'[13] In 1929, as he looked back over the previous half century, A.E. Garvie testified,

> Brought up as I had been in strict Presbyterian Calvinistic orthodoxy, including the belief in verbal inspiration, it can be understood how great was the shock, and how much need there was for adjustment between the new view and the old. . . . [W]hatever modification of views about the Bible itself the subsequent study of this progressive Biblical scholarship may have involved, my evangelicalism remained unshaken; and . . . it remains unshaken . . .[14]

Again, J.D. Vernon Lewis of the Congregational Memorial College, Brecon, who succeeded D. Miall Edwards as Professor of Christian Doctrine and Ethics, and was subsequently Professor of Old Testament and, for two years, Principal, wrote on biblical and devotional themes, but published no purely theological work. Yet he did as much as any to introduce Barth to Wales.

[11] A.J. Grieve, 'Congregationalism's contribution to theology. Some material for a bibliography', 359 n. 1.

[12] J. Young Evans, 'The new theology in Wales', 30.

[13] Thomas Lewis, 'Higher Criticism and Welsh preaching', 25. See further on the rise and reception of modern Biblical criticism, Willis B. Glover, *Evangelical Nonconformists and Higher Criticism in the Nineteenth Century*; Alan P.F. Sell, *Theology in Turmoil: The Roots, Course and Significance of the Conservative-Liberal Debate in Modern Theology*, ch. 2.

[14] A.E. Garvie, 'Fifty years' retrospect', 19.

By 1932 the Baptist T.R. Glover felt entitled to be jubilantly bullish: 'Today if you want a real old obscurantist college, you have to found one.'[15] In achieving this result, the part played by such believing biblical scholars as the Primitive Methodist A.S. Peake and the Congregationalist W.H. Bennett, should not be under-estimated. Similarly, there was a widespread feeling that the horror with which some had greeted the theory of evolution had by now been dissipated by the realization that, as the Unitarian James Martineau put it, 'neither of these two modern discoveries, namely, the immense extension of the universe in space, and its unlimited development in time has any effect on the theistic faith, except to glorify it.'[16] In a word, evolution came to be understood by most theologians not as an account of origins, but of the method by which God went to work.[17]

In some Congregational and Baptist circles there was a certain exhilaration deriving from the loosening of the fetters of a Calvinism deemed far too restrictive.[18] At first the relief was tempered, as in such writers as the Congregationalists E.R. Conder and R.W. Dale. Speaking for himself, Conder confessed to the Congregational Union Assembly of 1873 that 'Few, perhaps, inhaled with more satisfaction the freer air before whose breath a store of dry old phrases vanished like withered leaves, and the sacred Assembly's Catechism itself melted from off our children's minds like snow in spring time.' But while much had been gained, Conder felt it necessary to utter a cautionary word:

> Grant that our forefathers were too apt to substitute anatomical preparations of truth for its living presence. They loved to dangle before you the skeleton of the Gospel till all its joints rattled, when what you needed was the tone of her comforting voice, a Divine smile on her countenance, the warm grasp of her helping hand. But let us not forget that the anatomist's knife lays bare nothing but what is essential to life, health, and beauty. And the higher the life, the more complex the system in which it is embodied. Creatures which can be cut to bits or turned inside out, and live on all the same, are of a very low type. To the highest, the loss of a single vertebra would be death. The 'plan of salvation' is not the

---

[15] Quoted by E.J. Poole-Connor, *Evangelicalism in England*, 251.

[16] James Martineau, *The Seat of Authority in Religion*, 17.

[17] For biblical criticism and evolutionary thought see further Alan P.F. Sell, *Theology in Turmoil*, chs. 2, 3.

[18] For this story as it concerns Congregationalism, see Alan P.F. Sell, *Enlightenment, Ecumenism, Evangel: Theological Themes and Thinkers 1550–2000*, ch. 5.

'Glad Tidings'; the philosophy of religion is not religion; the most logical scheme of doctrine which Theology will ever frame will not take the place of the living word, by which souls are born again, and purified in obeying the truth. No! But nevertheless, a religious life strong in feeling and action, but intellectually feeble; a faith which is firm and simple as Trust, but as Belief is unintelligent, hazy, unable to distinguish doctrine from doctrine or truth from error – these are not worthy of the disciples of [Christ] . . . Nor is it in such characteristics that we can trace the features of the Church of the Future.[19]

Conder went on to point out that

The old Theology was not overthrown by argument. Calvinism is an iron ring of logic, which the hammer has not yet been forged that can break. It was burst asunder by the expansive force of love. The breaking point of the strain was the restriction it laid on an honest offer of salvation to all . . . [Possibly, Calvinists] were taking hold of the wrong end of the great problem of human salvation, in beginning with the eternal decrees of God, and the eternal covenant between the Father and the Son, instead of busying themselves with the end put into their hands by their Saviour's command – 'Go ye into all the world, and preach the Gospel to every creature.'[20]

John Angell James and R.W. Dale between them occupied the pulpit at Carrs Lane Congregational Church for most of the nineteenth century. The former served from 1805 until his death in 1859; the latter came as James's assistant in 1853, and continued until his death in 1895. In 1877 Dale recorded his opinion that many Congregationalists, James among them, thought that they were Calvinists:

[James] said to me once – raising his arm and clenching his hand as he said it – 'I hold the doctrines of Calvinism with a firm grasp!'

'But,' said I, 'you never preach about them.'

'Well,' he replied – with the *naïveté* which was one of the chief charms of his character – 'you know that there is not much about them in the Bible.'[21]

---

[19] E.R. Conder, 'The decay of theology', 70–71.

[20] Ibid., 72.

[21] R.W. Dale, 'On some present aspects of theological thought among Congregationalists', 5.

Construing Calvinism (tendentiously) as wedded to determinist philosophy,[22] whereas in fact it is a religious doctrine arising from gratitude at the way one has been divinely called and led, Dale argued that once the freedom of the will had been asserted, Calvinism could not but fall. At the same time he noted, and regretted, the fact that 'our faith has lost a certain grandeur, solemnity, and majesty, which belonged to the Augustinian and Calvinistic theology . . . If we could have the Calvinistic spirit, without the Calvinistic creed, it would be the regeneration of the Church and the salvation of the world.'[23] He is concerned that God's authority no longer impresses as it should, and that it is so hard 'to make men feel – whatever they may say – that sin is an awful offence, because committed against Him.'[24] Above all, he repudiates the sentimentality which surrounds the idea of 'an easy, good-natured God.'[25]

The personal turmoil which some who had been nurtured in scholastic Calvinism endured is epitomized by Robert Mackintosh, who regarded himself as a 'refugee' from the Free Church of Scotland, who 'fled to Congregationalism as a means of escape from outworn dogmas and creeds; but I resolved with God's help to be loyal still – or to be more loyal than ever – to the central faith of the Gospel . . .'[26]

In 1901 W.F. Adeney, Principal of Lancashire Independent College and Mackintosh's colleague, felt able to report that 'the Nonconformists have largely abandoned Calvinism, the Congregationalists almost entirely, the Baptists still clinging to some remnants of the system under the spell of Mr. Spurgeon.'[27] He thinks it to the credit of Calvin's 'merciless intellect' that 'Moderate Calvinism' has failed. P. T. Forsyth, likewise, was not slow to compose his obituary of Calvinistic scholasticism, and he did it, characteristically, in a too disjunctive way.

> The old orthodoxy laid on men's believing power more than it could carry. That orthodoxy, that Protestant scholasticism, was in its way

[22] See further Alan P.F. Sell, *Enlightenment, Ecumenism, Evangel*, 325–38.

[23] R.W. Dale, 'On some present aspects of theological thought among Congregationalists,' 6, 7.

[24] Ibid., 7.

[25] Ibid., 8.

[26] Robert Mackintosh, 'The genius of Congregationalism', 105. For Mackintosh see further Alan P.F. Sell, *Robert Mackintosh: Theologian of Integrity*.

[27] Walter F. Adeney, *A Century's Progress in Religious Life and Thought*, 116.

thorough. . . . It moved altogether if it moved at all. It attracted all-or-nothing spirits, whose tendency was to move like a prairie fire, covering the whole area but spreading only in one plane. It was comprehensive and acute rather than profound and subtle. . . . It had no atmosphere, no flexibility. And, great as it could be,[28] it came at last to be more vast than great. It brought to men more to carry than power to carry it. And like its predecessor, the medieval scholasticism, it was disintegrated by its own subtlety; it crumbled through its own acuteness; it died of its own insatiable dialectic; and fell of its own thin and ambitious imperialism.[29]

If Forsyth sees scholastic Calvinism collapsing under its own weight, as it were, Adeney attributes its demise to the new humanitarian temper of the age flowing down from Rousseau and the French Revolution.[30] In contrast to this, Calvinism, 'While prostrating itself before the awful Majesty of God . . . had no pity for man'[31] a statement, surely, which requires some qualification. In general, Adeney continues, Calvinism as well as feudalism went out with the cry, 'Liberty, equality, fraternity,' while in Scotland the poetry of Robert Burns gave it an added push, as did the theological writings of Thomas Erskine of Linlathen and John McLeod Campbell. Erskine 'broke the spell of Calvinism' by 'dwelling on the spiritual nature of redemption as a restoration to God and the true life of the soul, rather than mere deliverance from punishment.'[32] With the contributions of F.D. Maurice, Robertson of Brighton, the Congregationalist Baldwin Brown and others, the doctrine of God's Fatherhood has been made central in theology, displacing that of his sovereignty. Utterly repudiated is any idea that God's sovereignty is independent of morality, as if he were 'a sort of Sultan acting with pure caprice in choosing one for everlasting bliss, and relegating another to everlasting torment, on the Turk's plea that he "has a right to do as he will with his own."'[33]

---

[28] Forsyth did, after all, regard Thomas Goodwin as 'the apostle and high priest of our confession'. See his *Faith, Freedom and the Future*, 118.

[29] P.T. Forsyth, *Positive Preaching and the Modern Mind*, 84–85.

[30] My own preferred option is to think of the elevation of conscience and the right of private judgment flowing down from the Enlightenment as being that which prompted a much needed moral critique of *some expressions of* Calvinism. See Alan P.F. Sell, *Enlightenment, Ecumenism, Evangel*, ch. 3.

[31] W.F. Adeney, *A Century's Progress in Religious Life and Thought*, 122.

[32] Ibid., 125.

[33] Ibid., 130.

In the declining years of the nineteenth century few did more to establish the idea of God's fatherhood than the Methodist John Scott Lidgett. In his view this development amounted to nothing less than *The Victorian Transformation of Theology* – the title of his book of 1934; and his own major endorsement of the change was his work of 1902, *The Fatherhood of God in Christian Truth and Life*. The thesis of the latter is that 'on the one hand, the Fatherhood of God towards [Jesus Christ] is unique; and, on the other, the Fatherhood of God towards all men is determined in various ways by their relationship to Christ.'[34] Scott Lidgett's contemporary, the Unitarian scholar and Principal of Manchester College, Oxford, James Drummond, was among many others who elevated the concept of the divine Fatherhood:

> The doctrine of the fatherly character of God lies at the centre of the Christian revelation. Around this the other great doctrines of Christianity cluster, and from it they draw their vitality. Clearly to apprehend this doctrine is to hold the master-key which unlocks the mysteries of the kingdom of heaven, and admits the worshipper to the richest treasures of the Spirit. To explain it away, or to see it obscurely, or to thrust it into a subordinate position, is to miss the guiding light and vivifying power of our religion.[35]

Sailing still closer to the Trinitarian wind – at least terminologically – Drummond elsewhere declared that 'We can know the Father only through the spirit of the Son dwelling in our hearts by faith.'[36] Earlier still, with reference to 'the blessedness of a Father's presence,' Drummond declared that 'Not only through creation and through the voice of the Spirit in our conscience, but also through his Son God will still reveal himself to those who wait for his salvation . . .'[37]

Optimistic though many felt in the closing quarter of the nineteenth century, there were some who expressed grave disquiet –

---

[34] J.S. Lidgett, *The Fatherhood of God*, 2.

[35] J. Drummond, unreferenced quotation in the leaflet *Drummond* (Eminent Unitarian Teachers. 15), (London: The Lindsey Press, n.d.), 3 (but unpaginated); cf. his Hibbert Lectures, *Via, Veritas, Vita: Lectures on 'Christianity in its most simple and intelligible form'*, 170: 'the fundamental and characteristic idea of Christianity on [the doctrine of God] is that God is our Father.'

[36] Idem, *Some Thoughts on Christology*, London: Philip Green, 1902, 30.

[37] Idem, *Sermons on Christian Faith and Life*, London: Longmans, Green, 1879, 113–114.

especially concerning the state of systematic theology as such. In his address of 1873 Conder asked, 'is it not true that whatever place systematic Theology may maintain in the studies of our pastors, it has been for many years in steady course of disappearance from our pulpits; and that the number has been continually increasing among our hearers who account this disappearance a blessed riddance?'[38] Again, 'We have iconoclasts in plenty, but where are our architects? Good and solid work is being done in Bible interpretation . . .; but where are the Theologians at whose feet teachers of others will sit thirty years hence?'[39]

Twenty years on, in an address to the first meeting of the International Congregational Council, D.W. Simon, Principal of the Scottish Congregational College, referred ruefully to 'prominent ministers' who 'refer in tones of mock humility to their ignorance of Systematic Theology, or earn cheap applause by denouncing dogma and contrasting it with life;' and to 'leading laymen' who exclaim, 'We want practical preaching, not doctrine.' He noted that during the past 35 years, British Congregationalists had published only one systematic theology; that during the past 25 years only about 50 out of 600 Congregational publications were 'scientifically theological; and that out of upwards of 450 discourses by Congregational ministers printed during the last five years or thereabouts in *The Christian World Pulpit*, scarcely 30 were properly doctrinal.'[40]

In the year of Simon's lament, James Drummond sought reasons for the lack of interest in theology. He suggests that the exaggerated importance attached to it in the past is one cause of its decline. Another is that theology by itself is seen to be incapable of producing

---

[38] E.R. Conder, 'The decay of theology', 68.

[39] Ibid., 76. One hundred and twenty years on I found myself making the same point in my Aberystwyth Inaugural Lecture. See Alan P.F. Sell, *Testimony and Tradition: Studies in Reformed and Dissenting Thought*, 10. I return to the point in Lecture 4 below.

[40] D.W. Simon, 'The present direction of theological thought in the Congregational churches of Great Britain', 78. I suspect that part of the explanation for the dearth of systematics is that those theologians most capable of producing it were devoting themselves to apologetic tasks in relation to biblical criticism and evolutionary thought, and to such 'isms' as materialism, naturalism, positivism and neo-Hegelian immanentism – all of them in various ways deemed to be enemies at the gates. Most of the Nonconformist traditions were busy with apologetics in the second half of the nineteenth century. See further Alan P.F. Sell, *Philosophy, Dissent and Nonconformity*, ch. 5.

the religious life: 'The keenest theologian is not always the best Christian . . .'[41] Again, the fact of theology-inspired persecution has alienated the sympathies of many, and interest has been transferred to other matters, compared with which theological controversies 'present to us only the dismal barrenness of extinct volcanoes.'[42] Finally, new knowledge is undermining old theological foundations. In the light of all this some say, let us forsake theology and settle for religion. But, cautions Drummond, 'Religion always involves some kind of belief, and this belief is logically prior to the feeling of love or devotion which is associated with it.'[43] Thus, for example, Schleiermacher's positing of the feeling of absolute dependence as the ground of religion presupposes belief in that on which one depends. This is by no means to say that religion is founded upon dogma, for dogma is ratified and imposed by a constituted authority. Doctrines are formal and exact statements of what is believed and 'Theology is a system of doctrines, arranged in their due connection and subordination, and established by rational proof.'[44] Although religion cannot dispense with doctrine, for doctrines are accounts of what is believed, it can survive the fall of particular theologies. Drummond therefore feels able to end on a hopeful note.

> The final result of this present upheaval of thought will be, I cannot doubt, a fresh outpouring of the Spirit, not in signs and wonders, but in faith and love, and another onward step towards the realisation of the kingdom of God upon earth, and the establishment of that human brotherhood which Christianity has proclaimed, and Christendom denied. Well may we bear the temporary strife and anguish, if at the end we are to see the heralds of peace bringing glad tidings to the world.'[45]

Conder, Simon and Drummond could not have known that they were on the verge of a relative explosion of Nonconformist theology; for there was more Nonconformist activity in this field during the first 20 years of the twentieth century than at any period since that of the Puritans. In the three following lectures I shall adduce evidence to support this contention, but first it will be useful to

---

[41] J. Drummond, 'Religion and theology', 9.
[42] Ibid., 11.
[43] Ibid., 15.
[44] Ibid., 18.
[45] Ibid., 39–40.

view the Nonconformist theological landscape of the century as a whole.

II

Our brief glimpse of the nineteenth-century theological hinterland has sufficed to remind us that theology never arises from a vacuum. There is always a historical, intellectual and ecclesial context. Sometimes the events of history provide the stimulus to theological reflection; sometimes there is the need to come to terms with apparently or actually alien thought forms; sometimes there are doctrinal squabbles within or between the churches. There may be theologians who so live in the past that they wish only to reproduce Augustine, Luther, Calvin or whomsoever it may be; but close scrutiny of their work always reveals that they do not, because they cannot, exactly share the presuppositions of their chosen mentors; and to the extent that they embrace theological restorationism they may be denying the prompting of that very Holy Spirit in whom they otherwise profess to believe. None of which is to say that theology must be 'instant' in the sense that we have to re-invent it each waking morning. We are, inescapably, heirs of a tradition, and the balance between anchorage in the Gospel and openness to the times must ever be struck – always remembering that we can hear the gospel only in our time.[46]

The twentieth century provided Nonconformist theologians with both inner-family and external stimuli to theological endeavour. As to the former, in 1907 R.J. Campbell, minister of London's City Temple, caused a fluttering in Congregational dovecotes, and ripples elsewhere, with the publication of his book, *The New Theology* (how risky the terms 'new' and even 'recent' are in book titles). Repudiating both bibliolatry and ecclesiolatry, Campbell understands his New Theology to represent 'an untrammelled return to the Christian sources in the light of modern thought. But since its starting-point is a re-emphasis of the Christian belief in the Divine immanence in the universe and in mankind,'[47] modern thought – especially in its post-Hegelian immanentist form – seems to be the controlling factor. By 'God' Campbell means 'the one reality I cannot get away from, for whatever else it may be, it is myself.'[48] In a variety of other ways he

---

[46] See further, Alan P.F. Sell, *Testimony and Tradition,* ch. 1.

[47] R.J. Campbell, *The New Theology,* 4.

[48] Ibid., 18.

blurs the Creator-creature distinction which is so prominent in 'the Christian sources' and, notwithstanding the tradition that Jesus Christ is our Saviour from sin, he declares that Jesus 'came to show us what we potentially are.'[49] Indeed, when his spirit becomes ours, 'we, like Him, become saviours of the race.'[50] All of this is laid against the background of God's Fatherhood: 'God is not a fiend, but a Father . . . Why should we be required to be saved from Him?'[51] I had the impression that according to Christian tradition, it was sin from which we needed to be saved.

Many took up their pens against Campbell – Bishop Charles Gore among them.[52] From within the ranks of Congregationalism C.H. Vine gathered a collection of essays under the title *The Old Faith and the New Theology* (1907). Among the theologians who contributed papers were W.F. Adeney, D.W. Simon, R. Vaughan Pryce, and P.T. Forsyth, Principal of Hackney College. Of these the last, himself an erstwhile theological liberal, is the most pungent. He argues that the concept of immanence, on which the New Theology turns, is an inheritance from Greek and pagan thought, and that it has little to do with evangelical Christianity: it is monistic and evolutionary, and 'It does not go to the depths. It speculates about a Christ made flesh, but it never gauges the true seat of Incarnation – a Christ made sin. It is not a theology of Incarnation.'[53] In the same year the Scottish Congregationalist W.L. Walker, who had sojourned among the Unitarians between 1886 and 1893, published *What about the New Theology?* This temperate, judicious, work ran to two editions in 1907, and contained some incisive criticisms. Opinion in Wales, as represented by T. Charles Williams of Menai Bridge and J. Young Evans, was mutually contradictory. The former, explaining that Wales was intensely theological and tolerant, agrees with one in 'high authority'

---

[49] Ibid., 84.

[50] Ibid., 174.

[51] Ibid., 175. See also Campbell's *New Theology Sermons*. After returning to the Church of England, whence he had originally come, Campbell became Canon and Canon-Teacher of Chichester. In that capacity he published *Christian Faith in Modern Light*, a book which in places is astonishingly weak in argument – for example, on p. 35.

[52] See C. Gore, *The Old Religion and the New Theology*. For more on the intellectual context see Alan P.F. Sell, *Theology in Turmoil*, ch. 1; idem, *Philosophical Idealism and Christian Belief*, chs. 1, 2; and the Methodist Frederick W. Platt, *Immanence and Christian Thought: Implications and Questions*.

[53] P.T. Forsyth, 'Immanence and Incarnation', 48.

that 'the attitude of the Welsh public to the New Theology, as it is called, is much more liberal than the English.' The latter declares, 'The New Theology, as enunciated in the City Temple, the Welsh Nonconformists will reject . . .'[54]

Campbell subsequently espoused a more orthodox position and reverted to the Church of England in which he had been raised, finally becoming Canon and Chancellor of Chichester Cathedral. With hindsight we can see that the affair was little more than a nine days' wonder. It did, however, demonstrate the lengths to which liberal attenuations of the gospel could go; and it is not fanciful to suppose that such a scholarly liberal theologian as the Congregationalist C.J. Cadoux had the unreconstructed Campbell in mind when he admitted and regretted that there were liberals who emphasized the self-sufficiency of human beings, ignored sin and evil, and denied the Lordship, divinity and saving power of Jesus, and also his incarnation and resurrection.[55] This criticism is the more telling because it appeared in Cadoux's book, *The Case for Evangelical Modernism* (1938).

Among many more popular expressions of theological liberalism mention may be made of *The Working Faith of a Liberal Theologian* by the Congregationalist T. Rhondda Williams. He had found liberal theology to work in the lives of individuals and of society; he thinks that Wesley and Whitefield were held back by 'the incubus of a traditional theology' which 'prevented them from getting the full import and significance of their own truth';[56] and he is convinced that those who have felt the power of a liberal faith 'know that there is still more light and truth to break forth through the souls of men'[57] – though, unlike Pastor John Robinson, whose words he echoes, he does not mention the source of that light and truth as being the Word of God.

III

The liberal optimism in humanity (though not all liberals were equally optimistic), the notion that *we* are bringing in the Kingdom, the doctrine of God's Fatherhood-gone-sentimental: all of these ideas suffered a

---

[54] T.C. Williams, 'The influence of higher criticism on Welsh preaching', 21; J. Young Evans, 'The New Theology in Wales', 30.
[55] C.J. Cadoux, *The Case for Evangelical Modernism*, 8–9.
[56] T.Rhondda Williams, *The Working Faith of a Liberal Theologian*, 40.
[57] Ibid., xiii.

severe jolt with the onset of the First World War.[58] In 1902 Scott Lidgett could declare that 'The manifold influences of modern life have taught the neighbourhood and brotherhood of all men.'[59] In my copy of his book I find I have written an uncharacteristically sardonic marginal note: 'Wait for twelve years.' Prompted from without by the dire stimulus of war, in the light of which squabbles over the New Theology must have seemed domestic indeed, a number of theologians – Nonconformists among them – turned their thoughts to theodicy. Had they a prophetic word to address to a nation at war, and to a people many of whom were asking how could there be a loving and just God when such devastation was permitted? Three principals and one former principal rose to reply: E. Griffith-Jones of Yorkshire United Independent College, Adeney, who had retired from Lancashire College in 1913, S.H. Mellone of Manchester Unitarian College, and P.T. Forsyth of Hackney College.

Griffith-Jones's book of 1915 is thoughtful and wide-ranging. Entitled *The Challenge of Christianity to a World at War*, Griffith-Jones discusses the challenge of faith in the divine providence, which poses the question, 'what has the world of civilized men been doing with its God-given liberty that this calamitous war has come to pass?'[60] The challenge to civilization consists in showing the inadequacy of materialism; the challenge to morality consists in the demonstration that human beings are related to the Father-God revealed in Jesus Christ; the challenge to the home is to revive a healthy family sentiment; the challenge to nationalism is a regeneration of true patriotism; the challenge to militarism is the elevation of faith, hope and love as the solvents of all rivalries and the only secure bases of peace; and the challenge to religion is to recover its spiritual vision, to manifest unity in Christ, and to work for the healing not only of relations between the nations, but of those social ills which disfigure our own society.

W.F. Adeney was keen that people should sort out their ideas on this most perplexing question. To say that a calamity is a punishment is not to say that it is 'planned, and purposed, and produced by God.'[61] To think otherwise would be to fall into pagan anthropomorphism. This is not to deny that God is transcendent, it is to affirm that he is also immanent. But in the latter connection the peril is that of

---

[58] For the historical context see Alan Ruston, 'Protestant Nonconformist attitudes towards the First World War', in Alan P.F. Sell and Anthony R. Cross, eds, *Protestant Nonconformity in the Twentieth Century*, ch. 9.

[59] J.S. Lidgett, *The Fatherhood of God*, 279.

[60] E. Griffith-Jones, *The Challenge of Christianity to a World at War*, 24.

[61] W.F. Adeney, *Faith Today*, 18.

pantheism, and 'To say that everything that happens is a deed of God is pantheistic.'[62] The war was directly contrary to God's will, and was not sent or ordered by him. Why, then did he permit it? God does not give permission to war's promoters: it is an absurdity to speak of God's permitting an evil. Why, then, does he not prevent it? This would deny us the gift of freedom; there could be no sin; and non-theistic determinism leaves us with no moral order at all. Faith in God's providence is historically justified, and in our own lives we have experienced many blessings at his hand. But these appeals will not suffice the doubter. Our final appeal is to Christ for an assurance of God's goodness in the world. In his life, death and resurrection we have a redemptive gospel: 'It comes to us as a redemptive power offering this deliverance from evil by its own specific grace.'[63] As for the practical question of the action to be taken in time of war: we have to accept the paradox that while our faith repudiates war, it encourages people to participate in it. To be a warmonger is utterly unchristian; to counteract the mischief of war is not an unworthy act.

S.H. Mellone approaches the question from a different direction. He thinks it idle to speculate upon an alleged failure of Christianity as the cause of the war, though it is because people and nations are 'imperfectly Christianized' that such calamities as war descend upon us. War places substantial moral demands upon individuals and the nation, and in addition to the physical shock of war, there is the mental and spiritual shock. Thus,

> in the agony of war, we are learning the full horror of many things which were commonplaces in peace. We know now something of what it means to the nation that the most unholy trinity of mammon, strong drink, and lust should grind away the lives of unnumbered helpless children.[64] We made *progress* a watchword, though all history cries out against the notion of a gradual upward and onward movement of man . . . We made an idol of *science*; but now, many know what a few knew before – that science can do nothing but fulfil purposes set by human wills . . . Science proves herself the obedient and efficient servant of the will to destroy, as she is of the will to save. In *religion*, we had rejoiced at the departure of the 'age of dogma.' We supposed that a few broad and simple principles, the 'religion of all sensible men,' would suffice. We had lost the God of the old covenant, the God of the fire, of the

---

[62] Ibid., 21.
[63] Ibid., 71.
[64] Here speaks the Nonconformist conscience.

cloud, and of the thick darkness; and the God of the Cross of Calvary we had not found. Knowing that we must labour even for daily bread, we thought that faith in God would be cheap![65]

But perhaps the bravest words on the subject were uttered by P.T. Forsyth in *The Justification of God*. By 'brave' I mean that when many were wondering how God could be good and loving if all these disasters were happening, Forsyth came thundering out with the point: if God is *holy* love, and if human beings are as wicked as they are, what else should you expect but all this calamity? His reliance throughout is upon the redemptive and reconciling Cross which alone both saves us and satisfies God's violated holy love. A collage of his sentences will make his point:

> Our faith did not arise from the order of the world; the world's convulsion, therefore, need not destroy it . . . All is well with the world, since its Saviour has it finally and fully in hand. Victory awaits us because victory is won . . . The anomaly [here is his theological courage when many were perishing] is not that a God of love should permit such things as we see. In the egoist conditions of Europe and of civilisation everywhere, and with a God of holy love over all, the scandal and the stumbling block would have been if such judgments did not come . . . That God spared not His own Son is a greater shock to the natural conscience than the collapse of civilisation in blood would be. For civilisation may deserve to collapse, if only because it crucified the Son of God, and crucifies Him afresh. But if God spared not His own Son, He will spare no historic convulsion needful for His kingdom. And if the unspared Son neither complained nor challenged, but praised and hallowed the Father's name, we may worship and bow the head . . . It is a vanquished world where men play their devilries. Christ has overcome it. It can make tribulation, but desolation it can never make . . . The thing is done, it is not to do. 'Be of good cheer, I *have* overcome the world.'[66]

---

[65] S.H. Mellone, 'The moral equivalent of war',166–7.

[66] P.T. Forsyth, *The Justification of God*, 57, 78, 119, 194, 223, 166–7. Appalled by the way in which heirs of such a fine culture as the German – one from whose theological luminaries he himself had learned so much – could descend to such evil, Forsyth fired off *The Christian Ethic of War*. On the shadow side of temperate, this work dismayed many pacifists, and not pacifists only. It was never reprinted. The following works betoken a revival of interest in Forsyth's more central theology: Trevor Hart, ed., *Justice the True and Only*

IV

The theme of the providence of God was treated by Nonconformist theologians both before and after the First World War. In 1909 J. Oswald Dykes, who two years earlier had resigned the principalship of the Theological College of the Presbyterian Church of England, published his Cunningham Lectures under the title *The Divine Worker in Creation and Providence*. Dykes reviews his chosen doctrines in the light of the scientific advances of the preceding century, discusses the natural order and the place of humanity within it, and makes what to many older divines would have been a startling claim concerning providence.

> We shall not conceive of providence aright . . . if we leave room in its ordinary working for random or occasional interferences with the order of nature. In saying this I am not prejudging the exceptional case of miracles, centring in the history of redemption, some of them inseparable from it. These must stand or fall on their own proper evidence. I am thinking of the theory of special or exceptional providences, which hardly survives to-day.[67]

In answer to the question, 'Why is "the upward progress of humanity" so slow?' Dykes replies that human perversity and wickedness are the culprits. Nevertheless, God works ceaselessly on, and, after all, 'What is Providence but the age-long, worldwide labour for man's deliverance of the same Divine Lover of men Whose redeeming passion was consummated upon the Cross?'[68]

In 1925 Ebenezer Griffith-Jones, principal of Yorkshire United Independent College, published his two-volume work, *Providence – Divine and Human: A Study of the World Order in the Light of Modern Thought*. Twenty-five years earlier he had published *Ascent Through Christ*, a widely-welcomed book in which he reviewed facts pertaining to our redemption in the light of the then prominent principle of development. Now, in the aftermath of war he turns to providence, convinced that older writers were methodologically wanting. They so

---

Mercy: Essays on the Life and Theology of Peter Taylor Forsyth; Leslie McCurdy, *Attributes and Atonement: The Holy Love of God in the Theology of P.T. Forsyth*; Alan P.F. Sell, ed., *P.T. Forsyth, Theologian for a New Millennium*; idem, *Testimony and Tradition*, chs. 7, 8.

[67] J.O. Dykes, *The Divine Worker in Creation and Providence*, 264.

[68] Ibid., 285.

focused upon the providential God as to neglect the fact that many of the puzzles surrounding providence arise from 'purely human agency, which has disturbed the ideal course of events, and introduced abnormality into the divine plan from the beginning of human history.'[69] His guiding, evolutionary, theme is that whereas with all other creatures a departure from their proper upward path would have led to extinction, in the case of human beings God introduces a redemptive movement into the course of human history. In his second volume he traces the course of human history, arguing that God has placed human beings in an educative environment in which their providential function is to develop a world order consistent with, and in realization of, the divine purpose. It would seem that the evolutionary optimism which undergirded Griffith-Jones's thought – his substantial chapters on evil and sin notwithstanding – was falling out of fashion by 1925. At all events, it is recorded that the 'indifferent reception' accorded to this, his most substantial work, 'was a disappointment he felt keenly.'[70]

I have already referred to God's Fatherhood, and to Scott Lidgett's impressive book of 1902 on that subject. He was not the first Nonconformist in the twentieth century to lift the theme into prominence, however. In 1901 W.F. Adeney nominated Erskine of Linlathen and McLeod Campbell as the fountainheads of this development, and welcomed the way in which theology had taken a more ethical turn: 'it recognises the universal love of God as the central element of His character revealed to us in Jesus Christ, and His Fatherhood as the very highest conception of His nature that it is possible to attain.'[71] But Adeney is opposed to any sentimentalism with respect to God's Fatherhood which only wishes to dwell upon the kindly aspects of the divine paternity. For his Scottish mentors as for himself, 'the idea of the Divine Fatherhood is as far as possible from the notion of a mild, amiable paterfamilias, indulgent to the faults and foibles of his pampered family . . . The perfect father is one who knows how to keep his own house in order,'[72] and God's Fatherhood includes his sovereignty as an essential characteristic.

---

[69] E. Griffith-Jones, *Providence – Divine and Human: A Study of the World-Order in the Light of Modern Thought*, I, 8. Griffith-Jones's second volume, *The Dominion of Man*, was published in 1926.

[70] See his obituary by J.G.J. (probably John Gwyn James of Llandilo), *The Congregational Year Book*, 1943, 428.

[71] Walter F. Adeney, *A Century's Progress in Religious Life and Thought*, 131.

[72] Ibid., 128.

P.T. Forsyth is even more determined to avoid sentimentality, and his method is constantly to emphasize the truth that God's love is holy love.

> There is a kind of consecration which would live close to the Father, but it does not always take seriously enough the holiness which makes the fatherhood of the cross – awful, inexhaustible, and eternal, as full of judgment as of salvation . . . There was more fatherhood in the cross (where holiness met guilt) than in the prodigal's father (where love met shame).[73]

Whatever damage the First World War may have inflicted upon sentimental notions of God's Fatherhood, the concept itself survived the war.[74] As late as 1935 A.E. Garvie, Principal of New College, London, acknowledged his debt to his teacher A.M. Fairbairn's insight into God's paternal sovereignty, and wrote on *The Fatherly Rule of God* over all human affairs. He points out that 'In the combination *fatherly rule*, the adjective is protected against the weak sentimentalism which regards God's love as good nature, indifferent to sin, and the noun against the harsh dogmatism which has for so long and so often hidden the Heavenly Father's face from His earthly children.'[75] In the following year W.B. Selbie published his wide-ranging study of *The Fatherhood of God* which, though not correctly characterized as sentimental, is more genial and liberal than anything written on the subject by Forsyth. This impression emerges from Selbie's comments on the prodigal son. He says that the claim that in this parable we have the Christian gospel is denied only by those wedded to a substitutionary theory of the atonement. In his view, the loving Fatherhood of God and the sonship even of those who leave the Father's house are clearly proclaimed in the parable.[76] The truth of this need not be denied, but, as we have seen, Forsyth would rigorously have attacked the notion that this was all that needed to be said.

---

[73] P.T. Forsyth, *The Holy Father*, 5, 9.

[74] This is not to deny that, to this day, the concept of God's Fatherhood is a powerful one in the understanding and worship of the vast majority of the world's Christians. But it is not the energizing doctrine now that it was in the early decades of the twentieth century; and in some ultra-feminist circles it is variously queried, repudiated and scorned. See further Alan P.F. Sell, *Enlightenment, Ecumenism, Evangel*, 365–73.

[75] A.E. Garvie, *The Fatherly Rule of God*, 236.

[76] W.B. Selbie, *The Fatherhood of God*, 96.

V

We breathe a different air when we turn to the writings of two impressive Presbyterian theologians, John Oman and H.H. Farmer.[77] Both were successors of Oswald Dykes as principals of the Presbyterian, latterly Westminster, College, and Farmer became the Norris Hulse Professor of Divinity at Cambridge. The two publications of Oman which most concern us are *Grace and Personality* (1917) and *The Natural and the Supernatural* (1931). A running theme is that of the supremacy of the personal. There is no higher category, he argues, and the personal God is the highest being. God has created a world in which human beings are nurtured, but such nurturing must be by moral means. As he says, 'If morality without religion is apt to be slavery to accepted forms, religion without morality is apt to be slavery to accepted formulas.'[78] Accordingly, Oman repudiates all false authoritarianisms which deny personhood by obliterating the individual's moral freedom. God, the supremely personal authority, does not coerce, but draws out from people a free, obediential response, and this response, once made, enhances rather than diminishes the human person, who can then begin to express his or her true self. Religion, he argues in his later book, finds its origin in our immediate sense of the supernatural. In Christianity the supernatural is conceived as the personal God who graciously discloses himself to us within the natural order. So it is that 'religion must be a large experience in which we grow in knowledge as we grow in humility and courage, in which we deal with life and not abstractions, and with God as the environment in which we live and more and have our being and not as an ecclesiastical formula.'[79]

The major works of Farmer have a more obviously pastoral and ecclesial air than those of Oman, but they are no less concerned with the personal: indeed with the personal relations which should exist between God and human beings, and among human beings. If people are not in harmony with God, they are at odds with others and with the world around them. To Farmer, God is a 'living personal Will,' and 'It is of the essence of personal will . . . that it can only be known

---

[77] See further F.G. Healey, *Religion and Reality: The Theology of John Oman*; Stephen Bevans, *John Oman and his Doctrine of God*; G.F. Woods, 'Revised reviews: VI: John Oman's *The Natural and the Supernatural*'; F.G. Healey, *Prospect for Theology: Essays in Honour of H.H. Farmer*.

[78] John Oman, *Grace and Personality*, 66.

[79] Idem, *The Natural and the Supernatural*, 471.

to be real in and through concrete, historical situations and relationships where personal choices and decisions have to be made.'[80] In *The World and God* (1935) he seeks to face the fact that many have difficulty in reconciling belief in a personal God with their experience of the world as it is. Their perplexities focus upon providence, prayer and miracle. He discusses these in some detail and then proceeds to argue that for Christians it is supremely in the experience of reconciliation that they apprehend, immediately, that God is personal, and come to understand something of the meaning and purpose of history and the importance of the eschatological hope. The Christian's confidence is not a matter of strict demonstration, as he makes clear in *Towards Belief in God* (1942), but it is a matter of the coercive element in the experience and the pragmatic verification of it in the realities of life. But is it a groundless confidence? Farmer expounds the options thus:

> the Crucifixion of Jesus is either a great, grim, hoarse, derisive shout of *No* to the proposition that God is love, gathering into itself and summing up all those other evil things in human life which seem also to shout *No* to it; or it is a firm, steady, undefeated *Yes* penetrating, persisting through, all these other things. Who then is to decide which it is? The strange thing is – though it is not strange in view of the personal nature of God's dealings with us – the individual man must decide, must answer the question. And if the right answer be given, it is not the less of the inspiration of God because it is the man's own answer.[81]

In his Lyman Beecher Lectures, *God and Men* (1948), Farmer again emphasizes the personal. According to Christianity

> man is only distinctively man at all because, – whether he knows it or not, whether he likes it or not, – he stands right down to the innermost core and essence of his being, in the profoundest possible relationship to God all the time in an order of persons. If, *per impossible*, he could wrench himself out of that relationship, he would cease to be – MAN.'[82]

Human beings are, however, sinners, and Farmer understands by the finality of Christ 'His finality as reconciler in the personal world of God and Man.'[83] This is brought home to us above all in the Cross of

---

[80] H.H. Farmer, *Towards Belief in God*, ix.

[81] Ibid., 124–5.

[82] Idem, *God and Men*, 68.

[83] Ibid., 95.

Christ, which God used 'to reveal to men's sin-blinded eyes the true meaning of their life and destiny, and to redeem men into His kingdom.'[84] To the theme of the Cross I shall return in due course.

Since the Second World War a number of treatments of aspects of the doctrine of God have flowed from Nonconformist hands. In 1954 Charles H. Duthie, then Principal of the Scottish Congregational College, and subsequently of New College, London, published *God in His World*. Written as a Lent book, and with laypeople mostly in mind, it ranges widely and is inspired by Duthie's conviction that Christian evangelism is rooted in the doctrine of God. He reviews pantheism which ends by destroying the personality of God; teachings which clearly mark God off from the created order and then have difficulty in showing how the two can be related; and panentheism – the view that God 'contains' the world. To this last position he inclines, claiming that 'If the world and man are grounded in the being of God, we can understand . . . why it is that man cannot get away from God and is restless until he finds rest in Him.' It follows that 'The tragedy and irony of man's sin is that it is his repudiation of that which gives him the very power to repudiate.'[85]

The Congregationalist W.A. Whitehouse, then of the University of Durham, devoted his Riddell Memorial Lectures of 1959 to the question of the relations between science and Christianity – a question he addressed in a decidedly theological way.

> I am seeking only to bring out the distinctive content and characteristics of *Christian* faith, that this is God's world, with order and goodness in its making, an order and a goodness which can be seen as hints (or heard as echoes) of a glory in God which man has been made to share. The truth of this faith, or, if you prefer, its compatibility with human integrity, is open to be tested in appropriate ways. It is a truth which exposes itself for testing where Christians confess the same faith, not primarily by repeating or explaining or even justifying this classical statement, but by speaking and acting like men who believe what it says.[86]

But God's human creatures have rebelled against him, and hence 'The Lord who rules [creation] is the Lord who was crucified within it.'[87] To

---

[84] Ibid., 170.
[85] C.S. Duthie, *God in His World*, 55.
[86] W.A. Whitehouse, *Order, Goodness, Glory*, 20.
[87] Ibid., 24.

God's grace in Christ 'Gratitude is the characteristic response . . .; so that what one looks for in the world is anything which evokes in Christian men a gratitude which is all of a piece with the gratitude of the believer for the grace of his Lord Jesus Christ.'[88]

VI

In some quarters the older liberal optimism died hard. As late as 1923 the Congregational historian Albert Peel was confidently proclaiming the progress of the human race;[89] and the Welsh Congregational theologian D. Miall Edwards, a former student under Fairbairn at Mansfield, published a number of books and articles, including *Crist a Gwareiddiad (Christ and Civilization, 1921)* and *Crefydd a Diwylliant (Religion and Culture, 1934)* of which his continuing commitment to liberal theology and to social reform were among the inspirations. By now, however, other voices were beginning to be heard, and some felt that they could not ignore the prophetic word of the Swiss theologian Karl Barth, whose *Romans* was published in 1919. As is well known, Barth, nurtured in Calvinism, taught by Harnack and Herrmann, became convinced that neither the scholastic conservative theology of his youth nor the anthropocentric liberal theology of his mentors had a word for a world shattered by the First World War. Hence his recourse to the God who addresses his word to human beings in such a way as to demand a 'Yes' to it, and a 'No' to all attempts to translate theology into language about ourselves and our condition. According to Barth, we cannot any longer embark upon the enterprise of natural theology, for this would entail elevating our human intellectual constructions into interpretative norms; and, in any case, there is no analogy of being between ourselves and God; rather, there is an impassable gulf. This bold position gave rise to Barth's hostile reception of Emil Brunner's 'softer' position on natural theology;[90] and it also caused concern in a number of Nonconformist circles as we shall see.

Among early respondents to the early Barth was the Methodist Charles J. Wright of Didsbury College. It is his conviction that the Barthian challenge to religious experience derives from the sceptical view that 'man cannot by the constitution of his own spiritual, moral and rational nature come to know God,' and that 'Any theology

---

[88] Ibid., 76.

[89] A. Peel in *The Congregational Quarterly*, I, 1923, 230.

[90] See Emil Brunner and Karl Barth, *Natural Theology*.

which begins by denying the bond which unites God and man condemns itself to a perpetual inability to say anything about the Transcendent who is the object of religion.'[91] Another Methodist, J. Arundel Chapman, who taught at Handsworth, Didsbury and Headingley Colleges, also had reservations concerning the early Barth: 'Barth,' he writes, 'is scornful when he speaks of "religious experience"; God is the "Wholly Other"; "God in us" implies arrogance. Most of the religious seers of the past will, then, have to be convicted of this "arrogance", not excluding our Lord.'[92] Yet another Methodist could by no means be accused of not keeping himself up to date with theological trends. At the age of eighty-nine Scott Lidgett sallied forth with *God and the World. Essays in Christian Theism* (1943), in which he rebutted Barth's assertion of the discontinuity between human reason and divine revelation with the *tu quoque* argument that Barth's own position had been reached by a judgement of reason and one, moreover, which put him at odds with the Bible and the main line of the Christian tradition.

Within Congregationalism, A.E. Garvie viewed Barth with alarm, finding in his approach the ghost of Calvinism walking again. I say 'finding in his approach', rather than 'finding in his work', for on his own admission Garvie could not bring himself to study Barth's writings in detail when composing his book, *The Christian Belief in God*. 'Having given so much toil of mind and travail of soul to escape from Calvinism, I have no mind to return to its bondage,'[93] he declared. Nor did he mellow on this point with the passage of the years. In 1942 we find him advising that 'Neo-Calvinism which in some of its younger exponents is becoming an intolerant obsession must not be allowed to rob us to the gains which our more modern methods of dealing with the Holy Scriptures have taught us.'[94]

Against Barth's way of handling the Bible, C.J. Cadoux resolutely set his face. He takes Barth to task for holding that the Bible 'is the canon because it has imposed itself as such upon the Church, and invariably does so.' This he finds 'not only inadequate, but inaccurate and even absurd', for a canon has limits, and it took the church three

---

[91] Charles J. Wright, *The Meaning and Message of the Fourth Gospel: A Study in the Application of Johannine Christianity to the Present Theological Situation*, 193–4.

[92] J. Arundel Chapman, *Modern Issues in Religious Thought*, 56.

[93] A.E. Garvie, *Revelation Through History and Experience: A Study of the Historical Basis of the Revelation of the Godhead*, xii.

[94] Idem, 'Freedom of the Church in Christ', 113.

hundred years to settle those; and we do not 'get God on his own terms and not on man's, simply by taking over a traditional group of books, calling them "the canon of Holy Scripture", acclaiming their contents (in distinction from other literature) as "Revelation", and demanding "faith" in them as a Christian obligation.' This, he thunders, 'is an extremely superficial judgment.'[95] A related point was made, less belligerently, by R.S. Franks: 'No proof has even been given by Barth that the Word of God and his theology are equivalent, but his whole theology rests upon the sheer assumption that it is so: the Word of God is what he defines it to be and nothing else.'[96]

In 1940 Cadoux published *Christian Pacifism Re-examined*, one of the most learned volumes on its theme, though not without an occasional pugilistic, undefended, broadside of the kind to which some pacifists are on occasion strangely inclined: 'A theology like Barthianism,' he declares, 'which professes independence of philosophy, is bound to be arbitrary and unconvincing.'[97] Take that! In fairness to Cadoux, however, it must be noted that two years previously he had published *The Case for Evangelical Modernism*, in which, more temperately, he lodges complaints against Barthianism. While not unappreciative of its strengths, he nevertheless regards the phenomenon as a blind-alley. In particular he dislikes the Barthian passion for discontinuities rather than for distinctions: 'Natural Theology is one thing, revelation through Christ something totally other; and the difference between them is fundamental.'[98] He finds 'truly surprising' the way Barthians speak about religion: 'For them, religion is what man thinks about God; revelation is what God says to man – and the distinction between the two must be rigidly maintained.'[99] He further finds the Barthian emphasis upon sin morbid. Without at all denying the weight given to sin in the synoptic gospels, Cadoux feels that God's Fatherhood there takes precedence, and that 'The son's normal position is that, not of a sinner, but of a beloved child and member of the family circle; and when he sins, his sin is dealt with on that basis ... Jesus's great utterance that the Kingdom of God belonged to the childlike contradicts in my judgment any view of humanity which makes sin the *principal* item in the relation between man and God.'[100]

---

[95] C.J. Cadoux, 'Scripture and theology', 25.
[96] R.S. Franks, review of Daniel Jenkins, *The Gift of the Ministry*, 366.
[97] C.J. Cadoux, *Christian Pacifism Re-examined*, 46.
[98] Idem, *The Case for Evangelical Modernism*, 45.
[99] Ibid., 46.
[100] Ibid., 47.

More generally, 'If there is no way from man to God, why did Jesus bid men ask, seek, and knock, as the condition of receiving, finding, and having the door opened to them . . .?'[101] Cadoux further rebukes the inconsistency which he detects in the fact that on the one hand Barthians acknowledge the immanence of God, his presence in nature, and the inner witness of the Holy Spirit, whilst on the other hand they declare that God is revealed, not supremely but solely in Christ. As if all this were not enough, despite all that Barthians say about the historical character of God's revelation, they are comparatively indifferent to the historical facts of the earthly life of Jesus. The upshot is that Barthianism 'is not only paradoxical, but self-contradictory; it is needlessly dualistic, and bristles with false antitheses; it displays strong tendencies to obscurantism.'[102]

Gentler treatment of Barth flowed from other Congregational quarters. In his book, *By Faith Alone* (1943), H.F. Lovell Cocks, Principal of Western College, Bristol, showed himself sympathetically critical of Barth. His general view is that the earlier 'humanist theology is now in its decline, not so much because it has been shaken by the frontal attack of Barth and his school as for the reason that the harsh climate of our contemporary world has blighted it.'[103] He parts company with Barth most decisively in relation to the question of apologetics. He agrees that

> the best apologetic is in the end the proclamation of the Word, but is Barth wholly right in claiming that there is no room for any other? . . . We know the Gospel cannot be made acceptable to the natural man by any argument of ours, but some of his rationalizations of his refusal of grace can be exposed . . . Here natural faith, remaining discontinuous with saving faith, can yet be baptized into Christ and made to render valuable service to the cause of the Word among men . . . Not to establish saving truth but to clear away irrelevancies is the function of a legitimate Christian apologetic.[104]

This theme was resumed later by the Congregationalist Herbert Hartwell in *The Theology of Karl Barth* (1965).[105] The underlying issue concerns the point of contact between God and human beings. On this, some, Lovell Cocks among them, sought to temper Barth's disjunction with Emil

---

[101] Ibid., 48.

[102] Ibid., 54.

[103] H.F. Lovell Cocks, *By Faith Alone*, 9. For Lovell Cocks see Alan P.F. Sell, *Commemorations: Studies in Christian Thought and History*, ch. 13.

[104] Ibid., 118–9.

[105] See Herbert Hartwell, *The Theology of Karl Barth: An Introduction*, 184.

Brunner's conjunction. Querying the phrase 'point of contact' on the ground that God is in contact with us at every point, Cocks continues, 'Barth is right, surely, when he says that God must create His own point of contact with sinful man, and that we must take regeneration seriously. Yet Brunner is right when he urges that we cannot be accused of not taking regeneration seriously when we point out that it is man that is regenerated and not a stone or a fish . . . Faith is an activity of the whole man.'[106]

Though by no means uninfluenced by Barth, Hubert Cunliffe-Jones, Professor at Yorkshire United Independent College, Bradford, and subsequently at Manchester University, subjected Barth's strictures against natural theology to close attention in *The Authority of The Biblical Revelation* (1945). He first states Barth's objective: 'He is contending primarily that the God of Biblical faith is our sovereign Lord and that He remains free even in His Revelation to act towards us according to His will. God never in any way becomes an object of our mind so that we can take Him captive and bend Him to the service of our own desires.'[107] Cunliffe-Jones is the first to agree that there is an absolute claim of Christ upon us, 'but we do not honour that absolute claim by representing it as discontinuous at all points with the rest of human life.'[108] Admitting that in contrast with the light of the Christian Gospel, natural theology is 'a poor, frail, weak thing,' Cunliffe-Jones nevertheless insists that natural theology is 'the sign that man has been created in God's image and that God has mercy on man in never leaving him to be content with a godless existence.' Accordingly, 'it is the duty of Christian theology to implant a limited confidence in natural theology where none exists.'[109] In a word, Barth is 'over-emphatic in a good cause . . . The motive is a right one, but the contention is wrong. Indeed, if Jesus Christ is indeed Lord, there *must be* some natural theology . . . If man could repudiate entirely the claim of God upon him he would not be human.'[110]

---

[106] H.F. Lovell Cocks, *By Faith Alone*, 68–69.

[107] Hubert Cunliffe-Jones, *The Authority of the Biblical Revelation*, 80.

[108] Ibid., 81–82.

[109] Ibid., 82.

[110] Ibid., 83, 88. Cunliffe-Jones elsewhere regretted Barth's 'uncritical use of the penal substitutionary theory' of the atonement. This, he said, 'has been widely influential. A sign of its influence may be found in the brilliant but unconvincing insistence on penal substitution in the Christology of Wolfhart Pannenberg.' See 'The meaning of the atonement today', 119. For some pertinent observations upon Barth's tendency towards universalism and his extreme opposition to synergism, see Charles S. Duthie, 'Ultimate triumph', 202–6.

Barth's apparent denigration of human reason is what most disturbed Nonconformists of all stripes. In Robert Franks's view 'it is not enough simply to condemn reason and send it into a corner as a naughty boy, as the Barthians do. Reason has a way of coming out of the corner and behaving as an *enfant terrible*, whether we like it or not.'[111] He further predicted that

> Barth will in the end [not] be able to suppress reason. He says in his *Church Dogmatics* that there are fundamentally two types of Christian theology, the Pauline and the Apologist of the second century. Paul founded his theology on the inspiration of the Holy Spirit, the Apologists sought to equate Christianity and Logos or Reason. But in view of *Rom.* 1 and 2 it is erroneous to say that Paul did not respect reason: these chapters are the starting-point of all natural theology in the Christian Church ever since. And the Apologists began a work which is necessary if Christianity is to live and work in the world. I myself believe in a Logos theology, and think that the future of Christianity lies that way. I regard Barth as a great spellbinder, but I believe that the Church will presently free itself from the spell and return to saner ways of thought.[112]

It is hardly necessary to point out that, sixty years on, the spell has not, as yet, been broken. In some quarters, a thriving Barth industry implicitly cocks a snook at Franks. This does not, of course, prove him wrong.

Similar concerns were expressed by two Unitarian writers. In 1959, C. Gordon Bolam, noting that Barth recoils from the 'subjectivism' of liberal concepts of God, continues

> But it may be asked whether his 'objective' approach does not end in as great a difficulty where God is not merely remote but actually sundered from human communion. To speak of God breaking through to man by revelation is ultimately a counsel of despair, since revelation is subject to human interpretation and is not self-vindicating . . . The liberal is not projecting his subjectivism on to God, he responds with love to love.[113]

In the following year, Bolam's co-religionist, John Kielty, went so far as to say that Barth was, unintentionally, 'a close ally of the Communists, for he creates in masses of people a distrust of their own

---

[111] R.S. Franks, 'Trends in recent theology', 27.

[112] Ibid., 29.

[113] C.G. Bolam, 'Theological liberalism: a vindication', 135, 136.

powers and abilities.' He invokes the Orthodox theologian Nicolas Berdyaev in support: 'Karl Barth is the dehumanization of Christianity.'[114] With this level of near panic in the air, and after all the discussions of Barth to which I have alluded, it is as odd as it is strangely consoling that as late as 1955, Robert S. Paul could write an article under the heading, 'Congregationalism and Presbyterianism: X. Theological trends' without once mentioning Karl Barth.[115]

The Barthian theology found its way into Wales. Prominent among its pioneers there was the Congregationalist J.D. Vernon Lewis. Another was J.E. Daniel, who pitted Barth against the theological liberalism of D. Miall Edwards.[116] But few Welsh theologians were as acute in their critique of Barth as the Presbyterian Huw Parri Owen, Professor of Christian Doctrine at King's College, London. In 1971 he published *Concepts of Deity*. In his section on Barth he welcomes the way in which 'Barth consistently unites the idea of God as Being with the idea of him as personal; . . . maintains a true balance between the ideas of transcendence and immanence; . . . [reconciles] belief in God's creative love with belief in God's *aseitas*; . . . [and] Although Barth holds that we can know God only through Christian revelation, he makes a sustained attempt to articulate this knowledge in rational terms.'[117] But among a number of characteristically crisp negative comments is one in which Owen claims against Barth that even if it is true that Christianity differs in kind, not only in degree, from all other religions, and that a *saving* knowledge of God can occur only through Christ, these positions 'do not entail the view that all non-Christian concepts of God are totally false' – indeed many resemblances between Christian and non-Christian concepts of deity can be traced.[118] To Barth's underlying presuppositions (a) that if non-Christians cannot prove God's existence and have full knowledge of him they are idolatrous; and (b) that the doctrine of original sin entails total ignorance of God, Owen objects that one may hold that non-Christians 'possess a (logically) non-probative and partial knowledge of God,' and that all the doctrine of original sin entails is 'that apart

---

[114] J. Kielty, *British Unitarianism, Past, Present and Future*, 38, 39.

[115] See Robert S. Paul, 'Congregationalism and Presbyterianism: X. Theological trends', 2.

[116] See further, R. Tudur Jones, *Congregationalism in Wales*, 239–40; D. Densil Morgan, 'The early reception of Karl Barth's theology in Britain: A supplementary view', 504–27.

[117] H.P. Owen, *Concepts of Deity*, 104–5.

[118] Ibid., 107.

from Christ no man can have a perfect knowledge of God's nature or render *perfect* obedience to God's will.'[119]

Despite all the hesitations, the Barthian leaven worked its way into a number of Nonconformist pamphlets and articles, but few Nonconformists in the second half of the twentieth century showed themselves as indebted to it as the United Reformed minister Colin E. Gunton, Professor at King's College, London. Like his Nonconformist predecessors, he learned from Barth, but he was not a clone of Barth. Whereas in his early work, *Becoming and Being*, he contrasted Charles Hartshorne's process theology unfavourably with that of Barth, he subsequently tempered his Barthian zeal as influences as various as those of Coleridge, John Owen, John Zizioulas and Michael Polanyi worked upon him. I shall return to his Hartshorne-Barth book shortly, but for the present I note the modification of his position in his own words. In the preface to his *Theology Through the Theologians* (1996) Gunton writes, 'I have over the years attained a measure of distance from Barth's theology', a claim which is borne out in the ensuing essays; and in the preface to the second edition of *The Promise of Trinitarian Theology* (1997) he refers to his discussion in *Becoming and Being* of the logic of Barth's move from revelation to eternal God, and comments, 'I now believe that [Barth] failed to give adequate account of the distinction of the persons'[120] of the Trinity: a remark which suggests the increasing influence of a particular reading of the Cappadocian fathers upon Gunton's thought.

The upshot is that while some Nonconformist theologians – Scott Lidgett, Cadoux and Franks among them – were convinced that Barth's method was faulty, others were more sympathetic to his work. Even these, however, did not for the most part swallow him whole: Lovell Cocks and Cunliffe-Jones, for example, found Barth's opposition to natural theology too drastic, while Gunton became progressively dissatisfied with Barth at certain doctrinal points. F.W. Camfield, a student under Forsyth and later a DD of London University, came nearest to being a dyed-in-the-wool Barthian, but he became an Anglican. W.A. Whitehouse, on whom Barth was a formative influence, was one of the United Reformed Church's most respected theologians, but he did not write at length on Barth.

---

[119] Ibid.

[120] Colin E. Gunton, *The Promise of Trinitarian Theology*, xxv n.29. The reference is to *Becoming and Being: The Doctrine of God in Charles Hartshorne and Karl Barth*, 127–30.

VII

The 1960s, with their swinging theologies – J.A.T. Robinson's *Honest to God*, Harvey Cox's *The Secular City*, and the disparate offerings of the Death of God theologians (some of them erstwhile Barthians) – did little to prompt Nonconformist theologians to enter these lists – though the Methodist philosopher of religion, David A. Pailin, in *A New Theology?* (1964) contributed an account of the philosophical tributaries from Kant and Schleiermacher onwards which flowed into *Honest to God*, and the Baptist Keith Clements later provided an account of the debate surrounding that book in *Lovers of Discord* (1988). The Congregationalist Erik Routley wrote a jubilant review of Robinson's manifesto, which he soon said would have been more cautious had he read the *Observer* article published under the sensational title, 'Our image of God must go' before putting pen to paper;[121] and the Methodist Gordon Rupp, esteemed by many for his Luther scholarship, wryly remarked

> The Bishop of Woolwich sees a parallel between himself and Martin Luther, whose 95 Theses were also caught up in a publicity explosion. I wish him well. He has now only to be unfrocked, tried and condemned for high treason, to write four of the world's classics, to translate the Bible and compose a hymn book, and to write some 100 folio volumes which 400 years hence will concern scholars all over the world, and to become the spiritual father of some thousands of millions of Christians – to qualify as the Martin Luther of a New Reformation.[122]

For his part Rupp's fellow Methodist, C. Leslie Mitton, urged a balanced response to Robinson's tract.[123] But Routley and Rupp were primarily historians and Mitton was a New Testament scholar. In terms of book-length responses the theologians were largely silent, though in his Swarthmore Lecture of 1969 Maurice Creasey spoke lucidly and with reference to his own tradition in *Bearings, or Friends and the New Reformation* (1969). Perhaps the majority of Nonconformist systematicians endorsed the view expressed long before by E.R. Conder, 'the weathercock of fashion does but show which way the wind blows, not which way the world

---

[121] See *The British Weekly*, 21 March and 16 May 1963.

[122] E. Gordon Rupp, *The Old Reformation and the New*, 51.

[123] See C.L. Mitton, 'Honest to God', 276–9.

is moving. The real pioneers of progress are not always in the foremost ranks of change.'[124] But if that were their conclusion, one could wish that more of them had attempted to adjust the weathercock. It is not, of course, denied that some Nonconformist theologians paid considerable attention to Bonhoeffer and Tillich, on some of whose insights Robinson drew.[125] As for the secularization debate, the Presbyterian J.E. Lesslie Newbigin stands almost alone among Nonconformists with his popular discussion of the secularization theme: *Honest Religion for Secular Man* (1966).

VIII

The writings of the process philosophers and theologians have engaged the attention of some Nonconformists. As already mentioned, in an early work Colin Gunton took the prominent American process thinker, Charles Hartshorne to task. Gunton argues that 'In Hartshorne's theology we have a system of axioms, and both proof and concept follow logically from the basic insight that reality can be understood panpsychically as interrelated process, with God playing the parts of the supreme instance of process and at the same time the supreme explanatory factor in a rationalist system.'[126] He contends that the adoption of this system is in the nature of an act of faith, and that it places God under the control of cosmic forces which remove from him that genuine freedom which is God's by right. Hence we see clearly that 'the theology that wishes to stand on the intellectual feet of a philosophy is likely to remain a cripple.'[127] Those who acquiesce in such an arrangement as this make language concerning the incarnation, for example, merely a pictorial expression of truth the philosopher can more adequately frame in other terms.

The Methodist David A. Pailin, whose teaching career was spent at the University of Manchester, has, in a number of writings, shown himself to be much more sympathetic to process thought. He is not, however, uncritical of some aspects of it. For example, he queries Hartshorne's panpsychism, and observes that on some of his own concerns the process thinkers shed little light. He does, however,

---

[124] E.R. Conder, 'The decay of theology,' 67.

[125] See, for example, Daniel T. Jenkins, *Beyond Religion*; J. Heywood-Thomas, *Paul Tillich: An Appraisal*.

[126] C.E. Gunton, *Becoming and Being*, 216.

[127] Ibid., 222.

make much of the need for rational coherence, whilst recognizing that from the fact that a theory is coherent it does not necessarily follow that it accords with reality. He seeks 'a form of theological understanding that makes sense of the world in terms of God, where "God" is defined as the personally purposive ultimate being, rationality and value.'[128] It is not fanciful to suppose that Gunton would have regarded any resulting theology, so beholden to a particular philosophical approach, as crippled. In which case we should have had a fine case of theological tit-for-tat, since Pailin is inclined to slay foes – including Gunton, H.P. Owen and the entire brood of Barthians – without always according them adequate hearing.[129]

IX

Towards the end of the 1970s Christological questions came to the fore with the publication of *The Myth of God Incarnate* (1977). The general thrust of this collection of papers is that incarnational language is a mythological or poetic way of speaking of Jesus's significance for us. The Nonconformist contributors are John Hick and the Methodist Frances Young. In a follow-up volume, *Incarnation and Myth: The Debate Continued* (1979) they are joined by Lesslie Newbigin and the New Testament scholar, Graham Stanton, of the United Reformed Church. A further minister of the same church, Robert Crawford, published *The Saga of God Incarnate*, the revised edition of which appeared in 1987. More than one of the Nonconformist critics, while appreciative of the sensitivity of the 'mythographers' to those of other faiths, and fully aware of the 'scandal of particularity', nevertheless asked how far it is viable to dissociate incarnation from atonement in the way that their colleagues seemed to be doing.[130]

---

[128] David A. Pailin, *Probing the Foundations: A Study in Theistic Reconstruction*, 10. See also his earlier work, *God and the Processes of Reality: Foundations of a Credible Theism*.

[129] This, at least, is what I have presumed to say in a review of Pailin's *Probing the Foundations* in *Calvin Theological Journal*, XXXIII no. 1, April 1998, 215.

[130] I may perhaps mention that after the dust had settled I was myself emboldened to make a few remarks along this line in *Aspects of Christian Integrity*, 42–45.

X

In more recent years Newbigin entered into a missionary versus scholar debate with his fellow churchman John Hick over the question of the heart of the gospel in relation to religious pluralism. It is not the case that no earlier Nonconformist theologians had reflected upon the relations between Christianity and other faiths, but many of them had done so with the assumptions of Christendom in their minds, and under the inspiration of a post-Hegelian idealism which encouraged them to think of truth as one, of all religions having some glimpse of it, and of Christian truth as that to which all others pointed with greater or lesser degrees of clarity. Such, in brief, was the approach of A.M. Fairbairn, Mansfield College's first Principal, among others. A change of key is noticeable in twelve small pages in *What shall we say of Christ?*, published in 1932 by Sydney Cave, then President of Cheshunt College and subsequently Principal of New College London, who had served for ten years in India, and who had already published *Redemption, Hindu and Christian* (1919) and *Christianity and some Living Religions of the East* (1929).[131] Eschewing the condemnation by Christians of other faiths, Cave finds the decisive difference between them in the character of the god or gods they worship. He points out that the apparent modesty of the view that each race has the religion best suited to its needs can be a cover for racial superiority, but recognizes that serious thinkers also entertain the view that Christianity can no longer accord a unique place to Christ. He answers, 'It is not arrogance or ignorance which impels us to give to Christ a unique place. It is the conviction, born of faith and confirmed by knowledge, that in Him and Him alone has the character of God been fully manifested.'[132] Eleven years later, Hubert Cunliffe-Jones was even blunter: 'Whatever use God makes of the world's religions, in the last resort their witness to the nature of God is false, while the witness of the Bible to Jesus Christ is true.'[133]

In 1954 John Hick's (and Newbigin's) own teacher, the Presbyterian H.H. Farmer, made no bones about stating his assumptions thus: first,

---

[131] The former work is Cave's London DD thesis. He declined the opportunity of study in one of the ancient universities in order to sit under P.T. Forsyth at Hackney College. He was not the last Nonconformist to decline Oxbridge – a choice inexplicable to some, at least in England.

[132] Sydney Cave, *What Shall We Say of Christ?*, 222–3.

[133] H. Cunliffe-Jones, *The Holy Spirit*, 21. We may also note that in his apologetic work of 1932, *The Christian Belief in God in Relation to Religion and*

'God has made a unique and final revelation of Himself as personal in history through Jesus Christ and through the personal relationship to Himself which that revelation makes possible and calls into being.'[134] Secondly, there is a common defining essence underlying all genuinely religious phenomena. Thirdly, the Christian view of the living essence of religion is determined by what Christians believe to be 'God's self-disclosure in the Incarnation and in particular by His disclosure therein of His personal nature and His personal purpose towards man.'[135] Fourthly, 'whenever religion arises with some degree of spontaneous, creative, living power, it does so because at that point ultimate reality is disclosing itself as personal to man.'[136]

In a number of works[137] Hick has taken with the utmost seriousness the reality of multi-faith societies and the difficulties posed when religious believers make exclusive truth claims for their own religion – in particular, the claim that it is the only way of salvation. Can it be, he asks, that God has created millions of people whom he knows will forfeit salvation, often as a result of the accident of having been born in areas where *the* alleged truth is not known, or is not widely acknowledged? Deeming such a possibility objectionable, Hick turns towards a pluralistic solution. He builds upon a distinction (whose philosophical father is Kant) between the Real in itself and the Real as conceived and experienced by human beings; and he proposes that the truth claims of the several religions do not really conflict because they are claims about the way the Real is diversely manifested and experienced. This proposal constitutes what he calls his Copernican revolution in theology, a revolution which entails that we 'shift from the dogma that Christianity is at the centre to the realisation that it is God who is at the centre, and that all the religions of mankind, including our own, serve and revolve round him.'[138] He recognizes that the price of this hypothesis (his word) is the forfeiture on the part of all

---

Philosophy, A.E. Garvie had in mind throughout 'two dangers which the Christian theologian must avoid: (1) the isolation of Christianity from all other religions, and (2) the isolation of religion from the other interests and activities of human personality', p. 25.

[134] H.H. Farmer, *Revelation and Religion*, 23.

[135] Ibid., 27.

[136] Ibid., 28. See further, Christopher H. Partridge, *H.H. Farmer's Theological Interpretation of Religion: Towards a Personalist Theory of Religions.*

[137] See John H. Hick, *God and the Universe of Faiths; God has Many Names; Problems of Religious Pluralism; An Interpretation of Religion.*

[138] John H. Hick, *God and the Universe of Faiths*, 131.

religions of absolute truth claims; and that the standing challenge to his proposal is that it does not accord with the way in which the several religions perceive themselves, and is thus more of a recommendation that perceptions should change than a description of the intellectual or convictional status quo among the religions.

For his part, Newbigin understands the motivation which urges people to seek a basis of unity among the world's religions, but he repudiates Hick's approach, just managing, one feels, to stop short of using the word 'arrogant' to describe it. He writes

> What claims to be a model for the unity of all religions turns out in fact to be the claim that one theologian's conception of God is the reality which is the central essence of all religions. This is the trap into which every program for the unity of the religions is bound to fall. There is no real encounter. Hick's conception of God simply is the truth and there is no possibility that one of the world's religions can challenge it.[139]

Whereas the Christian's 'basic commitment is to a historic person and to historic deeds,' Newbigin continues, 'The other stance takes as its point of reference Transcendent Being.'[140] In this idealistic construction Hick places his faith, and no Christian can enter into dialogue with those who first propose that they surrender their own commitment to Jesus Christ for that of the idealist.

It cannot be said that other Nonconformist theologians have addressed this matter with the same amount of publicity as Hick and Newbigin (though it may be said that the criticisms of Hick levelled by H.P. Owen are more incisive than those of Newbigin[141]); but it reflects a certain credit upon the United Reformed Church that from its ranks have come two very different writers who have between them so clearly set the terms of what shall surely be one of the critical theological debates of the twenty-first century.

XI

As I conclude this bird's-eye-view of the landscape of Protestant Nonconformist theology in the twentieth-century I would simply remark that to date *ordained* Nonconformist theologians (I speak

---

[139] L. Newbigin, *The Open Secret*, 184–5.

[140] Ibid., 187.

[141] See the appendix to Owen's *Christian Theism. A Study in its Basic Principles.*

cautiously because since the laicizing of theology there may be theologians of whose denominational allegiance I am unaware) have not notably been inspired to publish book-length contributions to, or studies of, feminist versions of theology,[142] or to immerse themselves in the several theologies of liberation;[143] and it would be a gross exaggeration to say that any of them has been a significant proponent, or critic, of postmodern views.[144] What they have done is to offer studies, manifesting differing degrees of depth and a diversity of conclusions, of major Christian doctrines, and to some of these I now turn.

---

[142] I have referred to some aspects of feminism in *Enlightenment, Ecumenism, Evangel*, 288–9, 365–73. There does exist a *Feminist Theology Report* commissioned (in the 1980s?) by the Unitarian General Assembly. Arthur Long points out, however, that 'most of the material was taken from non-Unitarian sources – a sober reminder that Unitarians are not always as radical as they think they are.' See his paper, 'Unitarian thought in the twentieth century: a preliminary survey. Part 2', 458. Long notes that Ann Peart and Joy Croft were the main Unitarian contributors to the document. Peart has also written on female Unitarians in George Chryssides, ed., *Unitarian Perspectives on Contemporary Religious Thought*. Long himself hopes that 'all Unitarians now agree that we must not think of God wholly in masculine terms. But I also hope . . . that we will resist the suggestion that God has to be interpreted wholly in feminine terms. Nowadays, we must surely acknowledge that there is nothing wrong with calling God our "Heavenly Mother" – however strange that may still seem to some of us.' See his pamphlet, *Current Trends in British Unitarianism*, 28.

[143] For some brief reflections on liberation theology see Alan P.F. Sell, *Enlightenment, Ecumenism, Evangel*, 307–25.

[144] I could not avoid this subject in my work on Christian apologetic method. See, *Confessing and Commending the Faith: Historic Witness and Apologetic Method*, 132–48, 413–9, and *passim*.

Lecture 2

Doctrinal Peaks

The peaks in question are the doctrines of the person and work of Christ, the Holy Spirit and the Trinity.[1]

I

Near the beginning of the previous lecture I noted David Worthington Simon's lament at the sorry condition into which systematic theology had fallen. He did more than lament, however. Successively Principal of the Congregational colleges at Spring Hill, Birmingham, Edinburgh and Bradford, Simon published two sizeable works on soteriology. In the first, *The Redemption of Man* (1889), whilst rejoicing in the experienced fact of sins forgiven, he seeks an adequate account of the nature of forgiveness; in the second, *Reconciliation by Incarnation* (1898), he attempts to elucidate the manner by which forgiveness was achieved. Simon holds that in the most important sense God and man are already reconciled by the Cross: Jesus has finished his work. But the need to restore human beings is a continuing one, and the full realization of the kingdom of God is yet to be. He takes the fact of sin seriously, and does not balk at speaking of God's anger on account of it. Sin, he argues, does not adversely affect human beings only: God, construed as fully personal, suffers also. Christ bears God's wrath, but is not himself punished for our sins.

Simon does not rest with the personal relations of individuals only. There is a cosmic dimension to his thought which on the one hand is

---

[1] I am fully aware that this order may be queried. My own view is that the Trinity is the foundation and the climax of Christian theology. It is not, however, historically or in terms of the Christian's experience, the first to be articulated. For this reason, and also because of the revival of interest in the doctrine in the second half of our period, I place it where I do.

couched in Trinitarian terms, for 'Neither the "moral" nor the forensic view of the Atonement has any serious rational basis unless Christ be an incarnate Person of the Trinity';[2] and on the other, entails the working out of an undergirding cosmology designed to relate the Christian revelation to human history and the natural order as these are understood by historians and scientists. He writes that

> A cosmology is needed which shall do justice, alike to the facts which the science of nature has brought to light and established, on the one hand, and to the facts which may in general be designated spiritual on the other – a cosmology, in other words, among whose great moments shall be creation and evolution, freedom and conscience. The rectification of the relations of God and man, of man and God, and of man and nature, wrought out by the Logos or Word of God, in that, through the power of the Holy Spirit, He became incarnate, taught, lived, died, rose again from the dead and ascended on high, presupposes a specific origin, constitution and evolution of the cosmos in general, and of the earth in particular. Apart from a true rationale of the rise of the world there can be no true rationale of the redemption of the world. Given one cosmology, and redemption in the Christian sense – that is redemption in any sense – must seem from beginning to end irrational; given another cosmology, and a faith quickened and illumined intellect, its reasonableness will become increasingly evident.[3]

Some, including Robert Mackintosh, who adorned Lancashire Independent College – Simon's *alma mater* – with deep learning and dry wit for over thirty years, felt that Simon's underlying realistic philosophy which gave rise to his atonement-explaining personal relations as 'necessary biological effects, partly in the Divine and partly in the human constitution' prevented Simon from giving due place to ethical considerations.[4] As to Simon's style – and Mackintosh's: 'Simon . . . is a shirt-sleeved and carpet-slippered philosopher. Perhaps like others he derived from Germany a preference for shapelessness over that formal neatness which so often accompanies shallow thinking. But good style need not imply slack thought, and it is a great pity when form and substance are badly matched.'[5]

---

[2] D.W. Simon, *Reconciliation by Incarnation*, viii. For Simon see F.J. Powicke, *David Worthington Simon*.

[3] Ibid., 8–9.

[4] See Robert Mackintosh, *Historic Theories of Atonement*, 277.

[5] Ibid., 274.

In a lengthy paper published in 1897 the Principal of New College, London, R. Vaughan Pryce, expressed his deep concern that the penal substitutionary theory of the atonement had been expressed in such a way as to yield morally unworthy ideas of God: for example, that the wrathful God cannot restore the sinner until he has punished the innocent Son. With this has been coupled a 'highly artificial doctrine of imputed righteousness . . .'[6] Equally disturbing is the view that the only redemption required is 'redemption from ignorance, which is effected by knowledge, and not redemption from sin by any costly process of mediation.'[7] Pryce reviews the New Testament teaching on the necessity of Christ's death, and concludes that Christ

> died in order that the forgiveness of sins might be possible. He died in order that the flow of the life of God into the human soul might be possible. He died in order that evil might be vanquished ... The reader will not fail to observe the absence of certain ideas which have found a place in some modern systems of theology. There is nothing here about appeasing the anger of God. There is nothing here about the satisfying of an exacting creditor who will be paid to the uttermost farthing.[8]

Pryce next turns to such terms as propitiation, expiation, reconciliation and covenant. He finds that, 'As the Representative of the race, as the Prince of salvation, as the second Head of humanity, [Christ] fulfils the condition we could not fulfil, and at once pledges us, and enables all who believe in Him . . . to do what God's will requires.'[9] The incarnation does not mean that Christ became a man, but that he became the man – the Second Adam; and we are incorporated into him. The curse of the law (Gal. 3: 13) rests upon us because of sin, and from this curse Christ delivers us, 'Not by His becoming accurst of God in our place and stead, as some have dared to say, but by His dying as our Representative, Sponsor Surety, in the covenant of grace; by His so identifying Himself with us that He might "die unto sin once for all" for us. Here is the vicariousness of His death.'[10]

Pryce briefly traces the history of the doctrine of the atonement from Augustine down to the distortions which he is anxious to repudiate. He concludes that no doctrine of Christ's work is

---

[6] R. Vaughan Pryce, 'The redemptive work of the Lord Jesus Christ', 193.
[7] Ibid., 194.
[8] Ibid., 205.
[9] Ibid., 210.
[10] Ibid., 216.

acceptable which obscures its moral purpose: 'Its aim is to produce holiness.'[11]

The Methodist John Scott Lidgett published his substantial Fernley Lecture on *The Spiritual Principle of the Atonement* in 1897. He clearly states his objective thus: 'Our search will . . . be for the spiritual principle of the Atonement, considered as a satisfaction offered to God of the sins of the world.'[12] He reviews the biblical evidence, discusses a number of prominent earlier theories and, as we might by now expect, he sets his own contribution in the context of the Fatherhood of God. It is the Son who dies, and he dies for human beings who are the Father's rebellious children. Thus are sinners forgiven and adopted as sons; reconciliation with the Father is effected by our Head and Representative. By faith, which is at once God's gift and the 'supreme spiritual and moral act of which men are capable',[13] the death of Christ becomes our sacrifice: 'That which Christ uttered to God in His death, we by faith utter in Him . . .'[14] In a concluding chapter Scott Lidgett asks what bearing the atonement has upon the problems of social redemption and progress. He answers (as we might nowadays think, too optimistically): 'The fuller realisation of the filial spirit will have its immediate effect upon political, social, and economic interests, ordering them into growing conformity to the mind of Christ.'[15]

II

As the twentieth century opened, a collection of 18 articles originally contributed to *The Christian World* – nine of them by Congregationalists – was published. Two are of particular interest to us. W.F. Adeney, then Professor of New Testament Exegesis, History and Criticism at New College, London, and shortly to become Principal of Lancashire Independent College, fastened upon the distinction drawn by many, then as now, between fact and theory. In his sights are those, not least preachers, who suppose that they can appeal to the fact of the Cross in a manner devoid of theory. As Adeney says, 'The word "fact" has a tempting sound for the Englishman of Philistine proclivities.' He further explains that 'The life and death of the Saviour we take to be facts; the recovery of men and women from lives of shame and folly

---

[11] Ibid., 226.
[12] J.S. Lidgett, *The Spiritual Principle of the Atonement*, 9.
[13] Ibid., 408.
[14] Ibid., 407.
[15] Ibid., 415.

as far as this can be observed may also be set down to the category of facts. But the connection between these two series traverses a vast expanse of theory.'[16] Putting then current themes into perspective, he writes

> The history of the Church shows that in all ages the winning power of the Gospel has gone with a passionate preaching of redemption through the Cross of Christ. The Fatherhood of God, the Brotherhood of Jesus, the ethics of the Sermon on the Mount, our Lord's magnificent conception of the kingdom of heaven – great truths that have come to the front in our own day, and for the clearer vision of which we may well be thankful – have none of them evinced the missionary energy, the evangelising efficacy, that have been found to accompany the preaching of salvation through the Cross. We are told to look at facts. This is a fact, the significance of which cannot be gainsaid.[17]

Adeney proceeds to argue that the subjective aspect of the atonement – what is done for us – is properly understood only when viewed in the context of faith in the prior objective efficacy of Christ's saving work. Christ's obedience unto death was, according to Paul and Hebrews, of supreme value in the sight of God. The value of this to us, according to Paul, is that faith in Christ is union with him, and the work of Christ for us is never to be dissociated from the work of Christ within us.

Elsewhere Adeney discusses the end and object of redemption and the method and process of atonement by which the objective is attained. His first question is, 'From what did Christ come to redeem the world, and what supreme good did He thereby accomplish for the benefit of mankind?'[18] It is generally agreed, he continues, that since sin has undone the human race, it is from sin that we need to be redeemed. But there is more than one way of articulating the nature of the required deliverance. Is it, as in the writings of George Payne, Thomas Chalmers and others, a matter of the criminal's escape from just punishment? It came gradually to be seen that deliverance was needed not so much from punishment as from sin itself, and this has shifted the centre of gravity of atonement theology. It was further seen that there can be no punishment which is not attached to guilt; yet Christ was sinless, so how could he bear the punishment due to

---

[16] *The Atonement in Modern Religious Thought*, 144.

[17] Ibid., 146–7.

[18] Walter F. Adeney, *A Century's Progress in Religious Life and Thought*, 137.

us? A halfway house was reached by Payne when he contended that Christ was treated as if he were guilty, so that we could be treated as if we were innocent; but this provided no lasting resting-place for the doctrine. Now, under the influence of the idea of the Fatherhood of God it is understood that forgiveness does not follow the atonement as a reward purchased by Christ; on the contrary, the very provision of the atonement witnesses to God's forgiving love. God is not 'an implacable Being who required to be appeased by the blood of His innocent Son before He would consent to forgive a guilty world.'[19] Further, the Cross is now viewed not 'in solitary grandeur, but taken as the completion and consummation of a life-work.'[20]

The other symposium contribution to which I would draw attention is that by P.T. Forsyth. He sets out from the strong conviction that there will be no revival of religion unless there is a revival of personal faith in, and experience of, justification. The central revelation is concentrated in an atonement which has to do with sin and guilt. For this reason, 'The Church must always adjust its compass at the Cross.'[21] He proceeds to make a number of negative and positive points. Negatively, (*pace* Simon, for example), we have outgrown the idea that God has to be reconciled to us; that redemption costs the Father nothing; and that Christ took our punishment in a quantitative sense. 'We are only just escaping from the modern and sentimental idea of love which found no difficulty placed by the holy law of God's nature in His way of forgiveness,'[22] he continues; and we have outgrown the notion that God could not be forgiving until appeased by the blood of Christ. Gone is the idea that Christ made satisfaction to God's wounded honour or punitive justice: obedience rather than suffering rendered the needed satisfaction. We have learned not to separate Christ's obedient life from his expiatory death, and both modern scholarship and conscience advise us that Paul teaches that we are declared just, not made just. We know that we cannot have the fact of the atonement without a theory of it, and we further know that any such theory cannot be based on personal experience alone. Finally, we can no longer subscribe to the view that expiation and forgiveness are mutually exclusive ideas.

Positively, the Christian revelation concerns what Christ effected and not simply what he taught. We have a redemption which both

---

[19] Ibid., 142.

[20] Ibid., 144.

[21] P.T. Forsyth, *The Atonement in Modern Religious Thought*, 62.

[22] Ibid., 66.

judges and destroys sin and produces repentance in human beings: 'Love's awful moving cost in satisfying the broken law and maintaining its holy and inviolable honour, is the only means of producing such a sense of guilt as God can forgive.'[23] To put it otherwise, 'Salvation must be salvation not *from* judgment, but *by* judgment. Christ did not simply pronounce judgment, but effected it.'[24] Amendment on our part is not sufficient; any reparation must be made by God himself. Thus, 'The sacrifice flows from grace, and does not produce grace.'[25] As to the nature of the sacrifice, 'The principle of a vicarious Atonement is bound up with the very idea of Revelation, of love emerging into guilt. There is an atoning substitution and a penal; but a penitential there is not.'[26] Christ suffered because of our sin; but he did not undergo substitutionary punishment.

Forsyth elaborated upon the ideas here briefly expressed in many of his lectures and addresses – supremely in those gathered in *The Cruciality of the Cross* (1909) and in *The Work of Christ* (1910). Underlying all is his conviction concerning the nature of God's love as holy: 'To bring *sin* home, and *grace* home, then the *Holy* must be brought home. But that . . . can be done, on the scale of the Church and the world, only by replacing the *cross* at the centre of Christian faith and life, as an atonement not indeed to outraged dignity, not to talionic justice, but to this holy love.'[27] In all of this we see, 'not human nature offering its very best to God. It was God offering His very best to man.'[28] In other words, 'The real objectivity of the atonement is not that it was made to God, but by God.'[29] Moreover, Christ's work is of cosmic proportions: it involves the race.

At a time when many theologians – especially Anglican ones – were elevating the incarnation, Forsyth stood forth as *the* theologian of the Cross. The principle of atoning forgiveness was central for him for it created the Church. By contrast, the doctrine of the incarnation grew up very quickly within the Church: 'The doctrine of the incarnation grew upon the Church out of its experience of Atonement. The Church was forced to the deity of Christ to account for its redeemed

---

[23] Ibid., 78.

[24] Ibid., 81.

[25] Ibid., 82.

[26] Ibid., 84.

[27] Idem, *The Cruciality of the Cross*, 24.

[28] Idem, *The Work of Christ*, 24.

[29] Ibid., 92; cf. 99.

existence in Christ.'[30] But this strong emphasis upon the atonement in no way prevented his writing what some have regarded as his greatest work, *The Person and Place of Jesus Christ* (1909). Here, amongst much else that is of interest, he makes a sustained plea that we take the whole Christ of the New Testament: 'It is the whole Biblical Christ that is the truly and deeply historic Christ.'[31] There is no atonement in the teaching of Jesus – the Cross had yet to come. But the Cross having come, we see something of God's purpose in Christ, and to this the rest of the New Testament witnesses. We learn that 'With the person of Jesus comes a new religion, of which he is the object, and not simply the subject as its saint or sage.'[32] At the heart of the doctrine of the incarnation is the experience of the historic Christ. In this Christ 'we have the whole of God, but not everything about God, the whole heart of God but not the whole range of God.'[33] But this Christ was also pre-existent; his incarnation entailed a *kenosis*; and in humbling himself Christ realized himself (*plerosis*). Sensitively though he expounded his Christology, Forsyth never forgot that 'The mighty thing in Christ is his grace and not His constitution . . .'[34] Again, 'The knowledge of Christ is to know his benefits, taste his salvation, and experience his grace; it is not, as the academic people say, to reflect upon his natures and the modes of his incarnation.'[35] Not that this thought entirely inhibited Forsyth's authorial practice, as the book under discussion makes plain. Indeed, his conclusion contains the following affirmation:

> What we have in Christ, therefore, is more than the co-existence of two natures, or even their interpenetration. We have within this single increate person the mutual involution of the two personal acts or movements supreme in spiritual being, the one distinctive of man, the other distinctive of God; the one actively productive from the side of Eternal God, the other actively receptive from the side of growing man; the one being the pointing, in a corporeal person, of God's long action in entering history, the other the pointing of man's moral growth in the growing appropriation by Jesus of his divine content as he becomes a fuller organ for God's full action on man. The two supreme movements

---

[30] Idem, *The Cruciality of the Cross*, 50 n.
[31] Idem, *The Person and Place of Jesus Christ*, 169.
[32] Ibid., 114.
[33] Ibid., 257.
[34] Ibid., 10.
[35] Ibid., 221.

of spiritual being, redemption and religion, are revealed as being so personal that they can take harmonious, complete, and final effect within one historic person, increate but corporeal.[36]

Something of the range of Christological thought within Nonconformity will become clear if we place a Unitarian principal alongside Forsyth. In 1902 James Drummond of Manchester College, Oxford, offered some *Thoughts on Christology* in his Essex Hall Lecture. Drummond finds that some 'stand stiffly by the ecclesiastical dogma of the Incarnation, or the hypostatic union of two natures in one person through the miraculous birth of the God-man from the Virgin, with the resulting *perichoresis* and *communicatio idiomatum*,'[37] while others regard Jesus as the random product of physical evolution and deny all forms of Christology. Neither approach satisfies Drummond, but nor does a simple appeal to the Bible, which can no longer be regarded as infallible. His appeal therefore is to the Christian consciousness – a phrase 'which serves to express the peculiar form and quality of the religious spirit which is produced by Christianity.'[38]

Drummond argues that whereas subjective religious experience provides an insecure basis for proving the reality of a far-distant historical fact, there is a unity of spirit among Christians which transcends the centuries. The earliest experience of Jesus was as a teacher, a prophet; and he himself felt that he had a divine message to proclaim. What he taught, and what he was, go together in the ordinary Christian consciousness. To such a consciousness the slogan 'Christianity without Christ' is deemed inadequate. We have the sense of a permanent relation to Jesus. He 'is not so much a model, which we are to look at and copy, as a spirit of life which may diffuse itself, like a purifying atmosphere, through every variety of human vocation . . . Christ alone is the

---

[36] Ibid., 333–4.

[37] J. Drummond, *Some Thoughts on Christology*. Drummond had earlier published his Hibbert Lectures, *Via, Veritas, Vita*. He returned to the theme more fully in his *Studies in Christian Doctrine*, 252–316. See also the Christological remarks of S.H. Mellone of The Unitarian College, Manchester, in his *Converging Lines of Religious Thought*. In 1925 Mellone contributed a paper entitled, 'Unitarian Christianity in the 20th Century' to J. Estlin Carpenter, ed., *Freedom and Truth: Modern Views of Unitarian Christianity*, in which he branded 'Incarnation' an 'awkward Latinism not used by the Greek Fathers', and had recourse to Justin Martyr's notion of the *logos spermatikos*.

[38] J. Drummond, *Some Thoughts on Christology*, 14.

universal spirit to whom all Christians look, and whose life, whether dimly or clearly recognized, pulsates through the whole body, transforming and sanctifying men according to the measure of their faith.'[39] 'Christ,' he continues, 'has brought the love of God closer to human consciousness, and changed into a living sense of personal communion that large and vague belief with which men endeavoured to look into the infinite abyss of being . . .'[40] All of this is grounded in the fact that 'Jesus was a man in the full and complete sense of that word.'[41] Many call him Lord in the sense that he is the pre-eminent leader, the one by whose spirit alone society may be redeemed. Jesus may also be designated *the* Son of God for he founded the spiritual brotherhood of the sons of God. While the pre-existence of Jesus is not taught in even the most orthodox creed, he is not simply an earthly man, for 'The Spirit which was manifested in him was "the eternal Life," which weaves together the ages, which has ever dwelt in holy souls . . .'[42]

Whatever a Forsyth, or a son of Forsyth, might think of the anthropological and soteriological lacunae in Drummond's statement, his conclusion is beautifully written and, more to the point, is pastorally and devotionally suggestive.

> Everyone who believes and loves *has* this eternal life. But most of us walk in shadows, and are strangely blind to the mystery of our own being. We too have come from God, we know not how; we too, when our time arrives, must go to God; and meanwhile, as we move between two eternities, we must love unto the end; for he that loves abides already in God, and God in him. When these things are dim, and the earthly element in us threatens to swallow up the Divine, we turn in faith to the creative and illuminating soul who has been to us as the bread and water of life, and the peace of God steals gently into our hearts, and we feel once more that God is always nigh to man in order that man may draw nigh to him, and rest for ever in his love.[43]

In 1903 T. Vincent Tymms, Principal of Rawdon Baptist College, Leeds, delivered the Angus Lectures at Regent's Park College, then

---

[39] Ibid., 33, 35.

[40] Ibid., 39.

[41] Ibid., 43.

[42] Ibid., 56.

[43] Ibid., 57. For more recent, brief, exercises in Unitarian Christology (albeit some contributors have subsequently departed from that fold) see the symposium *Concerning Jesus*, edited by D.G. Wigmore-Beddoes.

in London. These were published in the following year under the title *The Christian Idea of Atonement*. Seeking to set matters in perspective, he points out that Christianity provides for more than salvation: 'Its most characteristic note is discipleship.' Accordingly, 'We are well assured that none will perish because of crude thinking, but the power of the Church to propagate her faith is largely dependent on her power to commend the great truths of the Gospel to the understanding as well as to the hearts of men.'[44] This work of commendation is made more difficult than it need be by crude thinking – above all by crude thinking about the atonement. Tymms therefore sets his face against the idea that vicarious suffering is to be identified with vicarious punishment, and he is concerned that 'This theory remains in the standards of numerous Denominations, and in the trust deeds of many churches and colleges.'[45] It wrongly pits biblical authority against enlightened morality, to the disadvantage of the former, whereas 'My own conviction is that the Christian idea of Atonement has no resemblance to the dogma commonly identified with this great word, and that the more severely the language of Scripture is examined the more vividly apparent it will be that the one is not merely a travesty, but a direct contradiction of the other.'[46] With such 'fighting talk' Tymms sets out his stall, and he proceeds carefully yet pungently to argue that from the Bible may be derived a doctrine of the atonement which asserts indeed that Christ is the propitiation for our sins, but which excludes 'every element which is incongruous with the Fatherhood of God, and with the spontaneity and freeness of His mercy . . .'[47]

In making out his case Tymms reviews a number of atonement theories, and is particularly critical of the antique but, unhappily, not obsolete ideas of Calvinism. He is staggered that 'writers of some eminence and of far-spreading influence still teach that out of the fountain of the Divine nature there flow the sweet waters of love and the bitter waters of hostility,' so that 'the difference between the reconciled and the unreconciled is not traced to the fact that the one class believes the truth about God and the other disbelieves it, but that God

---

[44] T.V. Tymms, *The Christian Idea of Atonement*, 3–4. Tymms was especially interested in apologetics. See his work, *The Mystery of God: Some Intellectual Hindrances to Faith*.

[45] T.V. Tymms, *The Christian Idea of Atonement*, 8.

[46] Ibid., 10.

[47] Ibid., 11.

is friendly to the one and hostile to the other.'[48] Ever alive to the movements of modern thought, Tymms finds that the 'The Christian idea of Atonement . . . links the Cross of Christ not only with the educational processes which prepared the way for its introduction in the fullness of time, but with all subsequent history, and with the prospective progress of mankind.' Hence our assurance 'that God's atoning work in Christ will never be allowed to fail, [and] that, in and through Christ, God and man will meet and abide eternally together, so that somewhere beyond the final tragedy of death, life will reign . . .'[49]

Not to be outdone by Congregational, Unitarian and Baptist principals, the Wesleyan W.F. Lofthouse, then a tutor and later Principal of Handsworth College, published *Ethics and Atonement* in 1906. His thesis is that

> right conduct, which it is the aim of ethics to analyse, springs from right relations between persons, and that a completely ethical society would embody the relations of members of the same family to one another. To restore these relations when broken, is the work of a personal reconciliation; – a reconciliation which cannot be accomplished by the person who has done the wrong, but only by the instrumentality of a third person, capable of occupying the positions of both injurer and injured alike. This process of reconciliation we have found, displayed at its fullest, in the accounts of the Atonement given in the New Testament.[50]

Lofthouse's teaching is undergirded by a covenant theology; he has much to say concerning the Mediator; he has shrewd criticisms to offer of the penal substitutionary theory of the atonement ('Christ did bear something for us; but it was not the punishment; it was the sin');[51] he trenchantly rebuts the heresy that the Father was angry with the Son, drawing support from R.W. Dale's Congregational Lecture

---

[48] Ibid., 174, 175. Calvinists, of course, are not slow to argue that the position Tymms complains of is a distortion of Calvin. I find it surprising that neither Robert Mackintosh, in *Historic Theories of Atonement*, nor T. Hywel Hughes (sometime principal of The Scottish Congregational College), in *The Atonement: Modern Theories of the Doctrine*, mention Tymms. The former does not refer to Scott Lidgett either.

[49] T.V. Tymms, *The Christian Idea of Atonement*, 436, 437.

[50] W.F. Lofthouse, *Ethics and Atonement*, 216–7.

[51] Ibid., 139.

on *The Atonement* (1875);[52] he contends that the atonement is made on behalf of the race,[53] and that, accordingly, it implies the pre-existence of Christ.[54] What some perceived as a deficiency in Lofthouse's treatment, namely his underplaying of the theme of sacrifice, was made good by another Wesleyan, Maldwyn Hughes in his work of 1924, *What is the Atonement? A Study of the Passion of God in Christ.*

Writing in a quite different style and, it must be said, with less discernment, another Baptist, Percy W. Evans, later to become tutor and then principal of Spurgeon's College, London, wrote on 'Christ's intellectual authority.' This authority, he declares, turns upon Christ's specific claims about himself, and especially upon the fact that he is the judge and Lord of conscience and of thought. He opposes D.W. Forrest's view that Jesus's knowledge was limited on the ground that 'if he is the same Being throughout, then He retains His divine attributes throughout, and amongst them Perfect and Unerring Wisdom.'[55] The authority of Christ, he continues, is not that of a voice from the past, but that of one known in our present experience. He proceeds to lambast Spiritualism for being 'a conspicuous example of lawless thinking',[56] and finally pronounces that the neglect of Christ's teaching on eternal destiny is among the causes of present-day lawlessness. One is left with the distinct impression that between Spurgeon's College in the 1920s and Rawdon College of two decades earlier there was, in terms of theological acumen, a great gulf fixed.

In 1924 Congregationalism's stalwart liberal evangelical C.J. Cadoux published *The Message about the Cross.* His subtitle described the work as 'A fresh study of the doctrine of the atonement.' Cadoux, like a number of those we have already considered, understands himself as writing in a context in which traditional atonement language has become meaningless to the modern mind. His objective, therefore, is not so much to review the familiar incidents of the story of the Cross, but to discern what the Cross meant to Jesus himself. He sets out from a comparison of Jesus with Deutero-Isaiah's suffering servant, finding that beyond all the parallels between them, the point of

---

[52] Ibid., 176.

[53] Ibid., ch. 10.

[54] Ibid., 284, 290.

[55] Percy W. Evans, 'Christ's intellectual authority', 25. For D.W. Forrest see Alan P.F. Sell, *Defending and Declaring the Faith: Some Scottish Examples 1860–1920,* ch. 8.

[56] Percy W. Evans, 'Christ's intellectual authority', 27.

difference is that 'In the old poems there is no suggestion that God himself shares, in any real way, in the sufferings of His Servant.'[57] He proceeds to discuss the Cross in Christian experience and, in a distinctly Abelardian way, he finds that the Cross convinces us of the being and goodness of God, convinces us of sin and of God's consequent suffering, and induces repentance, pardon and moral vigour. Passing to theological considerations, he hazards the suggestion that when some wish to make Jesus's death a condition of God's forgiveness, the truth intended is that 'forgiveness is impossible without the eternal presence in the Divine nature of that factor of which the self-sacrifice of Jesus is the grand manifestation within the limits of time and on the field of human history.'[58]

As for the extent of the atonement, Cadoux believes that while Jesus is potentially the Saviour of all people, our present human experience and the New Testament witness together prevent us from declaring that all will actually be saved, or that there is a 'cosmic salvation' irrespective of individual acceptance. Again, what we sow we reap; and thus forgiveness and reconciliation do not spare us the pains of hell, as used to be thought. Rather, they 'forestall the incurrence of future penalties by breaking the power of sinful habit in the present, and so preventing further sin.'[59] Concerning the God-ward reference of the Cross, Cadoux explains that 'The death of Jesus is the exhibition, under certain historical conditions, of the suffering which sin occasions to a loving and holy God.'[60] There is mystery here, which we shall never fathom; for 'The love of God is a vast immeasurable ocean; and it is no wonder that our soundings produce some puzzling results . . .'[61] There follows a chapter strikingly entitled, 'The saviourhood of the disciple,' in which Cadoux contends that human goodness and self-sacrifice have redemptive qualities in so far as they reveal God and are of God. Of such self-sacrifice Jesus's death is the first and best instance, and his victory over death is the guarantee of ours by participation in him. Cadoux turns finally to the ethical implications of the Cross, and here one of his deep commitments emerges: 'There is no escape from the fact that the Cross whereby we are saved owed its existence to the uncompromising pacifism of Him who dies

---

[57] C.J. Cadoux, *The Message about the Cross: A Fresh Study of the Doctrine of the Atonement*, 30.

[58] Ibid., 43–44.

[59] Ibid., 47.

[60] Ibid., 49.

[61] Ibid., 53.

upon it, and that the seed which caused the church of God to grow was the blood of pacifist martyrs.'[62] He concludes that 'God desires the co-operation of men who will grow to become more like Himself by becoming extremists in good-will.'[63]

English Congregationalism's most learned historian of doctrine, R.S. Franks, turned his attention to the atonement in his Dale Lectures of 1933.[64] The published version of his work contains an illuminating account of the influences upon him. He explains that his general position is that of a religious experience metaphysically justified. He was raised under the older evangelicalism, confronted modern biblical criticism as a theological student, and felt the need of a new basis for his faith. This he found in Ritschl and his disciple Harnack. From these he found a way out of the vexing problems of historical criticism, but it was Troeltsch who showed him that experimental theology devoid of an adequate metaphysical basis is insufficient. He was thus driven back to Schleiermacher. Troeltsch also directed him to C.H. Weisse who follows Schleiermacher's experiential path but combines with it a metaphysic indebted both to Hegel and to medieval theologians. A further ingredient was Karl Heim's insistence on the need to unify metaphysics and religion; and through Heim he came to Alexander of Hales, 'the true progenitor of the type of theology for which I now stand.'[65]

Franks defends an Abelardian view of the atonement, though unlike Hastings Rashdall, the Church of England's most prominent Abelardian, he cannot agree that God can suffer; and against F.C.N. Hicks's way of connecting the atonement with a 'catholic' view of the eucharist he pits the Protestant emphasis upon the moral, as opposed to what he calls the biological conception of the atonement. More particularly, against Hicks's strong Old Testament emphasis upon the blood-relationship between the clan and its God, and in face of Hicks's dwelling upon the concept of blood in the New Testament and his way of relating it to the Eucharist, Franks declares, 'Not life, but *love*, is the supreme word in Christianity. Life is what all religions

---

[62] Ibid., 85.

[63] Ibid., 92.

[64] Between the books of Cadoux and Franks, there appeared *Bannau'r ffydd*, Hughes, 1929, by D. Miall Edwards, Professor at Memorial [Congregational] College, Brecon. The chapters on the atonement are summarized by T. Hywel Hughes in *The Atonement: Modern Theories of the Doctrine*, 223–229. Edwards is broadly in the moral influence line of interpretation.

[65] R.S. Franks, *The Atonement*, x.

offer: the peculiarity of Christianity is that it interprets life through love.'[66]

After prolonged meditation Franks concludes that Abelard's doctrine brings us closest to the heart of the atonement: 'It is the doctrine that Christ reconciles men to God by revealing the love of God in His life and still more in His death, so bringing them to trust and love Him in return.'[67] The theory is, he thinks, wrongly called the moral theory, for it is supremely religious; and it is unfairly labelled subjective, for while it does concern the human response to God's love, 'it is in truth fundamentally objective, inasmuch as God, Christ, His Cross, and the Divine love are all the objects of human trust and responsive love.'[68] But in order that subjectivism be avoided, an appropriate method is required. This he finds in Anselm – in particular, in Anselm's way of addressing the problems of theology from a particular vantage point. Accordingly, Franks's project is to combine Abelard's insight with Anselm's method. Not the least important of Anselm's convictions is that theological pronouncements must be susceptible of rational justification. The medieval Franciscans distinguished between belief upon divine authority, and trust in the God who is truth. In the debate on this point Alexander of Hales was a catalyst, though he oscillates between the two options. By the time we come to William of Ockham's nominalism we find the whole of the subject matter of theology resting upon authority; and Franks finds Ockham *redivivus* in Barth's *Deus dixit*, and understands Calvin as the bridge between the two. The pitfall is that of so emphasizing the divine transcendence 'as to make a trust based on insight into His character impossible.'[69] It is noteworthy, Franks declares, that all that results from Anselm's theory is a possibility of forgiveness, and that Anselm, in order to show how Christ can save particular individuals, has to supplement his doctrine by reference to Christ's example and merit. This is tantamount to an admission on Anselm's part that his theory, omitting as it does all idea of subjective response to the work of Christ, is unsatisfactory as a basis for theology. We thus see that 'if law is made fundamental, any operation of grace is made impossible.'[70]

---

[66] Ibid., xv, quoting his review of F.C.N. Hicks, *The Fullness of Sacrifice*. Rashdall's work referred to is *The Idea of Atonement in Christian Theology*.

[67] Ibid., 2.

[68] Ibid., 4.

[69] Ibid., 20.

[70] Ibid., 26.

Franks proceeds to review the biblical teaching on the work of Christ and the traditional theories of the atonement, and then, in the wake of a discussion of Aquinas and Kant, he contends that 'The agreement of Authority and Reason which we seek is established, when we identify the Good Will . . . with the Divine Love as it is revealed in Jesus Christ. That fixes the principle of the experiential doctrine of the Atonement as at the same time the basis of a Christian metaphysic.'[71] It follows that against the Scotist doctrine of the pure unintelligibility of Christianity 'we must set that of an intuition of God as Love, an insight into His character as the highest ethical ideal, and a feeling of complete dependence upon Him for the realization not only of the ethical ideal, but also of all accompanying blessings that our composite nature requires.'[72] Not the least of those blessings is that of the forgiveness of sins. Indeed,

> It is the fact of sin that turns the doctrine of the Revelation of God's love through Christ into a doctrine of Atonement, and that changes the doctrine of the Church from one of a fellowship of saints into one of a fellowship of pardoned sinners called to be saints . . . Sin is only truly to be measured by the love which it rejects and refuses. It is failure to trust and obey God. . . . Nothing judges more clearly or consistently than love. It is the same love that judges us guilty sinners, when we rebel against it; and that removes our guilt, when in repentance and trust we return from our rebellion. The special name of the judgement that annuls the guilt of sin is forgiveness. . . . We cast no slight upon the moral law, when we accept forgiveness at the hands of God. We simply recognize love as the highest moral principle.[73]

To say that forgiveness is through Christ is to say that 'In Jesus [God's] love is *active*, seeking us even to the uttermost, coming where we are, finding us in the far country of estrangement whither our sins have brought us.'[74]

Franks concludes on a practical note. Whereas the older doctrine of atonement had a message for awakened, guilty sinners in whom the law had done its work, our problem today is deeper and more intractable. We have to do with those who have no sense of sin at all, but who suffer from a restless malaise. To these we must proclaim the

---

[71] Ibid., 119.

[72] Ibid., 131–2.

[73] Ibid., 151, 152, 155, 156, 157.

[74] Ibid., 165–6.

love that sought and seeks people – and not simply preach in the spirit of the atonement; we must exhibit the power of that love in our lives.[75]

In the middle decades of the twentieth century a number of popular, though nonetheless deep, works appeared on aspects of the atonement. In 1935 the Methodist W. Russell Maltby published his Cato Lecture, *Christ and His Cross*, a work which made a considerable impression upon many ministers and lay preachers. The burden of his message is that Jesus came to reveal God and save people from sin. Such a salvation can be by moral means only: 'Christ in His saving work will do no violence to the natures He has given us. His help, infinite as it is, must enter by the narrow door of our consent.'[76] Christ is joined to our sinful race, and he contends with our sin until we love it no longer. Having died on the Cross he rose again and is alive for evermore. We are to come trustfully to him, that he may 'take charge of us and of our infected and disordered lives.'[77] He personally grants forgiveness in which is our peace, and from which we derive the power of a new life.

Although writing for a general audience, Maltby does not hesitate to rebuke theologians with whom he disagrees. He seems especially tempted in this direction by Forsyth. He says that the simple believer meant something when he sang about Christ's bearing punishment in his stead; but such a believer's mind

> is not subtle enough to follow Forsyth's refinement and 'renounce the idea that Jesus was punished by the God who is ever well pleased with His beloved Son,' and yet believe that 'God must either punish sin or expiate it,' that 'He must either inflict punishment or assume it!' And when the same believer has learned that he must not set justice and mercy against each other he must learn next what seems to set holiness and love apart – for 'nothing but holiness can forgive; love cannot.'[78]

---

[75] In attempting to present the bare bones of Franks's theory I have not dwelt very much upon his adjustments to the thought of others. That he can be trenchant is exemplified by this (ibid., 184): 'When McLeod Campbell teaches that Christ made a vicarious confession of sin on behalf of humanity, we can only say that the conception violates the fundamental principles of moral personality.'

[76] W.R. Maltby, *Christ and His Cross*, 165.

[77] Ibid., 167.

[78] Ibid., 150, quoting earlier editions of Forsyth, *The Cruciality of the Cross*, 105, *Positive Preaching and the Modern Mind*, 333, and *The Work of Christ*, 129.

In 1938 H.H. Farmer's book, *The Healing Cross* appeared. This is a collection of expositions in four parts: Christ the Way; The severity which is good; The goodness which is severe; and The Healing Cross, in which Farmer seeks to present the message of the Cross in such a way that the eyes of his hearers are lifted from parochial preoccupations so that they may focus upon the place of the Christian fellowship in relation to the purpose of God in history. In proclaiming the message, the place of a reverent agnosticism must be allowed and the note of austerity must be struck: 'It must be a call which demands as well as succours, nay, succours because it demands, and demands because it succours.'[79] Finally, the message must set forth the Christian way in the only way it can be known – in the life of discipleship.

Nearly 30 years later Farmer published *The Word of Reconciliation*. The bulk of the work comprises a fresh interpretation of Christ's roles as prophet, priest and king, but there are more generally illuminating – and at least one *prima facie* startling – observations too. The latter is that 'Christ is able to be our Reconciliation, our Reconciler, because he is in his own person supremely, fully, *par excellence*, the reconciled man.'[80] He recognizes the problem: how can Christ be reconciled to God if he knew no sin and had no need of forgiveness? He replies, 'Christ is sinless, not because of negative avoidance of, or abstention from, this or that objectionable or prohibited behaviour, but because of a mighty, positive, utterly selfless love to men such as we in our sinful alienation from God and consequent alienation and separation from one another can hardly comprehend, much less share.'[81] No doubt; but one may still feel that the term 'Christ as *the* reconciled man' is a hostage to fortune, and that Luther's 'proper man' more aptly fits *the* human being. Such a one is absolutely in harmony with his Father, but no reconciliation is here in question, because none was needed.

Meanwhile, in 1957 Forsyth's pupil, H.F. Lovell Cocks, Franks' successor at Western College, Bristol, published *The Wondrous Cross*. At the heart of his exposition is this:

The Cross of Christ is the revelation of a divine love that is eternal. . . . Christ did not die on the Cross to turn God from hatred to love, or to buy from God a forgiveness that would otherwise have been denied to those who so sorely needed it. Christ did not die to make God love us;

---

[79] H.H. Farmer, *The Healing Cross*, viii.
[80] Idem, *The Word of Reconciliation*, 10.
[81] Ibid., 17.

He died because God has always loved us. . . . Our redemption equally with our creation is the work of the eternal Love. . . . It is the incarnate Son of God who dies on the Cross. If there has been no Incarnation there can be no Atonement. No *man* can redeem us . . .[82]

In the course of a lucid exposition, Lovell Cocks, like Franks before him, criticizes the ideas of vicarious punishment and vicarious repentance as being morally untenable; and, loyal churchman as he was, his pointed teasing breaks through from time to time: 'Let it be written in indelible letters in the offices of denominational headquarters and in all places where the leaders of Christian churches gather, that it was ecclesiastical vested interests that crucified the Son of God.'[83]

Three more substantial (in the sense of longer) books – all by Congregationalists – emanated from the middle years of the century, and these must at least be mentioned. The first, *The Cross and the Eternal Order* (1943), by Henry W. Clark, is a sustained reflection on the theme that 'the Atonement, in setting man right with God, sets God right with Himself.' That is, the atonement makes for 'a re-assertion of the purpose God eternally entertained.'[84] *An Approach to Christology* (1948) by Aubrey R. Vine is, as its sub-title indicates, 'An interpretation and development of some elements in the metaphysic and Christology of Nestorius as a way of approach to an orthodox Christology compatible with modern thought.' And in Robert Paul's *The Atonement and the Sacraments* (1961) the doctrine of the atonement is related to the sacraments of baptism and the Lord's Supper on the basis of historical and biblical studies, and in the context of a passionate ecumenical commitment which understands that 'in striving to reach the heart of the Atonement, we find ourselves worshipping at the same place, eating the same Bread, and drinking from the same Cup.'[85] Would that we did.

Although one thinks of the Methodist Vincent Taylor, Principal of Headingley College, Leeds, primarily as a New Testament scholar, it would be unforgivable not to mention his trilogy, *Jesus and His Sacrifice* (1937), *The Atonement in New Testament Teaching* (1940) and *Forgiveness and Reconciliation* (1941). On the basis of these careful studies he presented his own statement of what it all comes to in *The Cross of Christ* (1956). The Cross is a divine event which erupts in time, but

---

[82] H.F. Lovell Cocks, *The Wondrous Cross*, 17. Except, of course, *proper* man.

[83] Ibid., 39.

[84] Henry W. Clark, *The Cross and the Eternal Order*, 4.

[85] Robert S. Paul, *The Atonement and the Sacraments*, 268.

has eternal significance. Jesus understood himself as the Son of Man, the suffering servant, who offers himself as a sacrifice for sin. Not that he 'speaks of appeasing the anger of God, of placating Him and causing Him to be gracious to sinners. But He does use sacrificial ideas as a thought mould. . . . In His dying He expresses the sorrow and penitence which men *ought* to feel, and which in fellowship with Himself they *do* feel.'[86] Taylor proceeds to outline Paul's view of Christ's death: it is of cosmic significance; it concerns sin; its source is God's love; it is for the undeserving; and it is an enactment on behalf of sinners. He carefully observes that 'in St. Paul's teaching Christ's death is substitutionary in the sense that He did for us that which we can never do for ourselves, but not in the sense that He transfers our punishment to Himself, so that we have nothing to do but to accept His benefits.'[87] Again, in Paul's view the saving deed is the act of a representative, and his thought is influenced by, though not saturated with, sacrificial ideas.

Taylor next turns to Paul's understanding of the Cross in Christian experience, and discusses faith as trust, justification, reconciliation and sanctification; and faith as union and sacramental communion with Christ issuing in sacrificial living. From the letter to the Hebrews he draws the lessons that Christ's death is for us; it is a representative act; it is the one perfect sacrifice; and it is the prelude to Christ's high priestly ministry. There follows a discussion of the Johannine witness to God's love, humanity's need, the necessity of expiation, the concept of fullness of life, and the sacrificial motif. Following a brief review of atonement theories ancient and modern, Taylor offers his own statement of the matter. Human beings cannot save themselves: 'Only by the act of God in Christ can [man] attain to communion with God and to the knowledge of life in its fullness.'[88] His favoured word to characterize God's purpose is reconciliation. This is achieved by the Cross. Christ's saving deed is vicarious, representative, and sacrificial. It is the supreme revelation of God's love for humanity; it is an act of obedience to the Father's will to God's judgement upon sin.; and it 'issues in a ministry of intercession in which He voices our inarticulate penitence and desire for reconciliation.'[89]

As to our response: faith is trust in Christ; it is communal; it is both a spiritual venture and a gift of God; it is 'objectively controlled by the

---

[86] V. Taylor, *The Cross of Christ*, 21.

[87] Ibid., 31.

[88] Ibid., 87.

[89] Ibid., 95.

fact of Christ;'[90] and it is organically connected with life: '"Works" are the flowers of faith.'[91] The simplest exercise of faith suffices to bring us into a saving relationship with Christ – the ability to articulate a theory of the atonement is not necessary. Faith's response to Christ's saving work is immediate and complete; it entails a life of obedience and service – even of co-suffering with Christ; and it 'enters into, and receives, all the meaning of Christ's ministry on high.'[92] In drawing to a close, Taylor remarks, 'Perhaps our greatest need to-day, if we would rise above the poverty of much of our worship, is to experience once more the wonder of reliance upon Christ's ceaseless saving ministry, which is the true centre of Christian devotion and the abiding source of Christian living.'[93]

The liturgical note – and also the sacramental note which runs through Robert Paul's book – is struck again by John S. Whale in *Victor and Victim* (1960). Persuaded that neither ultra-transcendentalism nor naturalism will suffice, Whale argues for the holding together of eternity and time: indeed this is the presupposition of the gospel, 'that the eternal God was in the Man Christ Jesus reconciling the world unto himself.'[94] Christ's victory was wrought on our behalf, and hence it is good news for us. But Christ, claims Whale, is sacrificial victim too.

> At the Cross the sinless Son of Man was offering himself in perfect obedience as the atoning sacrifice for the sin of man. The Church of his Body is a monument to the fact that it was a representative sacrifice. We participate in his self-offering. The Lord's Supper or Eucharist is the special means of this participation: it is the Christian Passover.[95]

At the Cross sin is judged, and sin's penalty borne – the metaphor of penalty being indicative of the cost of our redemption from sin. But what of the scandal of particularity? Whale replies, 'It is one of the characteristic paradoxes of scripture that universality is the implicit logic of its strange particularity; "God so loved the world" is the outcome, in

---

[90] Ibid., 98.

[91] Ibid., 100.

[92] Ibid., 103.

[93] Ibid., 104.

[94] John S. Whale, *Victor and Victim*, 19.

[95] Ibid., 59. For Whale see Clyde Binfield, 'A learned and gifted Protestant minister: John Seldon Whale, 19 December 1896 – 17 September 1997', 97–131.

fact as well as in theory, of what begins as "You only have I known of all the families of the earth."[96] God's revelation is for all. So he proceeds to discuss the Church as the saved community, the sacraments, and the resurrection hope – this last construed corporately, not individualistically.

It is difficult to think of a significant book by a Nonconformist on the person and work of Christ published in the 20 years following Whale's. But in 1983 Colin Gunton came forth with *Yesterday and Today: A Study of Continuities in Christology*. It is a defence of orthodox Christology which finds in the incarnation not only the basis of reconciliation (because who the Saviour is determines what he can savingly do), but also the value of human life: 'That the Word became flesh speaks volumes for the value to God, and therefore the eternal value and importance, of human life in its temporality. It forbids the mistreatment of any member of the human family or any attempt to escape from human relationships in the various ways that have been, and are always being, invented by our fertility in evil.'[97]

In his work of 1988, *The Actuality of Atonement*, Gunton offers a treatment of soteriology. Disturbed by a perceived crisis in rationalism, and persuaded that metaphor, far from being redundant, is crucial to rational engagement with the world, Gunton begins by slaying some intellectual giants. Their good points notwithstanding, Kant transmogrified the Christian gospel into its opposite, for while 'Kant did see redemption taking place by means of a divine activity,' he claimed that 'God is to be found in human moral reason and action, not encountered as a personal creator and redeemer;'[98] Schleiermacher's emphasis upon feeling, which is understood as prior to thought, relegates religion to the supra-rational, and Schleiermacher is thus led to diminish Christian claims – not least, by evacuating the juridical aspect from his atonement theory; and Hegel's conceptual rationalism encourages him 'to treat evil as part of the order of things, a necessary if negative stage in the emergence of rationally self-aware beings.'[99] In face of these inadequacies, Gunton seeks 'to find a rationality which, because it is not rationalist, has better claim to express the truth of the doctrine [of the atonement]

---

[96] Ibid., 93–94.

[97] C.E. Gunton, *Yesterday and Today: A Study of Continuities in Christology*, 182.

[98] C.E. Gunton, *The Actuality of Atonement: A Study of Metaphor, Rationality and the Christian Tradition*, 7.

[99] Ibid., 19.

without detracting from the historical concreteness and fathomless depths of its object: specifically, to show that metaphor is both a pervasive feature of our language and that it is a way of telling things as they are.'[100]

Providing historical illustrations, he proceeds to discuss the metaphors of victory, justice and sacrifice, showing that all three are inherently relational. This leads him to adumbrate the Trinitarian basis of his case: 'the sacrifice which the victorious and risen Son makes to the Father *is* the perfected creation,' while 'It is the function of God the Spirit . . . to *particularize* the universal redemption in anticipation of the eschatological redemption.'[101] He insists that the focus of the atonement metaphors is always upon both God and the world, and upon the eschatological 'now' and the 'not yet'. Meanwhile, 'language takes shape, remains alive, in a community of speech,'[102] and the church is the community of reconciliation. He repudiates Constantinianism, suggests that the 'traditions of dissent' yield profitable insights concerning the way in which the Church may be both for and against the world, and contends that 'The church's proclamation will be seen to be merely political unless its own *polity* is given shape by the victory of Christ on the cross'[103] – in which connection he has in mind not so much church order as a non-racialist, family-supportive style of churchly life. In the development of this form of life the sacraments are of great importance, and the 'ecclesiological outcome' is that Christ and the Spirit 'create, in time and space, a living echo of the communion that God is in eternity.'[104] The eschatological unity of nature and grace, realized in Christ's atoning sacrifice, is the ground and inspiration of the Church's praise.'[105]

In his Didsbury Lectures, *Christ and Creation* (1992), Gunton returns to a theme to which I have already alluded. His case is that 'What is realised in the incarnate involvement of the Son in time and space is the redirection of the creation to its original destiny, a destiny that was from the beginning *in Christ*, for all creation is in and through the Son.'[106] This realization occurs through Christ and under the direction of the Holy Spirit.

---

[100] Ibid., 25.

[101] Ibid., 154, 170.

[102] Ibid., 173.

[103] Ibid., 183.

[104] Ibid., 199.

[105] Ibid., 83. See also my review of this book.

[106] C.E. Gunton, *Christ and Creation*, 94.

I turn finally in this section to two works by Paul S. Fiddes, Principal of Regent's Park Baptist College, Oxford. It is characteristic of his work that pastoral concerns are inextricably interwoven with theological considerations. This is clearly seen in *The Creative Suffering of God* (1988). Over against Don Cupitt, who declared that those who understand God as the fellow-sufferer with humanity destroy the value of God as a religious ideal; and in opposition to the Methodist Frances Young's view that the undue elevation of the Cross might deny God's involvement in other instances of profound tragedy, Fiddes seeks to speak consistently of 'a God who suffers eminently and yet is still God, and a God who suffers universally and yet is still present uniquely and decisively in the sufferings of Christ.'[107] In order to do this he invokes the concept of non-being as a symbol for the reality of the suffering God which, although it is a symbol only, 'does provide a focus for much of what we have discovered in this study about the suffering of the God who lives and yet experiences death.'[108] The employment of the idea of negativity further enables us to claim 'that God endures something analogous to our experience of death.'[109] But God is victor also: 'he negates the negation.'[110] Fiddes thus reaches his conclusion that

> we cannot and must not suppose that death only enters into the being of God in the cross of Jesus or that God only overcomes death there. Wherever trust in God is created, death ceases to be the instrument of hostile non-being. But in the cross of Jesus the encounter of God with death reaches its uttermost pitch, and so his suffering becomes most creative and persuasive. Here God goes furthest in speaking his word of acceptance to us, so that his offer can truly be named a 'new covenant', and through the cross he calls out a new word from us to him. In his humility, this is the conversation of the Spirit that God desires and suffers to create.[111]

In the following year Fiddes published *Past Event and Present Salvation.* He here argues that 'At the cross the relationships within the being of God himself were broken; that is, we can begin to express the belief that God stood in the place of alienation by saying that God experienced

---

[107] Paul S. Fiddes, *The Creative Suffering of God*, 3.

[108] Ibid., 261.

[109] Ibid., 262.

[110] Ibid., 263.

[111] Ibid., 267.

what it was like for a Son to be forsaken by his Father and for a Father to lose his Son. . . . But the cross assures us that because the love of God is stronger than death, the relationships within his being did not only survive, but emerged from death as altogether new.'[112] Indeed, at the point where we lose meaning, 'God gives the cross meaning, as he reveals himself to have been present there, making the further journey of discovery into his creation. . . . This past event has a creative power upon the present; as it grasps our imagination we find that we are being grasped by the living God.'[113]

III

Nonconformists are not alone in having produced few books during the twentieth century specifically on God the Holy Spirit. There is, however, a modest crop of volumes, of which one of the earliest is that by A. Lewis Humphries, Professor of New Testament Greek and Exegesis at Hartley Primitive Methodist College, Manchester. It is his Hartley Lecture entitled *The Holy Spirit in Faith and Experience* (1911). In his preface Humphries expresses gratitude for the exegetical work that has been done on the Spirit, but justifies his labours by proposing to focus on the underlying experience of the Spirit, and to do this with regard to modern developments in psychology. Nor are his sights confined to Christianity: 'For if the Spirit, *as realised in experience*, is simply God moving upon man for the bestowal of truth and life, there can be no presentation of the Spirit deserving to be called either scientific or Christian, which does not bring into one large synthesis the Spirit's operation not simply in some particular community of Christians, but in all who profess the Christian name, and in the broad field of the human race. A grievous wrong is inflicted on truth when the part is treated as if it were the whole.'[114]

Humphries examines the roots of the biblical teaching on the Spirit in the Old Testament, in non-canonical writings, and in the New Testament, where we see that 'The Holy Spirit acted upon Jesus, not to the suppression, but to the intensification, of the human.'[115] There follow studies of Pentecost, where the Spirit was manifested not for the first time, as Moberley supposes, but 'with a specific quality or

---

[112] Paul S. Fiddes, *Past Event and Present Salvation*, 218.

[113] Ibid., 220.

[114] A.L. Humphries, *The Holy Spirit in Faith and Experience*, v-vi.

[115] Ibid., 151.

potency;'[116] of the Spirit in the apostolic church; of spiritual gifts; and of the Spirit outside of Christianity – indeed, outside of religion and in paganism. In this last connection Humphries, while granting that 'it is doubtful whether New Testament writers viewed heathen faiths as in any way a sphere of the Spirit of God,'[117] argues that while the Spirit is everywhere active, the Christian experience of the Spirit belongs only to the Christian revelation. This contention leads him to discuss the Spirit and the Christian life, and here, as we might expect, he has emphases characteristic of Methodism within his sights. For example, 'It is the Spirit who, at the dawn of the life of sonship, supplies inward testimony to its reality – an element in the Apostolic teaching upon which Methodism has set due emphasis by its doctrine of assurance, the re-affirmation of which has been described as "the fundamental contribution of Methodism to the life and thought of the Church."'[118] In his final chapter Humphries briefly discusses some critical questions concerning the Spirit, and then becomes quite down to earth: 'in the organization of the Church and its detailed government can we not believe in, and make room for, the operation of the Holy Spirit?'[119] He looks for the time when the Church will seek, 'as her crowning equipment the full manifestation, first, within her and, then, through her, of that Spirit without which nothing is pure or strong, but in whom, and with whom the Church of Christ can fulfil the perfect will of her Lord.'[120]

In the same year, 1911, the Wesleyan, William Theophilus Davison, Principal of Richmond College, published *The Indwelling Spirit*. He disclaims any intention of presenting a systematic work on the Spirit but, setting out from the side of experience, not dogma, he understands that 'The Holy Spirit is God imparting Himself directly to the consciousness and experience of men.'[121] His apologetic interest is revealed in his desire to show 'the Christian doctrine of the Holy

---

[116] Ibid., 264.

[117] Ibid., 277.

[118] Ibid., 301, quoting H.B. Workman, in W.J. Townsend, H.B. Workman and George Eayrs, eds., *A New History of Methodism*, I, 19. Others find the heart of Methodism in the concept of holy living.

[119] Ibid., 362.

[120] Ibid., 363.

[121] W.T. Davison, *The Indwelling Spirit*, vii. Davison had earlier published a substantial volume on Christian ethics: *The Christian Conscience: A Contribution to Christian Ethics*, for which see Alan P.F. Sell, *Philosophy, Dissent and Nonconformity 1689–1920*, 164–6, 201–2.

Spirit meets the needs and claims of modern religious life better than certain philosophico-religious theorizings that ignore or disparage the teaching of the New Testament.'[122] His wide-ranging discussion encompasses many topics, among them the biblical witness, spiritual freedom, prayer in the Spirit, holiness, Christian mission and mystical religion. In his final chapter (as if anticipating criticisms of Tillich and Hick) he quotes the Scottish apologist, Robert Flint thus: 'Any philosophy which is in thorough earnest to show that God is the Ground of all existence must find it difficult to retain a firm grasp on the personality and transcendence of the Divine.'[123]

In a paper on 'The Holy Spirit and Divine Immanence' (1911) Davison reaffirms his points. He regrets the loss of transcendence in the thought of Spinoza, Hegel, John and Edward Caird, and T.H. Green, as well as in the writings of Eucken and the Modernists. He finds that immanentist-pantheizing tendencies are a feature of the revolt against deism. But monism will not suffice either, for 'A God who is not distinct from the universe, as well as present in the universe, is no God at all.'[124] By contrast with the foregoing lines of thought, theistic doctrine holds transcendence and immanence together, though with the former taking precedence. In the Bible this is shown supremely in the incarnation. It is the doctrine of the Trinity which makes it impossible to merge God with the universe or to sever him from it, while the progressive idea is preserved by the doctrine of the Holy Spirit, who 'shall guide you into all truth.'[125] But what of evil? Davison replies, 'God can only be immanent in such a world in proportion as He redeems it; that is, in holiest love and uttermost self-sacrifice judges the sin and saves the sinner.'[126]

In 1915 Thomas Rees, Principal of the Independent College at Bangor, published *The Holy Spirit in Thought and Experience*. Almost exactly half of the book concerns the biblical foundations of the doctrine. There follows a treatment of the development of the doctrine through Christian history with special attention to its relation to the doctrine of the Trinity in the early centuries, and to the Reformation concern to co-ordinate 'the witness of the Spirit in Scripture with its present witness in men's hearts as one undivided means of revelation

---

[122] Ibid., vii–viii.

[123] Ibid., 327. For Flint see Alan P.F. Sell, *Defending and Declaring the Faith*, ch. 3.

[124] *Idem.*, 'The Holy Spirit and divine immanence', 266.

[125] Ibid., 275.

[126] Ibid., 277.

and of all grace.'[127] Towards the end of his book Rees sounds a warning note.

> As philosophy no longer construes God in terms of essence and hypostasis, epistemology does not explain the origin and process of knowledge as inspiration and revelation, and ethics does not define the moral life as justification, regeneration and sanctification. These peculiar terms of the theology of the Spirit are being ousted from the familiar and effective language of our time, and, with them, there is danger than the force and quality of the particular facts they denoted may be lost to me.
>
> To replace them by a general doctrine of divine immanence, and by the abstract principles of general ethics will be to abandon the specifically Christian approach to the interpretation of the content of man's moral and intellectual life.[128]

The year 1928 saw the publication of the first edition of *The Christian Experience of the Holy Spirit* by the Baptist H. Wheeler Robinson. He sets out from Paul's threefold benediction in 2 Corinthians 13:14 and suggests that this is 'simply a more explicit form of that which Paul uses elsewhere, "The grace of our Lord Jesus Christ be with you all." When that is said, all is said, for the grace of Christ implies the love of God behind it, and the fellowship (of the whole group) with God created by the Spirit through that grace.'[129] Like a number of other theologians of his generation, Robinson brings psychological insights to bear upon his subject, and some of these are at least as questionable as is Robinson's antipathy, in the interests of personal experience, to older Calvinistic ways of discussing experience under the headings of effectual calling, justification, adoption and sanctification, and 'then, and only then', he complains, to faith and repentance.[130] It might be retorted that whereas the old order preserves the priority of prevenient grace in Christian reflection, faith and repentance might well be first on the lips of one announcing the gospel call in preaching or evangelism.

Be that as it may, Robinson proceeds to discuss the Holy Spirit in relation to the incarnation, the Church, the Scriptures, the sacraments,

---

[127] Thomes Rees, *The Holy Spirit in Thought and Experience*, 185. Not all the talk about personality, then rife, seems to have prompted Rees to query his use of impersonal pronouns for the Spirit.

[128] Ibid., 211.

[129] H. Wheeler Robinson, *The Christian Experience of the Holy Spirit*, 23.

[130] Ibid., 175.

the individual life and the Godhead. At the heart of his thesis is the claim that 'the very life-breath of the conception of the Spirit is unity of operation with the Father and the Son. As God was present in the world through Christ, so is God through Christ present in the Holy Spirit.'[131] Far from seeking to restrict the operations of the Spirit to the Church, Robinson welcomes the fact that 'most of us have now come to see in the vast evolutionary process a revelation of Spirit immanent in method, transcendent in Nature.'[132]

Short books on the Spirit by two Congregationalists may complete our sample. In 1943 Hubert Cunliffe-Jones, then Professor of Systematic Theology at Yorkshire United Independent College, Bradford, published *The Holy Spirit*. The Holy Spirit, he declares, 'is God communicating himself to us and enabling us to respond to him.'[133] Not indeed that the Spirit's guidance is known by us as an infallible truth. On the contrary, it is 'a human truth which we may reject and set aside and which can be known only in faith and prayer and as we have courage to witness to what we see.'[134] Belief in the Holy Spirit 'is the lynch [*sic*]-pin of Christian faith which makes the life, death, and resurrection of Jesus produce its real fruit in our lives.'[135] The Spirit is God himself at work in our hearts, and the Spirit witnesses to the risen and reigning Christ. From Forsyth, Cunliffe-Jones learns 'the evil of separating the Spirit from the Word;'[136] and he summons John Owen and others to his aid when discussing regeneration and sanctification. 'The work of the Holy Spirit in the human heart,' he writes, 'finds its completion in our eternal fellowship with the living God.'[137] There follow sections of the Spirit and the Church, the Spirit and the sacraments, and the relation of the Spirit to preaching: 'It is evident that the preaching of the word of God needs the work of the Holy Spirit, and that it is the reception of the Holy Spirit which enables the word of God to be preached with power. But it is equally evident that the hearing of the word of God in such a way that it brings forth fruit is also the work of the Holy Spirit.'[138] As for the Holy Spirit in the life of humanity at large, the manifestation is both

---

[131] Ibid., 121.

[132] Ibid., 225.

[133] Hubert Cunliffe-Jones, *The Holy Spirit*, 9.

[134] Ibid., 11.

[135] Ibid., 12.

[136] Ibid., 27.

[137] Ibid., 44.

[138] Ibid., 68.

limited and ambiguous. Nevertheless, Christians 'must believe in the transformation of all things under the guidance of the Holy Spirit, and strive to see that the essential Christian meaning is brought to bear on those great fields of human endeavour whose ambiguity needs positive direction if it is to subserve the well-being of human life.'[139]

Geoffrey Nuttall, of New (Congregational) College, London, widely esteemed for his scholarly work, *The Holy Spirit in Puritan Faith and Experience* (1946), published *The Holy Spirit and Ourselves* in 1947. He here seeks to assist 'the ordinary people of our churches to learn more of what is meant by the Holy Spirit.'[140] Accordingly, he provides some biblical background, showing that the character of the Spirit is the character of Jesus, and declaring, 'This experience of God's spirit in a personal way, this finding of the Spirit by the Spirit of Jesus, is the most momentous step forward along the whole road of our study.'[141] Like the gospel itself, the guidance of the Spirit may be known by all Christians, though the Spirit ever deals personally with people, and God does not override their personalities. Our problem is that we fail in trust, and do not have 'the humility to learn the way as we go.'[142] To walk in the Spirit is to accept the discipline of the Spirit, and to live in the community of the Spirit which is found wherever Christians gather to wait upon the Lord and together to follow their Guide.[143]

IV

During the latter years of the nineteenth century, W.F. Adeney contributed a paper on 'The Trinity' to the symposium *Studies in Christian Evidences*. He argues that the doctrine of the Trinity represents an attempt to coordinate the following facts of revelation: God is one; Christ is divine; God the Holy Spirit is within us. With reference to historical discussions he claims first, 'We cannot say that God is three in the same sense in which He is one.'[144] There are not three parts in God, and 'the three-foldness is more than that of three qualities.'[145]

---

[139] Ibid., 87.

[140] Geoffrey F. Nuttall, *The Holy Spirit and Ourselves*, vii.

[141] Ibid., 25.

[142] Ibid., 40.

[143] Ibid., 61.

[144] Walter .F. Adeney, in *Studies in Christian Evidences, Series I*, 130.

[145] Ibid., 131.

Secondly, we must not understand 'person' in Trinitarian doctrine in our modern sense of the term. Thirdly, 'To believe in the Trinity is not necessarily to believe in the equality of what are described as "the three persons".'[146] In this connection he finds the Athanasian Creed unintelligible; indeed, Athanasius himself is preferable, for he admits a certain subordination of the Son as one sent, and of the Holy Spirit who comes to us from God through Christ. The Bible gives 'a supremacy to God as the Father, from whom come the Son and the Holy Spirit.'[147] In answer to the question why we have three persons – not fewer or more – Adeney replies, 'Now I do not affirm that God only exists and acts as a Trinity. I venture to set no limits to the possibilities of the Godhead. . . . [W]e cannot assert that God is only a Trinity. But we can say that He is that, since He has come to us in a threefold way, which indicates that there is in Him at least a correspondingly three-foldness of Being and Life.'[148]

In 1909 Adeney published *The Christian Conception of God*, and here he returned to the theme of the Trinity. Though not the first doctrine to find its way into Christian experience, the Trinity is essentially Christian in two senses: it is true to the fact of genuine Christianity, and it is found in Christianity alone. He is aware of the pitfall of thinking in terms of three individualities in the Trinity, and of the dangers of ditheism and tritheism, and he finds help in the thought that monotheism does not mean that God is a monad. Positively, 'The doctrine of the Trinity has grown up as the least inadequate conception of the Godhead consistent with [the facts recounted in the new Testament].'[149] The essentials of the doctrine are the Fatherhood of God, the divinity of Christ, and the witness of the Holy Spirit – God has been 'pleased to reveal Himself to us in this threefold way.'[150] With cautions once again concerning the term 'person', Adeney finally resorts to mystery: 'There are distinctions; but they are ineffable distinctions.'[151] With what appears to be a parting shot at a large slice of the tradition, he declares, 'we cannot . . . assume that there was the same kind of distinction between the Father and Son before the Incarnation' as after it.[152]

---

[146] Ibid., 133.
[147] Ibid., 134.
[148] Ibid., 136.
[149] Idem, *The Christian Conception of God*, 227.
[150] Ibid., 242.
[151] Ibid., 245.
[152] Ibid., 245.

At the beginning of the twentieth century it was still possible to find works of controversy, however politely phrased, in which Unitarians would rebuke Trinitarians and vice versa – a pastime which became increasingly unfashionable as the century progressed. Consider, for example, Richard A. Armstrong's work of 1904, *The Trinity and the Incarnation*. He begins by listing four unreconciled beliefs of the average Englishman: Jesus is God; God is our heavenly Father; Jesus Christ is not our heavenly Father; there are not two Gods. In an endeavour to assist, Armstrong takes a long run at the contemporary problem. He outlines the New Testament teaching, and the history of the doctrine down to the Council of Chalcedon, whose creed 'for ever thrust the Arian theology outside the pale of orthodoxy. By a bold and uncompromising defiance of rationality, by divesting Jesus of every vestige of real humanity, by according to him every attribute of God, it strove to silence the controversies of two hundred years. It left Jesus Christ with a human nature only nominally human.'[153]

He then discusses a number of modern writers who either dissolve the three persons of the Trinity so as to leave them without significance, or they dissolve the unity of God into sheer fiction.[154] A.M. Fairbairn is among those in his sights. In *Christ and Modern Theology*, declares Armstrong, Fairbairn rests on the consciousness of Jesus as the true ground of theology: 'Thus, unless Jesus himself shows himself conscious of his own deity in the Gospels, the whole doctrine falls away.'[155] All we have are two or three doubtful texts in the Synoptics, and 'the utterances of the Christ of the Fourth Gospel, which, so the deepest criticism suggests, represent not so much the actual speech of Jesus as the mystic philosophy of the unknown disciple at Ephesus generations after the tragedy of Calvary.'[156] With his social Trinity Fairbairn leaves us with 'three several persons loving one another.'[157] Almost defeated, he sighs, 'Dr. Fairbairn, however, is a very technical and obscure writer, of whose meaning one can seldom be quite sure . . .'[158] He finds little consolation in R.J. Campbell's *A Faith for Today*, not least because he cannot think the thought 'He is Man without ceasing to be God; he is God without ceasing to be Man.'[159]

---

[153] Richard A. Armstrong, *The Trinity and the Incarnation*, 66–67.

[154] Ibid., 76.

[155] Ibid., 77.

[156] Ibid.

[157] Ibid., 79.

[158] Ibid., 82.

[159] Ibid., 92.

Furthermore, Campbell endorses Fairbairn's social Trinity, but having done that he contends that the three persons are not persons in our modern sense, but are self-manifestations of God, the one undivided personality – all of which seems to Armstrong utterly contradictory: God is not a society after all. Armstrong proceeds to challenge others, and then wonders why so illogical a belief should persist. He replies that an early recognition that in the person of Jesus was 'a new spiritual energy for the redemption of man'[160] was gradually bolstered as opposing views had to be met. By contrast with the doctrinal result, the teaching of Jesus reduces to this: 'God enters into communion with the soul.'[161] This, says Armstrong, is what the incarnation means.

In a more restrained, and a more searching, style, James Drummond revealed his predilection for what one might call a high Unitarian view of Jesus. 'Beholding the beloved Son,' he writes, 'Christians become conscious of their sonship. There is no revelation unless God, who commanded the light to shine out of darkness, shines in our hearts, and yet he gives the light of the Kingdom of his glory in the face of Jesus Christ.'[162] In an exposition of *The Pauline Benediction* (1897), he declares that 2 Corinthians 13:14 is 'the earliest expression of the great religious thoughts which underlie the doctrine of the Trinity. In this undogmatic form they are the common property of Christendom, of the Unitarian no less than the Trinitarian.'[163]

Drummond's most sustained discussion of the Trinity is found in his *Studies in Christian Doctrine* (1908). He rehearses the traditional Unitarian arguments against the doctrine: it is a late arrival on the scene; it is not stated in the New Testament; it is but an inference from scattered statements; the Bible's constant assertion of the unity of God does not sit well with it. Turning to the historical development of the doctrine he says that the fact that centuries had passed before the doctrine had attained its definitive shape is susceptible to more than one interpretation: it could have been present in embryo, or it could have been a novel departure from the simplicity of the ancient faith. He decides in favour of the latter option. While not denying that certain biblical texts concerning the Father, Son and Spirit do describe the Christian experience of communion with God, they do not imply the

---

[160] Ibid., 136.

[161] Ibid., 142.

[162] James Drummond, *The Christian Revelation of God: A Sermon preached on October 27th 1889, at the First Religious Service held in connection with the establishment of Manchester New College at Oxford*, 13.

[163] Idem, *The Pauline Benediction*, 7.

dogma of the Trinity. He dismisses the social Trinity as 'pure polytheism',[164] and surmises that that conception rests on an anthropological conception of God which assumes 'that what is necessary for the highest life of a finite mind must also be necessary for the infinite Spirit.'[165] Among other difficulties is that

> If each person has, or rather is, the whole of the Divine essence, and if that essence includes in its eternal nature a trinity of persons, then each person contains a trinity, to which in its turn the same argument may be applied; and thus we are conducted to an endless multitude. Or if, to escape this result, you say that each person contains *the* Trinity, then surely you fall into the error of confounding the persons; for if each person is in essence all three, there is no real distinction between them, and they become mere names without a difference. In this way the doctrine is self-destructive, and, whatever we may say, we are compelled in thought either to confound the persons or to divide the substance.[166]

Having presented further logical puzzles Drummond concludes: 'These difficulties cannot be evaded by calling the doctrine a mystery, before which our reason must sit dumb. The whole dogma is an attempt to translate mystery into that which is not mystery, and to present the eternal mode of the Divine existence in clearly cut intellectual propositions.'[167] Positively: 'We believe in God, the Father almighty, Maker of heaven and earth, and we believe in his sanctifying power in the souls of his children, and also in the holy Catholic Church and in the communion of saints, which are united into one Divine brotherhood through his all-pervading Spirit.'[168]

With nothing in the concluding sentence just quoted would P.T. Forsyth have disagreed. But, unlike Drummond, he felt that this belief led to, even required, the orthodox doctrine of the Trinity.

> All the metaphysic of the Trinity . . . is at bottom but the church's effort to express in thought the incomparable reality and absolute glory of the Saviour whom faith saw sitting by the Father as man's redeeming and eternal Lord, to engage the whole and present God directly in our

---

[164] Idem, *Studies in Christian Doctrine*, 149.

[165] Ibid., 150.

[166] Ibid., 157.

[167] Ibid., 158.

[168] Ibid., 162. Drummond here sails much closer to Christian orthodoxy than some latter day Unitarians would deem advisable.

salvation, and found the soul in Christ on the eternal Rock. . . . When that faith is raised from popular language and thought out, it means a doctrine of the Trinity, finding in the historic Son the Father's real gift of himself and his achieved purpose, and not a mere information nor a movement of willingness towards us. In Christ God did not send a message of his love which cost the messenger his life, but himself loved us to the death, and to our eternal redemption. . . . We have God in Christ as first hand, and seeing him we see the Father.[169]

In 1925 A.E. Garvie published *The Christian Doctrine of the Godhead*.[170] His sub-title both refines his theme and indicates his method: *The Apostolic Benediction as the Christian Creed*. In his Introduction he argues that Christian faith is based upon the fact of Christ: 'We must affirm on the ground of religious history and experience that there is an immediate contact and an intimate communion of man with God.'[171] Accordingly, 'Christian theology will be an exposition, commendation, and appreciation of the significance and value of that fact for faith.'[172] While by no means disparaging biblical and historical studies, his objective is constructive, and he confines himself to the object of Christian faith.

Launching forth in his characteristically orderly way Garvie's first section is on 'The grace of our Lord Jesus Christ'. He discusses the person and work of Christ, the apostolic experience and its interpretation,

---

[169] P.T. Forsyth, 'Faith, metaphysic, and incarnation,' 707, 708, 711. Though staunchly trinitarian, Forsyth did not treat the doctrine at length. See Alan P.F. Sell, *Testimony and Tradition*, 151–3.

[170] Garvie later gave a briefer, positive, account along similar lines in a series of lectures. See *Revelation Through History and Experience*. This volume includes an illuminating autobiographical Introduction and a Conclusion in which Garvie summarizes his *credo*. In a Preface he refers to some who had expressed surprise that in earlier writings, he had not taken account of Barth. He responds: 'Barth has not been needed to teach me the truth regarding the necessity and sufficiency of the Word of God . . . With all appreciation and gratitude for any service he may be rendering to bring thought back to the revelation of God and redemption of man in Christ, I must excuse myself from worshipping at his shrine; and as I am no iconoclast, I shall leave any Ephraim whom he has succoured to remain joined to his idol,' P. xiii. See further Garvie's autobiography, *Memories and Meanings of my Life*.

[171] A.E. Garvie, *The Christian Doctrine of the Godhead, or, The Apostolic Benediction as the Christian Creed*, 11.

[172] Ibid., 22.

and the dogmatic formulations of it. Under 'The Love of God' he treats the revelation of the Father, the relation of God to the world and to humanity, the problem of evil, and revelation and redemption. In Section III, 'The community of the Holy Spirit', he discusses the Spirit and the Church, and the Christian life and hope. A discussion of the Trinity completes his study. Well aware that he has throughout been expounding the doctrine of the economic Trinity, he now asks whether we may also speak of the ontological Trinity. The question is, 'Is God in His eternal nature as He has revealed Himself, Father, Son, and Holy Spirit?'[173] Garvie's answer is that 'If God has revealed Himself, the believer cannot admit that the revelation is concealment, that God makes Himself *appear* to man other than He *is*.'[174]

In passing, Garvie makes a number of pronouncements of interest, among them that

> Athanasius was right when he insisted on the *homoousion* to assert the unity of Christ with God, the Cappadocian fathers wrong when they allowed the term to be used with a tendency to tritheism. Much of the popular religious speech today, even in the pulpit, is tritheistic. There is a divine class to which Father, Son, and Holy Spirit belong, not a divine personal unity existing and manifested as Father, Son, and Holy Spirit. The task for constructive theology today is to recover the unity while not losing the reality of the differences within God which these descriptive historical terms express.[175]

A brisk review of some then current psychological and sociological theories encourages Garvie to observe 'a convergence of the two conceptions of personality as social and society as personal.'[176] Of these, the first helps us to understand unity-in-differences, the second, differences-in-unity. Indeed,

> We get the counterpart of the one substance of the creeds in social personality, and of the three persons in society as personal (as community) . . . As applied to God each of these conceptions must be raised to the height of perfection, God perfectly social in His personal activity, and God perfectly personal in His social relations, God perfect personality

---

[173] Ibid., 462.
[174] Ibid., 463.
[175] Ibid., 468.
[176] Ibid., 478.

and [*pace* Drummond] society in Himself, and the one because the other.[177]

Returning finally to the theme of the three persons in the unity of the Godhead, Garvie confidently declares,

> In the historical revelation (the economic trinity) the difference is more prominent than the unity. In the eternal revelation, which will consummate the historical, the unity will be dominant. There will not be absorption in a unity without any difference, but a unity in which all differences will at last be so harmonised as to make the unity perfect.[178]

In 1937 four professors at Wesley College, Headingley, Leeds, contributed lectures to a volume entitled *The Doctrine of the Holy Spirit*. Harold Roberts's contribution is entitled 'The Holy Spirit and the Trinity'. Skilfully blending theory and practice, he argues that 'If the theologian is faithful to his task, which is to interpret the content of the Christian Revelation of God in the light of the growing experience of the Church and not simply to examine archaeological remains, he will find that the doctrine of the Trinity makes his theology truly systematic and provides the only adequate basis for the life of devotion and service.'[179] Moreover, in the Trinity the theologian possesses 'a principle of interpretation that enables him to make sense of reality as a whole.'[180]

Roberts offers a brief analysis of some critical points in the development of Trinitarian doctrine. He cannot absolve the Cappadocians from harbouring tritheistic tendencies, and is much more sympathetic to the positions of Augustine and Aquinas with their emphasis upon the unitary consciousness of the Godhead in which 'three distinctive activities or functions have their ground.'[181] He is unimpressed by the social analogy which, as we saw, Garvie propounded, on the ground that it points in the direction of pluralism. His positive statement, non-susceptible to summary, is as follows:

> While recognizing that the nature of God defies verbal expression, we can affirm that the life of God is personal and that it constitutes a unity.

---

[177] Ibid., 479.
[178] Ibid., 480.
[179] Harold Roberts, 'The Holy Spirit and the Trinity', 109–10.
[180] Ibid., 110.
[181] Ibid., 113.

The Divine Nature has been made known to us in three activities which are not of accidental or temporary significance, but which derive from Its character as Eternal Love. These activities we may describe as creation, redemption, and inspiration, and, although they are distinctive in nature, they proceed from one and the same Being and are controlled by one and the same purpose. It is the Eternal Love of God that brought the world into existence, that offers itself for our redemption in the historic purpose of Jesus Christ, and that energizes within us so that we may respond to its holy appeal. Within each activity God Himself is to be found. The Creator of the world is none other than its Redeemer, none other that He who brings order out of chaos and by the inspiration of His own spirit banished the night of darkness and sin. In this sense, which preserves the fundamental intention of the Catholic Faith, we may with gladness declare, 'We worship one God in Trinity and Trinity in Unity.'[182]

Turning to the question of the Trinity in relation to Christian experience, Roberts affirms that 'There is no tenable explanation of the rise of Trinitarianism other than the determination to hold together the belief in the divinity of Christ, the unity of God, and the existence of the Christian community.'[183] Without compromising their inherited belief in the unity of God the apostles made their crucified, risen and ascended Lord the object of adoration. They were conscious of a power which brought them into a new relationship with God, and into a fellowship, the church, which they did not create.

In the doctrine of the Trinity Roberts finds the logical completion of theism:

> If we concentrate our attention on God the Father to the exclusion of God the Son and God the Holy Spirit, we inevitably begin to despair of ever keeping His laws, and a religion of grace is converted into a monotonous experience of frustrated effort . . . If, again, we worship the Son to the exclusion of the Father and the Spirit, we relapse into a pernicious form of ditheism which converts the Father into a Being whom nobody knows or wants to know . . . Finally, if we exclude the first and second persons of the Trinity and worship the Holy Spirit alone, our religion will deteriorate into that kind of immanentism which finds God everywhere in general but nowhere in particular.[184]

---

[182] Ibid., 118.

[183] Ibid., 119.

[184] Ibid., 125, 126.

Roberts concludes by exhorting his hearers and readers, in Paul's language, to put on the whole armour of God, 'and what is that but God in the fullness and richness of his being, Father, Son, and Holy Spirit?'[185]

In the sense intended by Roberts, this is something which, unsurprisingly, the Unitarian Herbert Crabtree was not at all inclined to do. On the contrary, in *The Doctrine of the Trinity* (1946) he contends that, no matter how helpful the doctrine of the Trinity may once have been, it has now been outgrown. It is metaphysically dubious and is couched in obscure terminology. Nor is Christ to be worshipped as God. Underlying his critique is a repudiation of dogma as such. To Crabtree, 'the Unitarian . . . believes that the only unity that matters – or is, indeed, possible – in the sphere of religion is to be found not in the acceptance of a formal creed or dogma, but in the spirit of charity, of tolerance, and of goodwill.'[186] We seem to have taken a significant step towards humanism from the position of a Drummond, or even a Mellone.

In 1953 R.S. Franks summed up a lifetime of reflection upon Christian doctrine in his book *The Doctrine of the Trinity*. He reviews the course of the doctrine's history from the New Testament to Barth and Leonard Hodgson. He reveals the long-standing tension within Christian doctrine between the *kerygma*, which underlines the unity of God, and the credal emphasis upon the distinction of the hypostases or persons, and shows that the development of the doctrine of the Trinity proceeded more quickly than that of the person of Christ, with its concern for the relation within him of humanity and divinity. Like Roberts, he finds the positions of Augustine and Aquinas more to his liking than the Cappadocian, but even so, 'The final result of the Patristic, followed by the Medieval, theology, was, therefore to leave a great hiatus between the doctrine of the Trinity and that of the Incarnation.'[187] With the modern period there comes the emphasis upon experience, and while some, R.C. Moberly and Barth among them, are content 'to revise the older position with its hiatus between a doctrine of the Trinity where the Persons are subordinated to the Divine Unity, and a doctrine of the Incarnation where this subordination is virtually ignored,'[188] others seek 'to get rid of the hiatus that vexes theology, either by adapting Christology to a firmly monotheistic

---

[185] Ibid., 128.
[186] Herbert Crabtree, *The Doctrine of the Trinity*, 31.
[187] R.S. Franks, *The Doctrine of the Trinity*, 194.
[188] Ibid., 195.

Trinitarianism, or by adapting Trinitarianism to the credal Christ-ology.'[189]

Franks's preferred method is to have doctrine judged by the *kerygma*, and this entails that doctrines be faithful to monotheism and to the real humanity of Jesus. From this standpoint he finds Leonard Hodgson's attempt to revive the social Trinity (which Franks traces back to Richard of St Victor) wanting on grounds of authority: John of Damascus and Augustine agree that what we know first is the divine unity, not the hypostases; reason: the social Trinity leaves us with no intelligible conception of God – it is 'too much like the unknown emergent of the future, that crowns the series of emergent unities in Alexander's *Space, Time and Deity*';[190] and experience: the Christian experience is not 'an experience of three distinct Divine Personalities. It is an experience of One God through Christ in the Spirit. Theology can analyse out of the experience the mediation of Christ and the power of the Spirit, but in the actual experience all is fused into communion with God.'[191]

In reaching his positive position Franks has recourse to Schleiermacher and Ritschl. He welcomes the way in which, in their Christologies, they both set out from the human Jesus, thereby adhering more closely to the *kerygma*. However, Schleiermacher's doctrine of the Trinity (God is the identity of nature and spirit, and the persons are phases of divine manifestation which do not touch the divine essence) requires to be corrected by Ritschl's insight that God is the Spirit who creates nature and finite spirits, and by Barth's insistence that God is as he reveals himself. But this recalls Aquinas, who taught that 'God eternally objectifies Himself in his Image and unites Himself therewith in the Love that is Himself.'[192] Accordingly, Franks concludes that 'the Christology of Schleiermacher must be combined with the Trinitarianism of Aquinas as reinterpreted by Barth.'[193]

No Nonconformist theologian did more in the last two decades of the twentieth century to place the Trinity in the centre of theological debate than Colin Gunton. So all-embracing is his Trinitarian vision (an analogy might be drawn with the centrality of the Cross in the writings of P.T. Forsyth) that it is difficult to place him in a study of this kind. I did manage to introduce his work on Barth and

---

[189] Ibid.

[190] Ibid., 196.

[191] Ibid.

[192] Ibid., 199.

[193] Ibid.

Hartshorne's views of God, and on the atonement in the appropriate places; and I could have treated his views on creation under the doctrine of God and his eschatology within the section devoted to that area of doctrine. But this would have been to falsify the scope of his work. I shall therefore simply list some of his works which bear upon the doctrine of the Trinity in the order of their appearance.

In *Enlightement and Alienation* (1985) Gunton claims that dualisms of various kinds are a product the Enlightenment, and that Kant is the major culprit here. These dualisms, whether of God and the world, faith and knowledge, the arts and the sciences, destroy the unity of the human being, for the mind becomes a disembodied spectator and the idea of the whole person in all of his or her relations is lost. The other error of the Enlightenment was to transfer the predicates of power, knowledge and glory, from God to humanity. The way to reverse this, says Gunton, is to revise the way in which the predicates, as applied to God, are conceived.

> To think of God as triune makes this possible, for the centre of Trinitarian thinking is that God defines himself, marks out for us his reality, through his Sonship. The power is the power of the cross, the knowledge the giving up of knowledge for our sake, the glory that of washing the feet of the disciples . . . The triune God, eternally one in the richness and variety of his being, has made himself responsible for our time by taking upon himself the burden of our alienation. That is why he is to be discerned at the heart of our existence.[194]

In a paper on 'Trinity, ontology and anthropology' Gunton pursues the notion of personhood in the light of the Trinity. He discusses the *imago dei* and suggests that 'Where the tradition tended to see our imagedness to consist in the possession of certain faculties, here the stress is on the ontology of personhood.' As to the question of human beings in relation to the rest of creation: 'The triune God has created humankind as finite persons-in-relation who are called to acknowledge his creation by becoming the persons they are and by enabling the rest of the creation to make its due response of praise.'[195] This theme is developed more fully in Gunton's book, *The Promise of Trinitarian Theology* (2nd ed. 1997).

---

[194] C.E. Gunton, *Enlightenment and Alienation: An Essay towards a Trinitarian Theology*, 154, 155.

[195] Idem, 'Trinity, ontology and anthropology: towards a renewal of the doctrine of the *imago dei*', 61.

What is needed is a theology which enables humankind and the world to be themselves, in the image of God and destined for the praise of God in their own ways, but as contingent and finite beings.

Within the broad framework of a Trinitarian theology, it becomes possible . . . to understand God and the world as related in otherness. It is one thing to be God, another to be the world. And yet the world can fulfil its created destiny only in relation to God. The theology of the Trinity provides, in this context, a way of embracing those relations to God we call creation and redemption within a conceptual framework which links the two without confusion, so that redemption is seen as the restoring and completing of that which was 'in the beginning.' That which was begun through the Son and in the Spirit, has its destiny in being returned, perfected, to the Father through their redeeming agency.[196]

At the dawn of the twenty-first century Paul S. Fiddes published his stimulating work, *Participating in God: A Pastoral Doctrine of the Trinity* (2000). Setting out from the realization that 'the early followers of Jesus had to rethink their understanding of the being of God because of their experience of God's acts among them', Fiddes develops a personal and relational understanding of the Trinity which seeks to avoid the perils of both modalism and pluralism, and which, through an 'epistemology of participation', conceives of God as 'an event of relationships.'[197] By virtue of these loving relationships within the Trinity, there is an analogy between human community and divine communion, and 'To engage in the relationships in God means that we are brought up against the challenge of the alien, the radically different, the unlike; but at the same time we have the security of experiencing a fellowship more intimate than anything we can otherwise know.'[198] Where we experience this fellowship, 'talk of God as Father, Son and Spirit comes alive.'[199] He proceeds to show how this happens in prayer, suffering, forgiveness, the facing of death, in relation to spiritual gifts, and in the sacramental life. Throughout, he seeks to complement the idea of the

---

[196] Idem, *The Promise of Trinitarian Theology*, 205. In his posthumously published collection of papers, *Father, Son and Holy Spirit: Toward a Fully Trinitarian Theology*, Gunton develops his trinitarian approach in relation to creation, the Holy Spirit, the sacraments of baptism and the Lord's Supper, and church membership.

[197] Paul S. Fiddes, Participating in God: A Pastoral Doctrine of the Trinity, 37, 38.

[198] Ibid., 55.

[199] Ibid., 56.

imitation of God with that of participating in God in pastoral experience. Here theological acumen and pastoral concern are blended in a manner characteristic of Fiddes's writings as a whole.

By neither Gunton nor Fiddes would the Unitarian Arthur Long be persuaded. Indeed, he allowed himself to greet the approach of Christianity's third millennium with a trenchant anti-Trinitarian blast. He was addressing his own communion, and first felt it necessary to persuade some of its members that his demolition task was worth undertaking. He reminds them that Unitarianism began as anti-Trinitarianism; that the rejection or questioning of the Trinity determined the Unitarian idea of God; and that the doctrine is no less vulnerable than it ever was. He refers to the incomprehensibility of the Trinitarian 'nonsense' in the Athanasian creed, and takes particular exception to the incarnation, which 'seems to make complete nonsense of the full humanity of Jesus, which even mainstream Christianity is obliged to affirm.'[200] He recommends that 'as Christian monotheists, let us . . . continue to put Jesus at the centre of our faith, seeing him as the supreme example of the way in which God, the Eternal Spirit of love and power, operated through human lives, revealing himself above all in the great Prophet-Souls of all ages.'[201]

V

I turn finally to what is probably the most comprehensive example of corporate theologizing across the range of Christian doctrine undertaken by any Nonconformist denomination during the twentieth century. In 1958, under the leadership of its General Secretary, Howard S. Stanley, the Congregational Union of England and Wales launched its project, 'The Next Ten Years'.[202] Eight commissions were established to report upon all aspects of the denomination's life: the nature of the Church; the faith as held by Congregationalists; buildings, rural areas and lay pastors; the nature, life and work of local Congregational churches; the missionary obligations of the Church; ministerial training; the denomination's influence in the life of the nation; and the Union's administrative concerns. Our particular concern is with the

---

[200] Arthur Long, *Current Trends in British Unitarianism*, 22.

[201] Ibid., 23. See also, A. Richard Kingston, *God in One Person*. The kernel of his case is that it is logically inconceivable that God should have become completely incarnate in one person at one point in history.

[202] See Howard S. Stanley, *The Next Ten Years*.

work of Commission II, a consideration of which will exemplify the way in which every attempt was made throughout the project to involve the local churches in the discussions.

The Commission began its work in 1958[203] and, in response to requests from the churches, its first task was to produce *A Short Affirmation of Faith*. This document, called in draft a 'Confession of Faith', and primarily designed as a teaching aid, was circulated to the churches during 1960; replies were sought by 31 October of that year; and the revised version was adopted by the Assembly in 1961. Seven hundred and fifty replies were forthcoming,[204] and that notice was taken of these is evident from a comparison of the draft with the final version. In the 'Confession' each clause is introduced by the words, 'We believe . . .'; in the *Affirmation's* first four clauses the introductory words are, 'We worship . . .', while the last two clauses retain the original wording. This change is indicative of the desire to make it clear that 'faith' is not merely a matter of intellectual assent, but of trust issuing in praise. Two clauses from the draft and the final version may be compared to reveal other amendments.

Confession

> We believe in the Divine Father. He created the world and sustains it with loving care. In wisdom and power He rules and overrules. He so orders the world that man can find peace only in trust and obedience, freely given. In compassion for a world disordered by man's misuse of his freedom, He sent His Son to be its Saviour and its Judge. The future of the world and its end are in the Father's hands.

Short Affirmation

> We worship God the Father. He created the universe and continually renews it. He rules the world in wisdom, and cares for all that He has made. He has made men free, but we find joy and peace only as we trust and obey Him. To a world disordered by men's misuse of freedom, He sent His Son to save them and to give them new life.

The principal difference here is that in the *Affirmation* the ideas of judgement and the world's future are reserved to the eschatological clause with which the document ends.

---

[203] The decision to proceed was taken at the meeting of the Congregational Council on 17–18 November 1958.

[204] *The Congregational Year Book* for 1960 lists 2984 local churches.

Confession

> We believe in the Church of the living God. The Church consists of all God's people whom Christ has gathered into one. In the Church on earth through Scripture, preaching, sacrament and mutual caring, God renews in every age the gift of His Son. The Church's calling is to bear witness to Christ, to claim all life for Him, and for His sake to love and serve all mankind.

Short Affirmation

> We believe in the Church of Jesus Christ. Christ has made all who trust in Him into one people in heaven and on earth. In the Church on earth, through Scripture, prayer, preaching, sacrament and mutual caring, God renews the presence of Christ and men's communion with Him. The Church's calling is to worship God, to bear witness to Christ in every land, to claim all aspects of human life for Him, and for His sake to love and serve all mankind.

There is a more strongly Christological flavour to the statement in the *Affirmation*, where the Church's first calling is said to be to worship God – a note missing from the 'Confession'. Missing from the *Affirmation* is the heritage-laden term 'gathered', as descriptive of the Church's nature, while there is a specific reference to the communion of saints in the *Affirmation* – something absent from the 'Confession'.[205]

Concurrently, Commission II worked on a longer *Declaration of Faith*, of which a draft was submitted to the churches in 1964. On this occasion only 150 replies were received, though some of them were substantial, and all were carefully considered. The revised version was submitted to, and adopted by, the Assembly of 1967. The Declaration is intended to do for its time what the *Savoy Declaration of Faith and Order* of 1658 did for its: to articulate the faith commonly held amongst the Congregationalists. The commissioners explain that

> The context of the present Declaration is a climate of uncertainty about Christian faith, within the Church as well as outside it. New causes for

---

[205] The 'Confession' was circulated by the Congregational Union in the form of a duplicated, typewritten sheet. The text of the *Short Affirmation* may be seen in *World Congregationalism*, III no. 8, May 1961, 22–23.

scepticism and unbelief have appeared with advances in knowledge
and experience during the past three centuries. In this period, too, God
has guided his Church towards new forms of Christian thought, and
these, though fruitful, have been unsettling.[206]

Undeterred, the commissioners set about their task, and outlined
their result in the Declaration's Preamble.

We affirm first the reality, the grace, and the triune being of God; we
declare our trust in him as sovereign over the universe; we declare our
belief that he has brought the Church into being to serve his liberating
purpose for all mankind; we declare our belief that he will accomplish
his purposes with grace and glory; we acknowledge what he requires
of us and of all mankind and affirm that he himself is enabling men to
fulfil this requirement.[207]

In his account of the project W.A. Whitehouse, who occupied the chair
for the second half of the Commission's life, explains that 'the
Declaration does not speak first and foremost about Jesus Christ but
about God. Its theism is thoroughly Christocentric – but it is *theocen-
tric* religion which is declared.'[208] This remark prompts the observa-
tion that like all such productions, the *Declaration* is properly the child
of its time, and its time was marked by the theology of the word and
by the biblical theology movement, most prominently represented on
the panel by John Marsh. Thus, while the presence on the panel of
such scholars as Nathaniel Micklem and Geoffrey F. Nuttall ensured
that perceived Barthian extravagances would be checked, the more
pro-Barthian influence of Hubert Cunliffe-Jones and of Whitehouse
himself is clearly detectable; though the matter is complicated by the
fact that such panel members as Harold Bickley and Lovell Cocks,
both students under Forsyth, and John Huxtable, who was closely
involved in the republication of Forsyth's works during the middle
years of the century, were equally committed to the objectivity of

---

[206] *A Declaration of Faith*, London: Congregational Church in England and
Wales, 1967, 3; reprinted in David M. Thompson, *Stating the Gospel:
Formulations and Declarations of Faith from the Heritage of the United Reformed
Church*.

[207] Ibid., 8.

[208] W.A. Whitehouse, 'Making the Declaration of Faith', 23. See also idem,
'What does Christian believing mean today?', 6–7. The Congregational *Union*
became the Congregational *Church* in 1966.

God's saving act, and out of sympathy with older anthropocentric optimism.[209]

Among many notable features in the *Declaration* is the strong statement that the presence of God the Holy Spirit 'is not confined to the Church; for even where the Spirit is not understood in relation to Jesus Christ, where his presence is undiscerned, where his very existence is denied, there too God works perpetually in the Holy Spirit to enlarge the possibilities of human life and to open the way for faith and sonship.'[210] There is a willingness to face things as they are – for example: 'We believe that God reigns over the universe. Plain evidence of his rule is not there for all to see . . .'[211] There is an affirmation of 'our Congregational conviction that the wholeness of Christ's universal Church may be present in local congregations, as well as in wider associations, where God gathers [there is the word!] people together in constant relationship for worship, for fellowship, for service and for witness to the world, under the care of Christ their Lord.'[212] As harbingers of theologies to come, there are substantial paragraphs on the proper use by humans of the physical order, and on our obligations towards other living creatures.

As Whitehouse explains, the most significant revisions of the first draft of 1964 were those concerning the section headed 'God is gracious,' to which strong paragraphs on God's generosity on creation and his forgiving love are added; a new paragraph specifically on God's providence is included, along with other amendments, in the section headed, 'God is sovereign over the universe'; and, whereas in the draft the Church was treated under two headings, 'God creates the Church' and 'God is sovereign over the Church,' in the final version the two sections are conflated and re-ordered, and the latter heading only is retained.[213]

---

[209] As is well known, Forsyth has been called a Barthian before Barth, though I think that this is an over-simplification. Their methods and styles were very different; Forsyth never cooled towards the sacraments in the way that the later Barth did; and, while Forsyth felt that in his time the primary apologetic task was within the church and not in relation to the 'world', he was not so hostile in principle to apologetics as was Barth and, indeed, from time to time he engaged in it. See further T. Hywel Hughes, 'A Barthian before Barth?', 308–15; and the essays by John Thompson and myself in Trevor Hart, ed., *Justice the True and Only Mercy*, of which the latter is reprinted in Alan P.F. Sell, *Testimony and Tradition*, ch. 7.

[210] W.A. Whitehouse, 'Making the Declaration of Faith', 21.

[211] Ibid., 22.

[212] Ibid., 34.

[213] Ibid., 14.

The *Declaration* was welcomed by many Christians of other traditions[214] and, if I may on this occasion offer my own opinion: in content
it constitutes probably the most significant document of its kind produced during this century from any quarter within the Reformed
family; and in its method of working, which involved consultations in
which all local churches were invited to participate, the Commission
– indeed all of the eight Commissions – demonstrated that the idea
that theologizing is the task of the whole people of God, if not perfectly realized in practice, can be very much more than a pipe-dream.

VI

I conclude this lecture by quoting a prayer:

> Grant, O Father, that we may seek not our own glory, but thine alone.
> May the world and self never come between us and thee, but with the
> holy simplicity of Christ may we listen for thy word; with single eye
> may we discern thy truth; and with pure heart may we cherish it; so
> that in the stillness and quietude of our souls we may have commun-
> ion with thee, and having ever clearer revelations of thy will, we may
> speak and act, not from ourselves, but under the leading of thy Spirit.
> So may we follow the Beloved into the kingdom of thy sons.[215]

This prayer might be thought to have more than a tincture of
Trinitarianism about it, but it was composed by the Unitarian James
Drummond. I could cheerfully offer this prayer – even more cheerfully if I were permitted to add the words 'and daughters' to its final
clause. I suspect, however, that a number of present-day Unitarians
would feel more ill at ease with it than I. This suspicion will be borne
out as I venture next into some ecclesiological thickets.

---

[214] Some of whom offered their reflections in several issues of *The British
Weekly*, May–June 1964.

[215] J. Drummond, quoted in *Eminent Unitarian Teachers, 15: Drummond*, 3 (but
unpaginated).

Lecture 3

Ecclesiological Thickets

How did the mainline Nonconformist traditions understand themselves in the twentieth century? How did they reach out to one another and to more distant communions during the so-called 'ecumenical century'? Is their traditional witness as Free Churchpeople still required, or even viable? These are the questions to be considered in this lecture.

I

Although 'Protestant' is a term which has suffered from being hijacked by those who perpetrate propositions containing the terms 'Rome', 'Babylon' and 'whore'; who spurn evangelicals who pray with Roman Catholics; and who place evangelicals who attend Roman Catholic funerals under a ban, there can be no shirking the fact that, *vis-à-vis* the Church at large, the English and Welsh Nonconformists are Protestants. That there are polemical precedents for anti-Roman scurrility dating from Reformation times cannot be denied. Suffice it to say that almost all of those Nonconformists of 'mainline' denominations who wrote on Protestantism during the twentieth century were concerned to emphasize the aspect of protesting *for* particular insights deemed biblical, any protestations *against* alien views standing, secondarily, as negative implications.[1] Moreover, most of these writers were ardently committed to the modern ecumenical movement.

---

[1] Though it must be granted that in his Christianity and Catholicism: A Vindication of Progressive Protestantism – a tome massive in bulk and massive in scholarship – the pacifist C.J. Cadoux came out fighting at a number of points. It would be interesting to review his case in the light of Vatican II and subsequent trends in Roman Catholic teaching and practice, but I cannot

I shall let P.T. Forsyth set the scene for us. In 1899 he published a lecture entitled, 'What did Luther really do?' The kernel of his answer, and the standpoint from which he criticizes the Roman Church is that

> What must control the Church, in actual practice and not mere theory, is the Word of God as the Gospel coming to the soul through faith, with the Church as a mere herald and medium and agent. Rob faith of its place and power, and the Church becomes not a medium but a media-tor, its minister becomes its priest, and its policy is not service but power. Faith is fatal to such a place for the Church. It is direct dealing of the soul with Christ. Christ is the object of faith, not a book, or a church. . . . The true authority over the soul and conscience is given through this faith. That authority is not the Church, but it is the effec-tual Word of God in the preaching of the cross, to which the conscience owes its life. And doctrine is just the best account we can give of this living faith in its living community.[2]

Three decades on, Forsyth's student, H.F. Lovell Cocks, published his account of the living faith of Protestants in *The Faith of a Protestant Christian* (1931). His emphasis upon grace, faith and the priesthood of all believers leads him to pull no punches with alternative positions. Thus, for example, he argues that 'Papal infallibility, like the Divine Right of Kings, is an instrument of despotic authority masquerading as an article of faith;'[3] and in connection with the Lord's Supper he

---

embark upon that large task here. Cadoux also published Roman Catholicism and Freedom. In referring to Cadoux's career in her article on him in ODNB, Elaine Kaye explains that the title 'professor' was 'a courtesy title used by contemporary theological colleges.' This, however, is not the case: the title was formal and official, and some of the chairs were named and endowed – for example, Cadoux's Mackennal Chair at Mansfield College. No doubt the title was originally used to witness to the Nonconformists' seri-ousness in providing higher education at a time when Oxford and Cambridge were closed to them. In that case the title, as well as being formal and official, was honourable. Perhaps Dr Kaye feels that the use of the title should be restricted to senior scholars in universities. But this would be to deprive not only English and Welsh Nonconformists, but also James Denney and H.R. Mackintosh in Scotland, Paul Tillich and Nels Ferré in the United States, and many more. I write this in the interests of historical accuracy: I do not think it a very Nonconformist thing to be unduly concerned about titles.

[2] P.T. Forsyth, *Rome, Reform and Reaction*, 135–6.
[3] H.F. Lovell Cocks, *The Faith of a Protestant Christian*, 17.

recalls a saying of his teacher: '"Conversion," says Forsyth, "is the true Transubstantiation." Not things, but persons, are the sacraments of grace.'[4]

If, as I have suggested, the twentieth-century Congregationalists spawned the majority of Nonconformist systematicians, while the Baptists were pre-eminent suppliers of Old Testament scholars between 1930 and 1970, the Methodists, as well as multiplying scholars determined to leave no equine hoofprint unexamined in their pursuit of Wesley, were, at least as importantly, to the fore in producing historians of the Reformation in the early years of the century, more especially in its middle decades, and intermittently thereafter. In justification of this claim it suffices to recall the work of H.B. Workman on Wyclif and Hus, Peter Stephens on Zwingli and Bucer, and Philip S. Watson, E. Gordon Rupp and Arthur Skevington Wood on Luther.[5] As might be expected, theological themes pervade these books. But for a concise statement of the essence of Protestantism as such, and one with which all the Methodists just named would have agreed, we may turn to Congregationalism's distinguished historian, Bernard Lord Manning. The Reformers, he informs us,

> relied on two main processes: first, they would remove from the Christian scene many unnecessary things which obscured the essentials; second, they would lay a new emphasis on the essentials. The truth as it is in Jesus was to stand clearer when competing growths were removed, and when its own outline had been cut with sharper tools. Protestantism, that is to say, is not the opposite of medieval catholicism: it is simply an improved kind of catholicism. Protestantism is not a negative thing. It is a positive re-statement of catholic truth.[6]

These words are as accurate and as fresh as when they were written in 1938.

---

[4] Ibid., 49–50.

[5] See H.B. Workman, *The Letters of John Hus*; idem, *The Dawn of the Reformation*; idem, *John Wyclif: A Study of the English Medieval Church*; W. Peter Stephens, *The Holy Spirit in the Theology of Martin Bucer*; idem, *The Theology of Huldrych Zwingli*; *Zwingli: An Introduction to his Thought*, Oxford: Clarendon Press, 1992; Philip S. Watson, *Let God be God: An Interpretation of the Theology of Martin Luther*; E. Gordon Rupp, *The Righteousness of God*; idem, *Luther's Progress to the Diet of Worms*; A. Skevington Wood, *Captive to the Word: Martin Luther, Doctor of Sacred Scripture*.

[6] Bernard Lord Manning, *Essays in Orthodox Dissent*, 51–52.

Manning's general approach is echoed in a number of works of the decade 1950–60. Of these the first is the important tract, *The Catholicity of Protestantinsm*. This was edited by the Methodists R. Newton Flew and Rupert E. Davies, whose committee included their fellow Methodists Kenneth Grayston, Philip Watson and Gordon Rupp,[7] together with the Baptists R.L. Child, P.W. Evans, and Ernest A. Payne, the Congregationalists H.F. Lovell Cocks, John Marsh, and Nathaniel Micklem, and the Presbyterians T.W. Manson and R.D. Whitehorn. The group had been convened in response to a request by the Archbishop of Canterbury, Geoffrey Fisher, who sought a Protestant response to the 'Catholic' statement he had commissioned entitled *Catholicity* (1947). The respondents begin by recalling that at the Second Diet of Spiers (1529) the designation 'protestant' was applied for the first time to those who opposed the rescinding of the decision of the First Diet of Spiers (1526), which had given some encouragement to evangelicals. The majority favoured not only the forbidding of Zwinglian teaching but also the arrest of Lutheranism. In their *Protestation* the minority group proclaimed

> fidelity to the Gospel, the Word of God contained in Holy Scripture, as the final court of appeal for the Church. The Gospel is God's Word in Christ, spoken in deed and in the power of the Holy Spirit, and the *Protestation* is a declaration of allegiance to our Lord Jesus Christ. This is positive enough. No movement as fruitful and abiding as Protestantism ever nourished itself on negations.[8]

The respondents proceed to argue that the term 'catholicity' means 'the presence of the living Christ' and 'the "wholeness" of the Gospel,' and they add that this wholeness is not fully possessed by any Christian communion.[9]

In 1954 Gordon Rupp reflected on *Methodism in Relation to Protestant Tradition*, and six years later he published *Protestant Catholicity*, a slim volume which includes his Scott Lidgett Lecture of 1959 entitled, 'The Protestant tradition and Christian unity.' He refers to his mentor Lidgett's argument in *Apostolic Ministry* (1909) that it is

---

[7] Though Rupp later confessed that 'I contributed only a name to the title page.' See his *Protestant Catholicity*, 41

[8] R. Newton Flew and Rupert E. Davies, eds., *The Catholicity of Protestantism, being a report presented to His Grace the Archbishop of Canterbury by a group of Free Churchmen*, 14.

[9] Ibid., 23.

a mistake to construe the Church's catholicity as 'the system of dog-matic truths which its ministry affirms, teaches and imposes,' or as 'the sphere within which . . . authority is exercised for the dispensing of ordered and external means of grace and for the guidance and con-trol of human conduct.' True catholicity 'consists in the fellowship of a great experience . . . fellowship with the saints though common access to God.'[10] Not the least entertaining section of this tract is Rupp's demolition of the Anglo-Catholic E.L. Mascall's view that the Reformation was an unfortunate mistake, and that what is required is a return to the original 'wholeness' of the Church; on which Rupp comments, 'Dr Mascall has not only sketched a valuable ecumenical programme. He has also unawares described the Protestant Reformation!'[11] Then comes the most important part of the lecture:

> This is no debating point, for it is the coherence of the Protestant tradi-tion which is in question between us. The dialogue between Catholics and Protestants can never be really fruitful until Catholics reckon, not with the salvation of individual Protestants, or the persistence in Protestantism of isolated Catholic truths, but with the Protestant Churches as societies, and with the coherence of its tradition as a whole.[12]

My way of putting the matter, reinforced in the light of personal expe-rience of formal international dialogue between the Reformed family and the Roman Catholic Church, is to say that the crucial question is whether, when referring to non-Roman Christian communions as churches, Rome is speaking theologically or sociologically; that is, are our churches truly gatherings of those who are saints by calling, or are they empirical institutions like schools, hospitals and public houses? There is an ambivalence in some dialogue statements which requires to be carefully scrutinized.

In 1955 John Whale published what has become a classic, albeit not, in the eyes of some, a flawless,[13] study of *The Protestant Tradition*. He is care-ful not to overlook the note of grace in the teaching of the pre-Reformation church, but claims that 'Protestantism has something more to say. It con-tends that, though the evangelical principle was thus asserted, it was

---

[10] E. Gordon Rupp, *Protestant Catholicity*, 34–35.

[11] Ibid., 44.

[12] Ibid, 44–45.

[13] See the reviews by Whale's fellow Congregationalists Geoffrey F. Nuttall and Horton Davies.

nevertheless largely neutralized by the two facts which were and are distinctive of the whole Catholic system: the powerfully active ideas of sacramental grace and saving merit.'[14] As to the former, 'Catholicism . . . interprets the grace of the Gospel, not as the attitude of God in Christ to sinners, but as "topping up the battery" of the soul.'[15] As to the latter, by conflating justification with sanctification, pardon is equated with purification – a process which ends only with death. Alluding to Bunyan's *The Pilgrim's Progress*, he declares, 'Christian must carry his burden on his back all the way from the cross to the Celestial City. There is no evangelical doctrine of Assurance here, even for the great Augustine. God in his distributive justice must fix his acceptance or rejection of men in accordance with the measure of their meritorious attainment, at the last.'[16]

Broadly united though they were on the major Protestant principles, the Nonconformists were no slouches when it came to showing how much scope for ecclesiological manoeuvre there was within the Protestant family.

II

A number of Nonconformists published general studies of the church during the twentieth century. Among them were John Oman's two works, *Vision and Authority* (1902, revised 1928) and *The Church and the Divine Order* (1911); P.T. Forsyth's study of *The Church and the Sacraments* (1917); the Presbyterian P. Carnegie Simpson's Chalmers' Lectures entitled The *Evangelical Church Catholic* (1934); and the Methodist R. Newton Flew's Fernley-Hartley Lecture, *Jesus and His Church* (1938). Taken all together these works exemplify the biblical, historical, systematic and missiological emphases which cannot be excluded from any rounded consideration of ecclesiology. To them may be added the essays of Lesslie Newbigin and Daniel Jenkins: respectively, *The Household of God* (1953) and *The Strangeness of the*

---

[14] John S. Whale, *The Protestant Tradition*, 48.

[15] Ibid., 50.

[16] Ibid., 66. Mention may be made of the Congregationalist (subsequently United Church of Canada) Kenneth Hamilton's book, *The Protestant Way*. This is a theoretical study which turns upon 'the Protestant contention that faith in revelation is the prime datum of the Christian life' (p. 239). Accordingly, dialogue between God and humanity is possible, as is that between human beings. By this means, spiritual values are communicated, though they are not susceptible of proof by objective demonstration.

Church (1955). It is not my purpose, however, to dwell upon such general studies, but rather to enquire into the particular ecclesiological self-understandings of the Nonconformist traditions which are here under review.

In the first half of the twentieth century Congregationalists, Baptists, Unitarians and Methodists were not backward in publishing works announcing their distinctive principles. Partly because of the widespread use of their Book of Order, which ran to seven editions between 1882 and 1964,[17] and partly because of their predominantly Scottish inheritance and sources,[18] the English Presbyterians were much less active in this field.

Turning first to the Congregational self-understanding, it is not surprising, given that their original *raison d'être* was ecclesiological, that Congregationalist authors should make much of the Church as God's calling, as one in Christ, and as manifested in local gatherings of saints. This theme is present in all of the works to be named, some of which are more triumphalist in tone than others, and a number of which make much of the claim that congregationalism (the lower case 'c' here admits the Baptists and others) accords most with apostolic church order. In 1902 there appeared a new edition of Albert Goodrich's *A Primer of Congregationalism* and a symposium edited by Dugald Macfadyen entitled *Constructive Congregational Ideals*. In 1904 J.D. Jones gave some *Reasons Why for Congregationalists*; in 1912 P.T. Forsyth brought out his *Faith, Freedom and the Future*; and in 1925 T.T. James held forth on *The Work and Administration of a Congregational Church*. The year 1924 saw the first appearance of E.J. Price's *A Handbook of Congregationalism*, a classic which was revised in 1945 and granted a new edition in 1957.[19] There followed A.D. Martin's *The Principle of the Congregational Churches* (1927) and W.B. Selbie's *Congregationalism* in the same year. The centenary of the Congregational Union of England and Wales was marked by the publication of *Essays Congregational and Catholic*, edited by Albert Peel, in 1931. Peel's *Inevitable Congregationalism* (1937) prompted the publication in the same year of Nathaniel Micklem's *Congregationalism*

---

[17] I am grateful to Martin Cressey for reminding me of the importance of this book, and of the fact that its history is summarized in the Preface to the 1964 edition. Its full title is, *The Book of Order: Being the Rules and Forms of Procedure of the Presbyterian Church of England*.

[18] For example, H.J. Wotherspoon and J.M. Kirkpatrick, *A Manual of Church Doctrine*.

[19] Price also published, *Baptists, Congregationalists and Presbyterians*, in which he outlines the polities of 'the three denominations'.

To-Day.[20] Elsewhere I have written that this was Micklem's 'reply' to Peel's *Inevitable Congregationalism*,[21] but Micklem says that his book is occasioned by Peel's 'welcome publication', but that he does not wish to enter into controversy with him. It is, however, tantamount to a reply, and it was so regarded by many. In the following year Peel published *Christian Freedom: The Contribution of Congregationalism to the Church and to the World*.

Bernard Lord Manning's highly important collection of *Essays in Orthodox Dissent* appeared in 1939, as did Leslie E. Cooke's '*Upon this Rock'. Congregationalism, Its Heritage and Task*. In the same year a manifesto was addressed *To the Ministers of Christ's Holy Gospel in the Churches of the Congregational Order*. It was drafted by Manning, revised by Micklem and John Whale, and also signed by Sydney Cave, Lovell Cocks, J.D. Jones, E.J. Price, and John Short. Emphasis was placed upon the importance of the visible, organized local church, and the resources of the Christian (especially the Reformation) heritage of witness. The signatories and their associates came to be labelled the 'Genevan' party.[22] In 1943 Nathaniel Micklem published *Congregationalism and the Church Catholic*, a manifesto of 'Genevan' Congregational catholicity. It must be granted that as well as their positive objectives, this group were concerned by what they perceived as the drift away from the historic faith of those who, under the leadership of the Reverend Thomas Wigley of Blackheath Congregational Church, London, had founded the Modern Free Churchmen's Union in 1932. They were perpetuating in the post-Barth era the older liberal theology, and Micklem was dismayed by their 'Re-statement of Christian thought' as published in *The Christian World* on 9 February 1933.[23] Finding neither the Trinity

---

[20] The second half of the twentieth century saw the publication of Harold Hodgkins, *The Congregational Way: Apostolic Legacy, Ministry, Unity, Freedom*, and Michael Plant and Alan Tovey, eds., *Telling Another Generation*. These are broadly representative of the views of those in the bodies responsible for their publication. See also Alan P.F. Sell, *Saints Visible, Orderly and Catholic: The Congregational Idea of the Church*; idem, *Commemorations*, ch. 14. For a pioneering account of the ecclesiology of the United Reformed Church see David R. Peel, *Reforming Theology*, 189–292.

[21] See Alan P.F. Sell, *Saints: Visible, Orderly and Catholic*, 97.

[22] For their influence upon worship, not least through the Church Order Group (founded 1946) see Alan P.F. Sell, *Testimony and Tradition*, 27–29.

[23] See the letter, 'A re-statement of Christian thought,' *The Christian World*, 9 February 1933, 7. The signatories were H.E.A. Condon, J.C. Harris, A.G.

nor redemption in the piece, Micklem rushed into print against its authors.[24] Albert Peel, the non-'Genevan', afterwards observed, in a statement skilfully blending puzzlement, humour and point-scoring, that 'most Congregationalists are not disposed to wander with the wizards on the Blackheath, nor do they propose to fall down and worship the dogmatic image which Nathaniel the Principal set up.'[25]

In 1945 C.J. Cadoux delineated *The Congregational Way*, declaring that since Congregationalism is open to all professed disciples, 'it is not a sect or connexion at all, but a body truly Catholic in character.'[26] Hence, among other things, the reluctance of Congregationalists 'to use the word "Church" of any group intermediate between the local company of believers and the Church Universal. There is thus, properly speaking, no such thing as "the Congregational Church" in a denominational sense.'[27] John Marsh's handbook *For the Church Member* came out in 1946.

While all of the authors mentioned were clearly singing in the same choir, they were not all taking exactly the same part, and occasionally a faintly discordant note was struck. For example, there were some, the historian F.J. Powicke and W.B. Selbie among them, who nominated spirituality as being the essence of Congregationalism. Ranged against them were P.T. Forsyth, Benjamin Nightingale and others, who opted for local autonomy, on the ground that spirituality was not the preserve of Congregationalism alone.[28] (I cannot forbear to interject that this is a contrived disjunction, for the gathering of the

---

Knott, F. Lenwood, K.A. Saunders and T. Wigley. I am grateful to Mr David Powell of The Congregational Library, London, for supplying this information.

[24] See *The Christian World*, 9 March 1933, 7.

[25] Albert Peel, *Inevitable Congregationalism*, 113. As a student I was despatched to conduct worship at a Lancashire church whose minister was of the Modernist sort. On the printed Order of Worship was the line, 'Reading from the Bible or other suitable literature.' I thought then, and I still think, that for Christian worship there is no literature which is suitable as an alternative to the Bible.

[26] C.J. Cadoux, *The Congregational Way*, 20.

[27] Ibid., 19. From 1966 there was such a thing.

[28] See F.J. Powicke, 'Historic Congregationalism in Britain', 269; W.B. Selbie, *Congregationalism*, 12; P.T. Forsyth, *Congregationalism and Reunion*, 46; Benjamin Nightingale, *Congregationalism Reexamined*, 18. The last was the reply of one church historian to another: to Albert Peel's *The Congregational Principle*. See further, Alan P.F. Sell, *Saints: Visible, Orderly and Catholic*, 77–83. For Powicke see idem, *Enlightenment, Ecumenism, Evangel*, ch. 1.

saints into fellowship by the Spirit through the Word and the exercise of the prerogatives of the local church under the guidance of that same Spirit are two sides of the same coin. If the gathering is done otherwise we do not have a church. If the autonomy is practised otherwise we do not have a church).

It is only fair to point out that elsewhere Forsyth seems to qualify his position on autonomy. While insisting that Congregationalism's 'religion is not spirituality but faith,' he continues, 'The interest of Independency is not so much the autonomy of the Church, far less of the individual, but of the positive Word and Holy Spirit . . . Its enemy is not an organised church, but a discrowned and deflated gospel.'[29] Forsyth's phrase 'the autonomy of the individual' reminds us that there was in the Congregationalism of the first half of the twentieth century – lingering still in some quarters – a quite rampant individualism which disturbed those concerned about Congregational catholicity, and even many of those who upheld the autonomy of the local church. C.H. Dodd described his experience of his home church at Pen-y-Bryn at the turn of the nineteenth century thus:

> There was behind us no great ecclesiastical organization and no clearly understood theology. Everything now depended on the individual. It was upon the basis of religious individualism that modern Congregationalism was formed out of the elements of the older Independency, and it is a different thing. I believe I lived in the last days when the great tradition of Calvinistic Dissent was still a force in the daily lives of men and women, and in the shaping of a society, and before I was grown up its power was gone.[30]

Dodd's experience may not have been universal among Congregationalists at the beginning of the twentieth century, but it was sufficiently widespread to become a further strand of the complex challenge which the 'Genevans' set themselves to address; and the fact that the churchmanship Dodd describes seems so alien to myself, and was so in the mid-century, when I was growing up, may, together with the introduction of such practical measures as the Home Churches Fund, be a measure of the degree of success that the 'Genevans' achieved.

---

[29] P.T. Forsyth, *Faith, Freedom and the Future*, 165.

[30] C.H. Dodd quoted in F.W. Dillistone, *C.H. Dodd: Interpreter of the New Testament*, 36.

However much they might disagree over 'spiritual *versus* autonomous', it became something of a habit for writers on both sides of the argument to extol Congregationalism as representing the true high churchmanship (as over against the claims of Catholics of other stripes). This tendency seems to have emerged during that period in the nineteenth century when pamphlets attacking and defending Anglo-Catholicism were flying in all directions. In 1897 Charles A. Berry addressed the Autumnal Assembly of the Congregational Union of England and Wales on 'The Churches of Christ and the Kingdom of God.' His address was reprinted in 1902 in the collection of papers gathered under the heading, *Constructive Congregational Ideals.* The subtitle of the volume is significant: *A Series of Addresses and Essays illustrating the Growth of Corporate Life and Feeling in the Congregational Churches during Forty Years, and the Significance of this Movement as a True Modern Development of Early Free Church Ideals.* In his paper Berry reminds his hearers of the well-known fact that he 'has claimed the title of High Churchman.' He reassures them that this has nothing to do with sacerdotalism, and continues:

> It is the affirmation of the Church, of the Church's privileges, powers, and duties, as against the individualist on one hand, who thinks he can complete his spiritual culture and fulfil his duty to Christ and human-ity without coming into associated fellowship; and on the other hand as against the priests, who have arrogated to themselves the functions and even the very name of the Church, and have insinuated themselves into dominion where they were under debt of service. But this affirma-tion of the Church as a Christ-ordained and Christ-equipped society, while it operates for the correction of these two dangerous errors, is inspired by considerations and emphasized for reasons much deeper than these.
>
> At the heart of it this revived enthusiasm for the Church is an attempt to recover the Church's spirituality, to save it from the blight of Erastianism . . . to differentiate it from the world in which and for which it is called to labour . . . It is zeal for the Kingdom of God which inspires this new devotion to the Church of Christ.[31]

In his article on 'Congregationalism' contributed to the *Encyclopaedia Britannica* (1910) the historian J. Vernon Bartlet put the point in a nut-shell: 'Congregationalism is essentially a high church theory, as distinct

---

[31] Charles A. Berry, 'The Churches of Christ and the Kingdom of God', 195–6. Cf. James S. Drummond, *Charles A. Berry, D.D. A Memoir*, 143–5.

from a high clerical one.'[32] P.T. Forsyth was equally to the point: 'Congregationalism . . . is High Church or nothing.'[33] J.D. Jones, eminent as a preacher and as an ecclesiastical statesman, could hardly contain himself:

> We Independents are high-churchmen, we are the highest of high churchmen, none hold such exalted views of the Church and its prerogatives as do we, for we believe that the Church is the body of Christ, His feet, His hands, His eyes, His lips, it is His visible representation to the world; it is by means of His Church that Christ speaks and acts in the world today; by it He proclaims His Gospel; through its agency He works for the redemption and healing of this stricken world; by the voice of the Church He declares to the penitent the forgiveness of sins.[34]

The point was reiterated, less dramatically but no less earnestly, by John Marsh in 1943.[35]

Again, the Genevan party distinguished between any two or three gathered as comprising a church (for two or three gathered Anglicans would not constitute a Congregational church) in the interests of the classical marks of the Church: the preaching of the word, the administration of the sacraments, and right ordering. Some who were not of the 'Genevan' camp were happy to agree with those who were, that the Church Meeting is not a democratic assembly in the sense of 'one person, one vote, and government by the majority decision' but a credal assembly[36] witnessing to the Lordship of Christ over the whole of churchly life and service, where the objective is the mind of Christ and unanimity in him. J.D. Jones spoke for many when he said, 'People sometimes talk of the Congregational Church Order as a democracy. The word has done us untold harm';[37] ten years later A.E. Garvie declared that 'The plea that Congregationalism has the

---

[32] J.V. Bartlet, 'Congregationalism,' 928 (b).

[33] P.T. Forsyth, *Faith, Freedom and the Future*, 215.

[34] J.D. Jones, *Congregational High Churchmanship: Three Discourses delivered during his Visit to Australasia*.

[35] John Marsh, 'Obedience to the Gospel in terms of churchmanship and church order', 56.

[36] See further, H.F. Lovell Cocks, *A Church Reborn: Address from the Chair of the Congregational Union of England and Wales delivered in Westminster Chapel, London, on May 15th 1950*, 21.

[37] J.D. Jones, *Congregational High Churchmanship*, 13. Cf. P.T. Forsyth, *The Church and the Sacraments*, 12–13.

advantage of being a more democratic mode of Church government leaves me icily cold';[38] and in *The Church Meeting and Democracy* (1944) and *Congregationalism: A Restatement* (1954) Daniel Jenkins elaborated upon the point.[39]

Many church polity and related themes were separately discussed in a series of pamphlets published by the Congregational Union of England and Wales during the 1940s and 1950s – among them *Church Membership* (1947), *50 Questions about Congregationalism* (1951), *The Church Meeting* (1952), *Worship* (1952), *The Meaning of the Communion Service* (n.d.) and *Our Heritage of Free Prayer* (n.d.). Of these the first was in its sixth printing by 1954.

A further long-standing difference of opinion among Congregationalists concerned the idea of the catholicity of the local church in relation to the question of the place of wider foci of churchly life. The 'Genevans', frequently invoking John Owen, were willing to accord a more formal place to assemblies than some of their 'local autonomy' colleagues; though long before they came on the scene we find William Hewgill declaring that 'It is worshipping a fetish to say the Congregational Union can never be anything else but a talking assembly.'[40] The 'Genevans' were for wider assemblies not simply because they were useful, but because they were right and theologically justifiable. On this matter they spoke with a somewhat different accent from that adopted by Peel and Cadoux. Thus, where Peel extolled the freedom and autonomy of the local church, Daniel Jenkins reminded his readers that 'It is [its] emphasis upon the particularity of the Church, much more than its emphasis on freedom, which is, perhaps, the greatest contribution of Congregationalism to the life of the whole Church.'[41]

These considerations re-surfaced when Commission I, one of the commissions set up under the review of denominational life, *The Next Ten Years*, proposed that Congregationalists enter into a national covenant and acknowledge themselves to be a national churchly body rather than a voluntary union. Some saw this as a threat to cherished local autonomy; others felt that the proposals did not sufficiently safeguard scriptural principles; and still others, like myself, agreeing with

---

[38] A.E. Garvie, 'The Free Churches in England', 132.

[39] See also Daniel T. Jenkins, *The Nature of Catholicity*, 110–111. The lament of R.F. Horton, minister of Lyndhurst Road, Hampstead, echoes down the years: 'They do not know what a Church Meeting is. In fifty years I have failed to teach them.' Quoted by Albert Peel, *Robert Forman Horton*, 186.

[40] W. Hewgill, 'The confession of a County Union secretary', 206.

[41] Daniel T. Jenkins, *Congregationalism: A Restatement*, 44.

those who held that in the Bible there is no 'third Church' between the local church and the *una sancta*, agreed after discussion that provided that Church Meetings were properly safeguarded and the mutuality of *episcope* as between the several foci (not levels!) of churchly life were assured, it would be in order to speak of the Congregational *Church* in England and Wales on the understanding that this was an expedient called for because of the disunity of the empirical Church, and that the Congregational witness to catholicity would not thereby be impaired. After considerable debate the majority of churches in the Congregational Union of England and Wales covenanted together to form the Congregational Church in England and Wales in 1966.[42]

Equally persuaded by the gathered church idea, the Baptists (however graciously some of them treat paedobaptists – even in some cases, and in the line of John Bunyan, receiving them as members of local Baptist churches without prescribing immersion) differ from the Congregationalists principally in their witness to believers' baptism as being the only proper baptism. Their self-descriptions, in which both themes are given due prominence, include *Baptist Principles* (1925) and *The Life and Faith of the Baptists* (1927) by H. Wheeler Robinson, Principal of Regent's Park College; Ernest A. Payne's *The Fellowship of Believers* (1944); and Arthur Dakin's *The Baptist View of Church and Ministry* (1944). In *The Gathered Community* (1946), Robert C. Walton argued that 'Believers' Baptism . . . represents the final logic of Separatism. It is the symbolic representation of the principle of the gathered church, whose members have each made their individual profession of faith.'[43] In 1947 (in a work which ran to five editions) Henry Cook made no bones about *What Baptists Stand For*, and in accord with Congregationalists of similar persuasion he lamented that among Baptists 'it is not understood as it ought to be that Baptists are High Churchmen in the best and truest sense of that much-abused term'[44] – a reference to the polity of the church of baptized believers gathered under the Lordship of Christ alone. It would seem that, also like the Congregationalists, the Baptists had some difficulty in persuading some of their number of the true significance of Church Meeting; for in the statement *The Baptist Doctrine of the Church*, approved by the Union Council in 1948, the following passage occurs:

---

[42] See further Alan P.F. Sell, *Saints*, 112–115; and idem, *Testimony and Tradition*, ch. 12.

[43] R.C. Walton, *The Gathered Community*, 168.

[44] Henry Cook, *What Baptists Stand For*, 32.

The church meeting, though outwardly a democratic way of ordering the affairs of the church, has deeper significance. It is the occasion when, as individuals and as a community, we submit ourselves to the guidance of the Holy Spirit and stand under the judgments of God that we may know what is the mind of Christ.[45]

Of particular interest is the symposium *The Pattern of the Church: A Baptist View* (1963) to which the contributors were Neville Clark, Alec Gilmore, W.M.S. West (who also published *Baptist Principles* in 1969), and Stephen F. Winward – all of them then in pastoral charge, though Clark and West subsequently became principals – of the South Wales Baptist College, Cardiff, and Bristol Baptist College respectively. Equally alive to the New Testament background, the Baptist heritage, worship, polity and the ecumenical vision, this book is, in its general flavour, most nearly on a par with those of the Congregationalists Manning, Micklem and Jenkins. None of them emulates Percy W. Evans's provocative denial that infant baptism is baptism at all.[46] Far from it: Morris West, for example, though a loyal Baptist, was a model of committed and sensitive ecumenical endeavour.[47]

Over the years some Baptists, including George Beasley-Murray and R.E.O. White have cautioned against a too individualistic under-standing of baptism on the part of Baptists. The setting of Baptist polity firmly within covenant soil, and with reference to the saints' participation in the triune communion of God by Paul Fiddes, and Nigel G. Wright's argument that the idea and reality of God's covenant undergirds the Baptist understanding of, and commitment to, the Trinity, the biblical witness, the Baptist tradition and mission represent two endorsements of this.[48] Another is Anthony R. Cross's substantial work, *Baptism and the Baptists: Theology and Practice in the*

---

[45] *The Baptist Doctrine of the Church*, 3.

[46] See Percy W. Evans, et al., *Infant Baptism To-day*.

[47] See J.H.Y Briggs, ed., *Faith, Heritage and Witness: A Supplement to The Baptist Quarterly Published in Honour of Dr. W.M.S. West*.

[48] See Paul S. Fiddes, *Tracks and Traces: Baptist Identity in Church and Theology*; Nigel G. Wright, 'Covenant and covenanting', 287–90. Not unrelated to the theme of covenant are recent reflections upon children in relation to Baptist ecclesiology. See Paul Martin and David Tennant, 'Believers' baptism, the fellowship of believers and faith development', 96–104, 121–31. For the historical background see Ernest A. Payne, 'Baptists and Christian initiation', 147–57.

Twentieth Century (2000).[49] A third is seen in the revival of Baptist interest in baptism as a sacrament, in which connection Anthony Cross can even entitle a paper, 'The myth of English Baptist anti-sacramentalism.'[50] Mention should be made of Brian Haymes's thoughtful pamphlet, *A Question of identity: Reflections on Baptist Principles and Practice* (1986), and of the attractive series of leaflets, *Baptist Basics* published by the Baptist Union for church members and enquirers.

Until recently, as far as I have been able to discover, there has been little detailed *theological* writing upon Baptist associations and the Baptist Union in so far as these have significance in a communion which prizes local autonomy.[51] Among Baptists who see a need for such reflection is J.H.Y Briggs, who makes the standard point and utters a cautionary word:

> Within Baptist church structures, the associations and the Union have only such powers as are covenanted to them by the member churches . . . The vulnerability of the Union to theological disaffection is apparent, as for example in the Christological debate of 1971,[52] in the questioning of the Union's membership of the World Council of Churches, and more recently in the emergence of new authority structures in those churches which accept the full thrust of restorationism.[53]

---

[49] See also Anthony R. Cross, 'Baptists and baptism – a British perspective', 104–21.

[50] See Philip E. Thompson and Anthony R. Cross, eds., *Recycling the Past or Researching History? Studies in Baptist Historiography and Myths*, ch. 7. See also Anthony R. Cross and Philip E. Thompson, eds., *Baptist Sacramentalism*, and a further volume under the same title to follow.

[51] Though for the excitements surrounding the founding of the Union see Peter Shepherd, *The Making of a Modern Denomination: John Howard Shakespeare and the English Baptists.*

[52] The reference here is to the debate (and discord) engendered by an address delivered at the Baptist Union Assembly in 1971 by Principal Michael Taylor of Northern Baptist College on the subject: 'The incarnate presence: how much of a man was Jesus Christ?' Taylor proposed a degree Christology, to which a number took exception. See further, Peter Shepherd, *The Making of a Northern Baptist College*, 231–4.

[53] J.H.Y. Briggs, 'Double affirmations: Baptists since 1945', 61. See also the brief but wide-ranging paper by Keith G. Jones, 'Rethinking Baptist ecclesiology', 4–18. For a friendly view of Baptists 'through the keyhole', see Alan P.F. Sell, *Testimony and Tradition*, ch. 2.

In our discussions of Christology and the Trinity we have already come face to face with major Unitarian doctrinal distinctives, and these are rehearsed also in their several apologies and handbooks. Among the earliest was Alfred Hall's *Beliefs of a Unitarian* (n.d., but 1910) which spawned further reprints until 1932. There followed W.G. Tarrant's *Unitarianism* (1912), in which the author found Unitarians characterized by their resistance to any final definition of 'Unitarianism'; and S.H. Mellone's *The Religion of Authority and the Religion of Reason* (1924). Mellone commends Unitarianism for being rational and scriptural, open to free enquiry, and grounded in spiritual experience; denounces the 'religious impressionism' of liberal evangelicalism,[54] regards Anglo-Catholicism as dangerous because it is 'the work of an unregulated priesthood',[55] and is deeply concerned by the growth and influence of Roman Catholicism. In face of such threats, he declares, it will not do for Unitarians simply to extol the freedom of the isolated individual soul, neither must they let freedom run wild: they must show 'that our inheritance of spiritual liberty can be made the foundation of a real Church life, and that public Worship means something more than sitting listening to the opinions of a particular man.'[56]

By now Unitarians were wondering how they might express their wider fellowship in organizational terms. Of all the heirs of Old Dissent, and long after Wesley had bequeathed the Arminian Methodists both a gospel and a constitution, the Unitarians were the last to gather themselves into a national body. This they finally did in 1928, when they constituted their General Assembly of Unitarian and Free Christian Churches. If the former part of the name indicates those who thought of themselves in the line of Rational Dissent, the latter part attempts to accommodate those, like Martineau, who had been opposed to denominational labels and structures as such.[57]

In *Unitarianism: Essays and Addresses* (1939) by J. Lionel Tayler, we find, in addition to chapters on Unitarian history and doctrine, a sermon on 'Cheerfulness of spirit and its cultivation.' In 1945 a commission appointed by the General Assembly produced its report entitled

---

[54] S.H. Mellone, *The Religion of Authority and the Religion of Reason*, 12.

[55] Ibid., 13.

[56] Ibid., 18.

[57] See further, and also for an 'insider's' reflections on this subject, Arthur Long, 'Unitarian thought in the twentieth century', II, 247–60; II, 445–64. For a brief account of the theological-cum-ecclesiological trends within Unitarianism see Roger Thomas, 'When is a Unitarian not a Unitarian?', 107–118.

A Free Religious Faith – and the faith envisaged was of the liberal *Christian* sort.[58] A symposium edited by Kenneth Twinn entitled *Essays in Unitarian Theology* was published in 1959. This was intended as an update of the 1945 General Assembly Report. The latter had not been innocent of dissenting statements, and by 1959 the degree of unanimity among Twinn's authors was so reduced that a collection of individual essays was the only practicable outcome. John Hostler's *Unitarianism* appeared in 1981. Whereas Hall's 1910 volume remains among the most comprehensive as covering Unitarian belief, practice and polity (though, unlike Hall, some latter-day Unitarians would find it more difficult to regard Unitarianism as a form of Christianity), the themes of Hostler's study are reason, freedom, the humanity of Christ, the authority of conscience, the welfare of man, the autonomy of the individual, and the importance of Unitarianism. At the time of writing the most recent example of this genre is *The Elements of Unitarianism* (1998) by George Chryssides. He discusses Unitarian history, doctrine and witness within a global perspective, and is at pains to point out that modern Unitarianism, being creedless, is hospitable to, among others, those of an atheistic or Buddhist turn of mind, as well as to those who continue to regard themselves as Christians.

It is difficult to resist the feeling that the attempt to pin down present-day Unitarianism is akin to that of arresting an Heraclitean flux. If that remark should appear as the puzzled remark of an outsider, let it be noted that many Unitarians themselves share the sense of puzzlement. In his lecture on *Current Trends in British Unitarianism*, Arthur Long declares that 'One of the foremost characterics [*sic*] of Unitarianism as a movement . . . is a considerable measure of diversity – a diversity sustained by an undergirding unity.' As the lecture proceeds the impression is gained that the diversity is more apparent than the basis of the unity.[59] Indeed, Long himself discerns eight categories within current Unitarianism: Liberal Protestant Christianity, Existential Unitarianism, Non-Christocentric Theism, the All-Faiths approach, Non-Theistic Humanism, Unitarianism as Social and Religious Protest, and New Age Unitarianism.[60] James Drummond, as

---

[58] See Arthur Long, 'Unitarian thought in the twentieth century', II, 445–50.

[59] Arthur Long, *Current Trends in British Unitarianism*, 8.

[60] For analogous diversity among the British Quakers see Martin Davie, *British Quaker Theology since 1895, 1997*; John Punshon, *Letter to a Universalist*, 1989; idem, 'The significance of tradition. Reflections on the writing of Quaker history', 77–96. For an outsider's reflections see Alan P.F. Sell, *Enlightenment, Ecumenism, Evangel*, 66–69.

we saw when discussing the Trinity, was able to be more precise as to the essence of Unitarianism. But he died in 1918.

Since Arminian (no less than Calvinistic) Methodism was born and nurtured in the soil of the Evangelical Revival we shall expect that its distinctives are primarily religious and evangelistic rather than ecclesiological. Indeed, according to Bernard E. Jones, it was not until the last quarter of the nineteenth century that 'the Wesleyan Methodist society was becoming self-consciously a church,' and, as David Carter notes, 'the term "church" was not officially applied to it until 1891.'[61] Unsurprisingly, the experimental emphasis is ineradicable from Methodist self-studies. In *The Roots of Methodism* (1903) W.B. Fitzgerald traces Methodism's story, explains its polity, and discusses its faith – its message to all (*contra* Calvinism), and its emphasis upon the changed life, experience and Scripture. In *Methodism* (1912) H.B. Workman adopts a broadly similar approach, though venturing into America and other parts, and so does W. Bardsley Brash in his book of the same title published first in 1928. Brash has just eight pages on polity, but a whole chapter on Methodism as a missionary church. In his Fernley-Hartley Lecture, *The Spirit of Methodism* (1937), Henry Bett discusses the Methodist contribution to religion, theology, literature and society; and his further work, *What Methodists Believe and Preach*, was in its fourth printing by 1952.

In July 1937 the Methodist Conference meeting in Bradford approved a statement on *The Nature of the Christian Church according to the Teaching of the Methodists*. The authors set out from the nature of the Church as shown in the New Testament; they emphasize the continuity of Methodist with the Church of the ages, whilst at the same time acknowledging its debt to the Protestant Reformation; and they conclude with seven affirmations. These may be summarized thus:

1. The Church is appointed by God to witness by life and word to the gospel's redeeming power.
2. The Church is 'a redeemed society of believers' which shares the gift of the Spirit and enjoys that communion with God the Father which is granted through the forgiveness of sins through our Lord Jesus Christ. The Church is called to 'show forth Christ in daily life'

---

[61] B.E. Jones, 'Society and church in Wesleyan Methodism, 1878–93', 134; David Carter, 'The context and content of mid-Victorian Wesleyan ecclesiology', 225. See also, John Munsey Turner, *Conflict and Reconciliation: Studies in Methodism and Ecumenism in England 1840–1982*, ch. 5.

and, 'as a sacramental society, to testify that ordinary life may be holy.' The gospel is to be carried to the world.

3. The several 'Churches' are 'but a partial and imperfect embodiment of the New Testament ideal. They are already one in Christ Jesus; they have not to create that unity . . . it is the gift of God.'

4. The Christian life is lived in a fellowship which honours word and sacraments.

5. The Methodist Church carries the marks by which the Church has been known from apostolic times: the word of God, the sacraments, the profession of faith, the ministry. Living faith is to be exhibited by church members.

6. The Church is to evangelize and to serve society by caring for the needy and combating 'disease and poverty, ignorance and vice'.

7. 'Since the Gospel brings victory over sin and death, God has knit together the whole family of the Church in heaven and on earth in the communion of the saints . . .'[62]

In 1938 W.E. Sangster, disturbed by a perceived lack of evangelistic zeal and passion for holiness, announced to all who would listen that *Methodism can be Born Again*. He takes a kindly view of the Oxford Group Movement, and suggests that its notes of fellowship, assurance, holiness and personal evangelism are characteristic of genuine Methodism and need to be recovered by it. In *Methodist Churchmanship and its Implications* (1946) H. Watkin-Jones examines Methodist doctrine, worship and evangelism in the light of the catholic nature and mission of the Church; R.H. Copestake writes for young people and adherents in his pamphlet *The Methodist Way* (1951); and in his book Methodism (1963), Rupert E. Davies sets *Methodism* in its historical and global context, and discusses its future prospects.

A number of books on specific Methodist distinctives remain to be noted, in addition to that of Humphries on the Holy Spirit, to which I referred earlier. The first is C. Ryder Smith's *The Christian Experience: A Study of in the Theology of Fellowship* (1926). The clue to his approach is given in the sub-title, for he draws upon the growingly influential group psychology of the day to argue that 'the Christian experience harmonizes with the rest of human experience, and completes it.'[63]

---

[62] *The Nature of the Christian Church according to the Teaching of the Methodists*, 38–40.

[63] C. Ryder Smith, *The Christian Experience: A Study in the Theology of Fellowship*.

Two years later, the theme of Wilfred R. Wilkinson's Hartley Lecture was *Religious Experience: The Methodist Fundamental* (1928). He answers his own question concerning the fundamental question in religion thus: 'It is the possession of a religious experience. To know God in Jesus Christ is the one thing needful. Where that is, nothing else matters seriously.'[64] Religious experience, being contact with God, gives us the assurance that God is, that we belong to him, and that the values we seek are real. It is progressive, and it is enriched by Christian fellowship. Other Methodists who wrote on Christian experience include H. Maldwyn Hughes, *The Theology of Experience* (1915), E.S. Waterhouse, *The Philosophy of Religious Experience* (1923), and A. Victor Murray, *Personal Experience and the Historic Faith* (1939). Nor, at the more popular level, should we overlook the considerable impact of the preaching and writing of Leslie D. Weatherhead, the title of whose book *The Transforming Friendship* (1928) sufficiently indicates the main motivation of his work, namely that of nurturing in his hearers and readers the experience of the reality and life-trans-forming capability of Jesus Christ.[65] In 1952, from a more historical perspective, Arthur S. Yates published *The Doctrine of Assurance* with special reference to John Wesley. Finally, in a recent perceptive paper, Clive Marsh has construed experience in terms of the outworking of redemption (understood as participation in Christ by the Spirit) in the individual, the Church and society. 'Redemption,' he insists, 'is a fundamentally social experience.' He regrets that as it has become more self-consciously ecclesial, Methodism has 'taken its working-out of the experience of redemption away from the workplace and family.'[66]

Mention must now be made of *The Doctrine of Christian or Evangelical Perfection*, published by H.W. Perkins in 1927, and of the learned work of R. Newton Flew of Wesley House, Cambridge, on the same subject: *The Idea of Perfection in Christian Theology: An Historical Study of the Christian Ideal for the Present Life* (1934). Taking his bearings in the New Testament, Flew proceeds through Christian history with

---

[64] Wilfred R. Wilkinson, *Religious Experience: The Methodist Fundamental*, 7.

[65] For Weatherhead see John Travell, *Doctor of Souls: A Biography of Dr. Leslie Dixon Weatherhead*.

[66] Clive Marsh, 'Appealing to "experience": what does it mean?', 130. The immediately following paper in this collection brings the theme of the social into relationship with the Methodist idea and practice of connexionalism. See Philip Drake, 'Joining the dots: Methodist membership and connected-ness', 131–41.

a view to showing that when the term 'perfection' is not used as if it were synonymous with 'sinlessness', but is construed as concerning life in the kingdom of God, the doctrine of perfection is central to Christian thought. Among many other illuminating things, Flew shows that 'for Quakerism and Methodism . . . the driving power was a doctrine of holiness and that both arose in the form of a reaction against the conventional piety of the day.'[67] His conclusion is that

> The doctrine of Christian perfection – understood not as an assertion that a final attainment of the goal of Christian life is possible in this world, but as a declaration that a supernatural destiny, a relative attainment of the goal which does not exclude growth, is the will of God for us in this world and is attainable – lies not merely upon the by-paths of Christian theology, but upon the high road.[68]

In his comprehensive work, *Doxology* (1980), Geoffrey Wainwright returns to the fountainhead, Wesley, whose position on entire sanctification or perfect love he encapsulates thus: 'Negatively formulated, it was the condition in which no sinful attitude or action was deliberately entertained or committed. . . . Positively formulated, perfection meant for Wesley the pure love of God and neighbour.'[69]

Between them, the books just noted epitomize what John Munsey Turner has called 'a deep and fundamental controversy among Methodists about Methodism's nature. Is its *raison d'être* a holiness group, a leaven within the life of the church? Is the "grand depositum" really the doctrine and practice of Scriptural Holiness or was Methodism the re-assertion of religious experience as the key feature of Christian living; a way of turning the flank of the Enlightenment's attack on Christianity?'[70] Far be it from me to pose as a referee in this matter; but if by grace one *experiences holy living*, and if one's *religious experience* is of the *holy*, is such a strong disjunction appropriate? Or does my question simply betoken an uncomprehending – even an unsanctified – mind?

---

[67] R. Newton Flew, *The Idea of Perfection in Christian Theology: An Historical Study of the Christian Ideal for the Present Life*, 399.

[68] Ibid., 397.

[69] Geoffrey Wainwright, *Doxology: The Praise of God in Worship, Doctrine and Life*, 461.

[70] J. Munsey Turner, 'Victorian Values – or whatever happened to John Wesley's scriptural holiness?', 165.

III

If the Nonconformists were not slow to articulate what they perceived as their denominational distinctives, some of them were equally keen to bring those insights to bear upon matters ecumenical. This is not the place to rehearse the origins of the modern ecumenical movement; and I shall not refer to ecumenical engagement 'on the ground'.[71] It will suffice to note some of the recurring theological issues which inner- and inter-confessional dialogue raises. I shall therefore refer to some examples of relevant writings published by Nonconformist theologians, and to some documents to which they contributed; for a good deal of ecumenical theology has, appropriately enough, taken the form of 'committee theology' – a term which is sometimes employed pejoratively and not always justly to indicate something bland, vacuous, innocuous. I shall speak first of relations within and between the Free Church traditions, and then of their theological contribution to the wider ecumenical movement. In limiting myself to the contributions of theologians I stick resolutely to my last; I by no means underestimate the importance of contributions by biblical scholars,[72] church historians and the noble army of ecclesiastical statesmen and women to the ecumenical enterprise.

As with ecclesiology in general, so with ecumenism: a number of Nonconformists published works in favour of Church unity understood not as entailing uniformity, and not as something which Christians create. Rather, the unity of the Church is given in and with the gospel: on the ground of the Son's saving work, the Father calls out by the Spirit one people for his praise and service. Given that there are divisions within the empirical Church – supremely at the Lord's table – the challenge is to address those factors and challenge the sectarian attitudes which prevent the manifestation of the God-given unity. This general line runs through *The Reunion of the Church* (1948; revised 1960) by Lesslie Newbigin; *Christian Reunion: Historic Divisions Reconsidered* (1971) by John Whale; and two short works by John Huxtable: *Christian Unity: Some of the Issues* (1967) and *A New Hope for Christian Unity* (1977). It is also the case that some within the

---

[71] For which see John A. Newton, 'Protestant Nonconformists and ecumenism'.

[72] The work done by an ecumenical group of biblical scholars under the leadership of C.H. Dodd on *The New English Bible* had the unifying effect of taking them behind their denominational 'small print' to the texts acknowledged by all.

Free Churches have dissented from this approach, generally on the conservative evangelical ground that since the only proper unity is unity in the truth, and since the truth is found in Scripture, we may not unite with those whose interpretation is deemed to be defective.[73] This has, however, been the stance of a minority in the denominations under review, and while God is not necessarily on the side of the big battalions, and although pamphlets have fluttered on inerrantist breezes from time to time, I am not aware of a substantial contribution along this line from the ranks of the Baptists, the Methodists or the United Reformed Church and its forebear traditions. Accordingly, I turn to these traditions, beginning with the Methodists; and I shall add a note on the rather different ecumenical experience of the Unitarians at the end of this section of my lecture. We shall see as we proceed that some who are not in principle opposed to ecumenism are not necessarily inclined to adopt every scheme that is put before them.

If to John Wesley his parish was the world, the casual observer of nineteenth-century Methodism might gain the impression of an assortment of adjacent fields. By the later decades of the century, however, a measure of ranching had already occurred, and in 1907 the Methodist New Connexion, the United Free Methodists and the Bible Christian Church came together in the United Methodist Church. Of the three constituents, the first two had seceded from Wesleyanism, the last had grown up independently. In 1932 the United Methodist Church, the Primitive Methodist Church, whose origins were in early nineteenth-century camp meetings (frowned upon by the Wesleyan Conference of 1807) and the Wesleyan Methodist Church were united.[74] This is not the place to recount the false starts and the polity-blending discussions which preceded union; my point is simply that whereas continuing disunity would have placed Methodism in an ambiguous position in future ecumenical discussions – even supposing that such discussions had been possible at all, the 1932 union equipped Methodism to play its full part in such activity. A most informative account of this as it

---

[73] I have considered this argument in *Enlightenment, Ecumenism, Evangel*, 286–8.

[74] See A.W. Harrison, B. Aquila Barber, G.G. Hornby and E. Tegla Davies, *The Methodist Church: Its Origin, Divisions, and Reunion*. See also Henry Smith, John E. Swallow and William Treffry, eds., *The Story of the United Methodist Church*; and the handsome volumes: B. Aquila Barber, *A Methodist Pageant: A Souvenir of the Primitive Methodist Church*, and R. Newman Wycherley, *The Pageantry of Methodist Union*.

relates to Britain is found in David Carter's book, *Love Bade Me Welcome: A British Methodist Perspective on the Church* (2002). It must, however, be granted that the 1932 union also brought together some who found themselves uneasy bedfellows when subsequent ecumenical discussions were in progress. I diplomatically allow a Methodist to make the point. Referring to what he calls 'high' and 'low' tendencies within Methodism, Bryan S. Turner writes

> The union of Methodism in 1932 had the effect of high-lighting the divergence between the two wings. Methodists with a free-church background feared that union would be bought at the cost of the importance of the local chapel and its laity; 'high' Methodists feared that union would be detrimental to Wesleyan sacramentalism, the position of the ministry, and the strength of the Connexion.[75]

At this point I leave matters internal to Methodism in order to sketch the context of ensuring discussions. In 1946 Archbishop Geoffrey Fisher invited the Free Churches to consider taking episcopacy into their systems, and Anglican-Free Church meetings ensued. Participants included the following Free Church theologians: Nathaniel Micklem and Lovell Cocks (Congregationalists); R. Newton Flew and Harold Roberts (Methodists); and R.D. Whitehorn (Presbyterian). A report entitled *Church Relations in England* was published in 1950, but the initiative eventually ran aground on the issues of episcopacy and priesthood. In view of the persistence of this stumbling block down the decades (and in relation to dialogues with other Christian communions in addition to those with the Anglicans), and by way of showing that there was no smoke without fire, I select from many other similar statements Canon Sansbury's honest words of 1954. He writes, 'It must be emphasised that Apostolic Succession, whether in the Tractarian form, or in the later restatements of the doctrine, is held widely and sincerely in many sections of the Anglican communion to be of the *esse* of the Church.' A Free Church person would have needed to be living on another planet not to have suspected that very thing; but by stating the position from the pen of an Anglican, I hope to dispel any suggestion that Free Church challenges to the notion that (contrary to the canon law of the Church of England) the historic episcopate is of the *esse* of the Church[76] were directed against a man of straw.[77]

---

[75] B.S. Turner, 'Discord in modern Methodism' 159.

[76] C. Kenneth Sansbury, 'Episcope in the Anglican communion', 27.

[77] See further, Alan P.F. Sell, *Aspects of Christian Integrity*, 93–97.

The same issue was raised in discussions between the Church of England and the Church of Scotland. These had begun in the 1940s, and at that time the Presbyterian Church of England and the Episcopal Church in Scotland sent observers to the talks. A further round of meetings followed, with the four churches having equal status as full members of the consultation. The Presbyterian Church of England sent four representatives, of whom one was the theologian R.D. Whitehorn. Another was Mr John M. Ross, the author of an undated pamphlet entitled *Presbyterian Bishops*? In the course of the conversations the concept of 'bishops in presbytery' was canvassed, and the Presbyterian party were concerned to ensure that, 'the laity and the presbyterate were fully linked with the Bishop in the doctrinal and spiritual decisions of the Church, and that the Church had such independence in spiritual things as, for example, to be able to reform its liturgy, or have its Bishops appointed on the recommendation of the Church including lay representation.'[78] Almost 50 years on an Anglican-Presbyterian church order embodying these principles remains to be achieved. It is difficult to say whether, in informed circles,[79] episcopacy or the establishment question is the primary cause of the stalemate.

I return now to the Methodists. The Free Church-Anglican conversations having broken down, in 1953 the Methodists alone made initial approaches to the Church of England concerning the possible resumption of conversations, and two years later the Methodist Conference authorized these. This led to what was probably the most significant occasion of inner-Methodist discord in the second half of the twentieth century. An Interim Report appeared in 1958, and thereafter the momentum increased. Finally, in 1968 the scheme of union was published.[80]

In the meantime, however, sometimes quite vociferous opposition to the direction being taken was voiced within Methodism (and also, it goes without saying, within the Church of England, but that is not my concern here) especially following the publication of the pamphlet *Conversations between the Church of England and the Methodist Church* (1963). In July 1963 proponents of unity gathered under the banner, 'Towards Anglican-Methodist Unity', and published their

---

[78] *Relations between Anglican and Presbyterian Churches: A Joint Report*, 17.

[79] I allude here to the anti-bishop frenzy stirred up by the *Scottish Daily Express*.

[80] *Anglican-Methodist Unity: Report of the Anglican-Methodist Unity Commission, Part 2: The Scheme*. For the reflections of a scholarly Methodist on the union proposals see J.M. Turner, *Conflict and Reconciliation*, ch. 10.

convictions. In response to this, another party, The Voice of Methodism, came into being; it pledged to uphold the evangelistic and doctrinal principles of the Methodist Deed of Union of 1932, and 'to seek the fellowship of ALL Christians without uniformity of Worship or of Organisation.'[81] While it is reasonable to suppose that the majority of those who sympathized with this movement were former Primitive and United Methodists, one of its leading lights was the former Wesleyan A.E. Clucas Moore. Nor should we forget that as early as 1919 the Wesleyan W.T. Davison had published a pamphlet on *The Historic Episcopate* in which he observed that the crucial question was whether the bishop's authority was from above, or from the community of faith, and warned that Free Church people must not commit themselves to monarchical or oligarchical principles – even in the cause of Christian unity.[82]

Fifty-four years on, similar and substantial dissent was articulated by four of the twelve Methodists on the Anglican-Methodist Commission: the New Testament scholar C. Kingsley Barrett, the philosopher Thomas Jessop, the Principal of Cliff College Thomas D. Meadley, and the Old Testament scholar Norman Snaith – none of them erstwhile Wesleyans. On his own account Barrett articulated one of the principle objections to the scheme.

> It must be clearly understood that what is involved in the proposals . . . is not merely the relabelling of Methodist chairmen of districts, but the full acceptance of the historic episcopate, which includes the belief that the Church of the present day is linked with the Church of the apostles and that the sign of this is a continuing succession of bishops. This idea is very bad history and worse theology . . .
>
> Because the Church of England sincerely believes in this historic episcopate, the report requires that something be given to Methodist ministers which they did not get when ordained within the Methodist Church. . . . I believe that this amounts to reordination which I, as a Methodist minister, could not accept. I believe that my present ordination is a proper and sufficient one.[83]

The evangelical Methodist New Testament scholar Howard Marshall was even more pointed:

---

[81] See A.E. Clucas Moore, *What is The Voice of Methodism?*
[82] See W.T. Davison, *The Historic Episcopate.*
[83] An undated cutting from *The Guardian.*

If the historic episcopate is not a necessity for unity according to Scripture, if indeed it is a doctrine which has been frequently associated with and productive of false doctrines of sacrifice and priesthood, it cannot be assumed that Methodist dissentients are likely to take the historic episcopate into their system. They may accept episcopacy, indeed they already have it, but they cannot accept the historic episcopate, and they cannot go through a ceremony which is designed to make some (not all) Anglicans believe that they will then possess something which they themselves would repudiate.[84]

Norman Snaith was in general accord that 'the Anglican exclusive claim is definitely wrong . . . Modern Anglicanism is a sect, and I believe it is wrong for a Christian to become a member of a sect.'[85]

In 1962 Rupert E. Davies of Didsbury College, Bristol, published *Methodists and Unity* – a fair-minded book in which he gave one more page to 'What Anglicans may dislike about Methodists' than he gave to 'What Methodists dislike about the Church of England'. While not taking exception in principle to episcopacy, he queries why one particular variety of it was deemed necessary for the Church's well being: 'Why is the historic episcopacy, but not, apparently, soundness of doctrine or holiness of life, *necessary* (though all are, of course, desirable) for the fullness and wellbeing of the Church?'[86] He does not, however, address the position held by many Anglicans that in episcopal ordination within the historic succession *potestas* is conveyed to ordinands which is not available to anyone else, and which is deemed to guarantee the 'validity' and 'regularity' of sacramental ministry.[87] Gordon Rupp, a member of the conversations panel, was similarly silent in those of his pro-union salvos that I have been able to track down.[88]

---

[84] I. Howard Marshall, 'Strange prospects for reconciliation', 16.

[85] Norman Snaith, in the fifth of a series of comments on *Conversations between the Church of England and the Methodist Church*, 197, 199.

[86] Rupert E. Davies, *Methodists and Unity*, 72.

[87] For an example of an Anglican who did not hold the disputed view see James Packer, in J.I. Packer, ed., *The Church of England and the Methodist Church*, 28: 'The idea that episcopal ordination adds something to a man's ministerial commission which he would not otherwise have reflects a superstitious institutionalism which is, perhaps, the Anglican occupational disease; certainly the Bible will not justify it.' Gordon Rupp made merry with this document in his *Consideration Reconsidered*.

[88] For example, 'A dissentient view of the dissentient view concerning Scripture and Tradition', 187–92; idem, 'Meadley's medley', 154–6.

The Presbyterian T.W. Manson did make the point, however, in his devastating attack on Bishop Kenneth Kirk's understanding of the episcopate. He contends that the one 'essential ministry' in the Church is 'the perpetual ministry of the Risen and Ever-Present Lord Himself';[89] and that

> we ought seriously to consider whether it would not be a good thing to dispense with the misleading term "Apostolic Succession," which carries with it the idea that someone has died and left his rights and property to someone else. Ought we not to be laying the whole emphasis upon the fact of continuous life, unflagging strength, and unceasing work? And if we do that, can we find, and need we seek, any other basis of continuity than the Risen Christ Himself?[90]

It is always painful for those of closely related denominations to see their friends passing through the agonies of discord. And certainly the Baptists, Congregationalists, Presbyterians and Unitarians were not inclined to rush into print with dire warnings to the Methodists, or even with much encouragement to them. But the editor of *The London Quarterly and Holborn Review*, John T. Wilkinson, invited a representative of each of these traditions to offer some 'Free Church Comments upon the Anglican-Methodist Conversations'. Two of the commentators were his own colleagues in Manchester: W. Gordon Robinson, Principal of Lancashire Independent College, and Principal Fred Kenworthy of the Unitarian College. Standing firmly in the tradition of historic Dissent (and not at all reluctant to regard himself as a Unitarian *Christian*) the latter argued obliquely with reference to the establishment principle that 'A truly ecumenical church must surely bear witness to those truths within Christianity to which the historic dissenters have constantly and courageously borne witness. . . . It will be the opinion of many that no truly catholic church will arise in their despite.'[91] Noting that Congregationalists already had a record of entering into unions in Canada and South India, Robinson could only point out that the proposals in the Anglican-Methodist report *Conversations* 'have been received by Congregationalists with less than enthusiasm and with more acceptance of the "Dissentient View" than of the main part of the report.'[92] He continues:

---

[89] T.W. Manson, *The Church's Ministry*, 100. Cf. his *Ministry and Priesthood: Christ's and Ours: Two Lectures*.

[90] Ibid., 54 n.

[91] Fred Kenworthy, 'A Unitarian comment', 299.

[92] W. Gordon Robinson, 'A Congregationalist comment', 294.

With regard to the conception of the ministry, there is disappointment that *Conversations* seems to indicate a wholesale acceptance of the so-called historic episcopate, a toying with an idea of priesthood which is alien to the Free Churches, a danger of the acceptance of the necessity of reordination, and a possible resultant pre-occupation with the validity of episcopal ordination and the invalidity of any other kind to the ultimate exclusion of all but those episcopally ordained.[93]

Four years later John Huxtable, than whom no Congregationalist was a more committed ecumenist, returned to the theme in connection with the draft of the Service of Reconciliation which had been circulated.

It rests on an uneasy compromise because a crucial issue has not been faced. What the Methodists have to offer the Anglicans is not unambiguously comparable with what the Anglicans have to offer the Methodists. Methodists do not question Anglican orders. At least some Anglicans question, or even deny, Methodist orders . . . Unless two doctrines of the ministry in question can be more clearly seen to be different but not mutually inconsistent ways of accepting a commonly held conviction, it is difficult to see how a satisfactory service can be arranged.[94]

It is not at all inconceivable that in writing as they did, both Robinson and Huxtable had Bernard Lord Manning looking over their shoulders, as it were. In 1930 Manning told the Fifth International Congregational Council that

The Supper of the Lord is either celebrated or not celebrated. The Body and the Blood of Christ are spiritually received or they are not received. We simply do not know what an irregular or an invalid celebration is. We do not deal in percentages with the grace of God . . .[95] When we can botanise about the Burning Bush, either it has ceased to burn or it has been consumed.

Two years later Manning was even blunter:

The entire conception of *validity* and *regularity*, *invalidity* and *irregularity*, applied to the means of grace and to the action of the Body of

---

[93] Ibid., 295.

[94] W. John F. Huxtable, *Christian Unity: Some of the Issues*, 67.

[95] Bernard Lord Manning, *Essays in Orthodox Dissent*, 116, 117.

Christ, is both ludicrous and blasphemous. If God acts at all He cannot act invalidly or irregularly; and if God be not acting in the Church there is no action; for the Church has no meaning whatever as a human society apart from God's action.[96]

There is no need to pursue the later stages of the 1960s debate. When *The Scheme* secured the requisite vote from the Methodist Conference, but failed in the Anglican Synod of 1972, many Methodists, and not a few Anglicans, were deeply distressed, and other Free Churchmen could only sympathize with their sorrowing friends. At the same time, some of the latter could not suppress their private feeling that it is dangerous to leave Methodists and Anglicans alone together in a room lest the Methodists are too easily persuaded; and some may even have been reminded of Bernard Manning's prophecy of 1933: 'We cannot doubt that the Anglicans will offer sooner or later very favourable terms to the Methodists. They would meet the Methodists everywhere, except on the fundamental issue. The Methodists would have to admit that full salvation comes by bishops alone – but anything else that they want they would get.'[97]

The posing of 'what if' questions is a pleasant but finally unproductive pastime; but one Methodist afterwards reflected that 'The development of a full schismatic state of affairs in the 1960s was . . . forestalled in Methodism by the Anglican rejection of *The Scheme*.[98] That schism had been a real possibility had the union taken place was certainly the view of Norman Glanville of The Voice of Methodism: 'It would be an immense help,' he wrote in 1964, 'if the Report on the Conversations could be withdrawn before an irrevocable step towards union is taken, which would certainly bring Methodism, as we know it, to an end, and open up wounds which would take a long time to heal.'[99] In fact, however, wounds were inevitable whatever decision had been taken. This was also to be the experience of the Congregationalists to whom I shall turn shortly.

But for the present I must note two further, more broadly ecumenical matters. First, in 1964 some five hundred people representative of twenty-five denominations gathered in Nottingham under the auspices of the British Council of Churches for the First British Conference on Faith and Order. Among those present was a scattering of church

---

[96] Ibid., 75.
[97] Ibid., 145.
[98] B.S. Turner, 'Discord in modern Methodism,' 159.
[99] Norman Glanville, *Why We Still Say No*, 1.

historians, a few biblical scholars, and four Methodist and three Baptist theologians. The conference members sought one Church renewed for mission by an agreed date. They famously declared, 'We dare to hope that this date should not be later than Easter day, 1980.'[100] Easter day 1980 came and went, and to this day such a manifestation of unity in Britain eludes us. Secondly, whereas in Wales the Church in Wales, the Presbyterian Church of Wales, the Methodist Church, the United Reformed Church and a number of Baptist churches had entered into a covenant for unity in 1975, in England a proposed Covenant promoted by the Churches' Unity Commission, whose executive officer was John Huxtable, failed when the Synod of the Church of England rejected it in July 1982.[101] Following his retirement, Huxtable ruefully reflected thus:

> I came to the sad conclusion that no matter what the Church of England might say in all sort [sic] of discussions, when it came to decision-making there was a system of voting that more or less ensured that the extreme Catholic and the extreme Evangelical wings could combine to leave things as they were. . . . Ever since Geoffrey Fisher's sermon about taking episcopacy into non-episcopal systems, his own conduct of affairs, as many will remember from his voluminous correspondence, reveals a horror of the Church of England ever becoming different. . . . It is to be the bridge Church over which no traffic ever flows. I hate writing this . . .[102]

A happier outcome, from Huxtable's point of view, was the formation of the United Reformed Church by the union of the majority of the English and English-speaking Welsh Congregational churches with the Presbyterian Church of England in 1972.[103] At the time this was sometimes trumpeted as the bringing together of two traditions which had stood side by side for three hundred years. In a sense this

---

[100] *Unity Begins at Home: A report from the First British Conference of Faith and Order, Nottingham, 1964*, 78.

[101] See *The Failure of the English Covenant: An Assessment of the Experience of the Churches' Council for Covenanting*. For some Quaker reflections on the ecumenical road travelled see *Unity in the Spirit: Quakers and the Ecumenical Pilgrimage*.

[102] W. John F. Huxtable, *As it Seemed to Me*, 71.

[103] For a sketch of Congregational-Presbyterian relations through the centuries see Geoffrey F. Nuttall, 'Relations between Presbyterians and Congregationalists in England', 1–7.

was true, for there was a remnant of seventeenth-century Presbyterians in north-east England and Stafford, who had not become either Congregational or Unitarian during the eighteenth century. But the bulk of the membership of the Presbyterian Church of England comprised Scots and people of Scottish extraction, whose forebears had come to England following the union of the English and Scottish Parliaments in 1707, with a further significant influx during the nineteenth century.[104] The churches they established, together with the surviving orthodox English Presbyterian churches – 63 congregations in all – were gathered into the Presbyterian Church *in* England in 1842. An English Synod of the United Presbyterian Church of Scotland was constituted in 1863. The two bodies united to form the Presbyterian Church *of* England in 1876. The 1972 union was, nevertheless, the first union in England and Wales that crossed traditional confessional boundaries.

An initiative taken at the Presbyterian General Assembly of 1939 towards closer relationships between themselves and the Congregationalists was thwarted by the onset of war; but in 1943 the Presbyterian Laymen's League urged the General Assembly to consider conversations regarding possible union with the Congregational Union of England and Wales, and this overture was made in 1945. By 1947 draft proposals were ready (the Congregationalists having taken care to ensure that both Micklem and Peel were among their representatives), but by 1949 it was concluded that they did not command sufficient support to justify further negotiations at that stage. A covenant to foster closer cooperation was, however, decided upon, and this was brought into effect in 1951. In 1963, by which time, it will be recalled, the Congregationalists were contemplating a national covenanted body to be known as the Congregational *Church* of England and Wales, conversations with the Presbyterians were resumed and the union was consummated in 1972.[105] Hubert Cunliffe-Jones was the leading

---

[104] For the doctrinal development here alluded to see Alan P.F. Sell, *Dissenting Thought and the Life of the Churches: Studies in an English Tradition*, ch. 5.

[105] For the steps towards union see Arthur L. Macarthur, 'The Presbyterian road to 1972', 4–7; Ronald Bocking, 'The United Reformed Church: background, formation, and after', 7–17. See also Arthur L. Macarthur, 'The background to the formation of The United Reformed Church (Presbyterian and Congregational) in England and Wales in 1972', 3–22. Among articles written on the occasion of union see John Huxtable, 'The United Reformed Church', 4–6; and the very thoughtful contribution by Stephen Mayor,

theologian on the Congregational side during the early stages of the conversations, while the Presbyterian theologian Martin H. Cressey did sterling work throughout as secretary of the Joint Committee. The latter afterwards wrote,

> It was early agreed in the Joint Committee that the New Testament senses of the word 'church' were two – the universal church and the local church. To call denominational bodies 'churches' is to reveal . . . 'that the failure and weakness of the Church have in particular been manifested in division which has made it impossible for Christians fully to know, experience and communicate the life of the one, holy, catholic, apostolic Church.' It was sharing this understanding of the

---

'Congregationalism and the Reformed tradition', 196–208. Mayor is rightly concerned that the Congregational debt to the radical Reformation be not forgotten; on which see also Alan P.F. Sell, *Dissenting Thought and the Life of the Churches*, ch. 20. At one point, however, I demur. He writes, 'even in the classical Congregationalism of the seventeenth century there was little sense of the wholeness and authority of the Church Catholic' (p. 202). But in 'The Institution of Churches and the Order Appointed in them by Jesus Christ', which was appended to *The Savoy Declaration of Faith and Order* (1658) (in D.M. Thompson, *Stating the Gospel*, 112) we read, 'Besides these particular churches, there is not instituted by Christ any church more extensive or catholic entrusted with power for the administration of his ordinances, or the execution of any authority in his name' (clause 6). But this is because the particular (local) church is the Church catholic; but if that is so every other local church is also the Church catholic. Accordingly, as Mayor concedes on the following page, 'In the classical Congregational era of the seventeenth century, churches did not act in major issues, such as calling a minister, without a good deal of local consultation by letter and by messenger.' Hence, when Pope John Paul II used to say that communion with the Bishop of Rome is a visible sign of the catholicity of the Church, I would say that gathering with the saints in worship and Church Meeting is a visible sign of the catholicity of the Church. See further, Alan P.F. Sell, *Testimony and Tradition*, 225–226. For a classical seventeenth-century Congregational statement see John Owen, *A Discourse concerning Evangelical Love, Church Peace, and Unity* (1672), in *The Works of John Owen*, edited by William H. Goold, 82: 'this is the church catholic visible, whereunto they all universally belong who profess the invocation of the name of our Lord Jesus Christ, their Lord and ours . . .' Cf. ibid., 78. For the retrospect of one who did not go forward into The United Reformed Church, but continued with the Congregational Federation, see Trevor Watts, 'History in reverse: reflections on the events of 1972', 20–26.

local church and the universal church that empowered the negotiators.[106]

I may add that it also calmed those Congregationalists who in the 1960s were seeking, and shortly received, a more accurate ecclesiological statement in justification of the change from Congregational Union to Congregational Church.

The objective was the inauguration of a new church benefiting from two traditions, rather than the cobbling together of two existing constitutions. Accordingly, it was not appropriate to approach The United Reformed Church's *Basis of Union* in a spirit of 'hunt the ecclesiologies', so that one could say, 'This was theirs; this was ours.' It was nevertheless clear that in terms of polity each party had to learn from the other. Twenty years ago, when attempting to view the polity in relation to the Congregational heritage, I reflected as follows:

> The first clause of the *Basis of Union* makes it plain that the Church is the calling of God. The second and sixteenth affirm (albeit not in these words) that the Church comprises saints: its members are Christ's redeemed people; the third declares that the Church is catholic; the fourth makes clear that its apostolicity is in the gospel and (by implication) is not of the sacerdotal kind. None of this is out of accord with the Congregational idea of the Church; and John Robinson would have been quite at home with the sixth clause: 'Christ's mercy in continuing his call to the Church in all its failure and weakness has taught the Church that its life must ever be renewed and reformed according to the Scriptures, under the guidance of the Holy Spirit.' Here is that 'founded freedom' which Congregationalism prized so highly. Sainthood and catholicity are there; so too is orderliness. The Church is an ordered society (and at this point former Congregationalists have been challenged by the Presbyterian understanding of the eldership), but at its heart there remains the *Church* Meeting. But all is now set within a fresh and determined context of corporate *episcope*, whose excitements and challenges will occupy the new Church for some years to come.[107]

---

[106] M.H. Cressey, 'Notes on the theology of union: theological aspects of the formation and process of The United Reformed Church before and after 1972', 22. He quotes from the original version of the *Basis of Union*, in *The Manual of the United Reformed Church*, 11, clause 7.

[107] Alan P.F. Sell, *Saints: Visible, Orderly and Catholic*, 116–7.

Clause eight of the *Basis of Union* declares that the uniting partners 'see their union as a part of what God is doing to make his people one, and as a united Church will take, wherever possible and with all speed, further steps towards the unity of all God's people.'[108] Within ten years they had begun to realise that aspiration, for in 1981 they were joined in union with the Re-formed Association of Churches of Christ,[109] Martin Cressey now serving as a United Reformed theologian on the Joint Committee, with Philip Morgan and David M. Thompson being prominent representatives of the Re-formed Association of Churches of Christ.

From the time of their origins, the Churches of Christ had been characterized by two predominant motifs: a restorationist approach to church polity, and an ecumenical vision. These came into conflict from time to time, and secessions resulted in the United States. In Britain some churches became isolated from the main group, and it was those of a more 'main line' ecumenical persuasion who entered the union: I employ the qualification 'main line' because some of those who remained outside the union on evangelical grounds regarded themselves as ecumenical in the sense of being at one with all those who share the evangelical faith. A standard account of *What Churches of Christ Stand For* was published by William Robinson in 1926. Among other works, Robinson also published *Essays on Christian Unity* (1923), and unlike most who have written on that subject, he also produced a work entitled *Everyday Chemistry* (1919). The Churches of Christ had in 1941 made overtures to the Baptist Union, but discovered that their fellow believer Baptists were in some cases receiving members who had not been baptized, and of this they disapproved. They received a more favourable response from The United Reformed Church, as Philip Morgan, their leading ecclesiastical statesman, has recalled.[110]

A significant theological issue on which the uniting parties had traditionally disagreed was that of baptism. After appropriate discussion it was agreed that both paedobaptism and believer baptism would be

---

[108] *Basis of Union*, 1973, 12.

[109] 'Re-formed' because the 1976 union proposals, while they had secured the legally required majority at the United Reformed Church Assembly in 1977, failed to reach the required target among the Churches of Christ. Success came consequent upon the reorganization of the latter body. See further, David M. Thompson, *Let Sects and Parties Fall: A Short History of the Association of Churches of Christ in Great Britain and Ireland*, 195–97. The historian David Thompson served as secretary of the Joint Committee.

[110] Philip Morgan, '1972 and Churches of Christ', 23–29.

available in the united Church, and be understood as 'a unique part of the total process of initiation'; and that a conscience clause would safeguard the position of those unable to accede to this. It was resolved that

> When baptism is administered at an age of responsibility, upon profession of faith, the baptized person at once enters upon the full privileges and responsibilities of membership. When baptism is administered to an infant, upon profession of faith by his parent(s), he is placed under the nurture of the Church that he may be led by the Holy Spirit in due time to make his own profession of faith in Christ as his Saviour and Lord, and enter upon the full privileges and responsibilities of membership.[111]

Since the Churches of Christ had both local elders authorized to conduct worship and preside at the Lord's Supper and travelling evangelists (many of whom became settled as pastors), the question of ministry and eldership in the United Reformed sense was a further significant matter for debate. Eventually a system of trained ministers and differently-trained auxiliary ministers, many of them in secular employment, was devised, with Churches of Christ elders having the choice of becoming auxiliary ministers (and being offered appropriate training as necessary) or of continuing as ordained elders but now in the United Reformed sense of the term, or of continuing to exercise the privileges of ordained Churches of Christ elders 'for such a period as shall be determined by the District Council.'[112] It remains only to add that in 2000 the majority of the churches of the Congregational Union of Scotland united with the United Reformed Church.

During the nineteenth century the Baptists, no less than other Nonconformists, began to take what we nowadays recognize as denominational shape. For them, one aspect of this development was the drawing together of Particular and evangelical Arminian Baptists, the latter being the heirs of Dan Taylor's New Connexion of General Baptist churches (1770). This rapprochement occurred following the abandonment by the Union of its Calvinistic statement of faith in 1832.[113] The Strict and Particular Baptists[114] remained, and the Gospel

---

[111] *Negotiations between The United Reformed Church and the Re-formed Association of Churches of Christ: Revised Proposals for Unification*, 11.

[112] Ibid., 13.

[113] See further, Ernest A. Payne, *The Baptist Union: A Short History;* Peter Shepherd, *The Making of a Modern Denomination.*

[114] For whom see Kenneth Dix, *Strict and Particular: English Strict and Particular Baptists in the Nineteenth Century.*

Standard Baptists[115] emerged, outside of the Union. During the twentieth century, while there were informal links between the English Strict and Particular Baptists (or Grace Baptists), the Gospel Standard Baptists, and the Baptist Union, the presence of both particular and evangelical Arminian doctrinal strands in the heritage of the Baptist Union, as well as the open table practice of many of its member churches, and the ecumenical commitment of a sizeable proportion of them, has thus far prevented such a coming together as the Methodists have experienced – if, indeed, the question has been raised at all (and if it has, I and those Baptists I have consulted are quite unaware of it). Even within the Baptist Union there are differences of view as to the propriety of participating in the quest to manifest that unity which is given in and with the gospel; and this notwithstanding the fact that for centuries there have been local union churches in England comprising Baptists and Congregationalists.[116] Nevertheless many Baptists have made substantial contributions to the ecumenical movement in England and Wales, including some of their prominent theologians. Thus, for example, Morris West served the British Council of Churches (which was constituted in Baptist Church House in September 1942) from 1963 onwards, while Leonard G. Champion chaired the Council's Mission and Unity Department from 1967–69.[117]

Behind West, Champion and others lay J.H. Shakespeare's pioneering quest for wider unity. He adumbrated his vision and left readers in no doubt as to his commitment in his book of 1918, *The Churches at the Crossroads*. In the wake of the First World War, and in connection with the Lambeth Conference's 'Appeal to all Christian People' (1920), he raised the possibility of conversations with the Church of England. His stoutest opponent in this was T.R. Glover and, as between some of the Methodists and Anglicans 40 years later, the crux of the problem was episcopacy. Glover insisted that nothing resembling re-ordination would be permitted; Shakespeare could not see how episcopacy could be threatening provided it were constitutional (cf. bishops in presbytery as pondered by Presbyterians) and not

---

[115] For whom see S.F. Paul, *Historical Sketch of the Gospel Standard Baptists*.

[116] For the longer history of 'Baptist-Congregational relationships' see Ernest A. Payne, 216–26.

[117] For these details and many others see Anthony R. Cross, 'Service to the ecumenical movement: The contribution of British Baptists', 107–22.

prelatical.[118] He later opined that he did not think episcopacy 'too great a price to pay . . . for the incalculable blessing of fellowship.'[119] The initiative ran into the ground, much to Shakespeare's personal distress. The question of *episcope* did not, however, evaporate; on the contrary, towards the end of the century, and in the wake of discussion of the World Council of Churches' document *Baptism, Eucharist and Ministry* (1982) a number of Baptists have considered the matter as it bears upon their own fellowship, not least as represented by Area Superintendents.[120] Of these, J.F.V. Nicholson gathered adjectives to characterize the pattern of *episcope* among the Baptists. It is, he wrote, 'corporate, collegial, personal and diverse, flexible, charismatic.'[121] Not surprisingly, 'sacerdotal' was not among the adjectives which dropped from his pen.

In addition to their relations with one another, and with others in this country, the Congregationalists, Baptists, Presbyterians and Methodists have played their part in the wider ecumenical movement in diverse ways. Building upon such co-operative ventures as the British and Foreign Bible Society and the Evangelical Alliance, and in the wake of the spread of the gospel through their missionary bodies, global organizations of confessional families began to develop, of which the first was the Alliance of Reformed Churches throughout the World holding the Presbyterian System (1875), followed by the World Methodist Council (1881), the International Congregational Council (1891), the Baptist World Alliance (1905), and the Disciples Ecumenical Consultative Council, which first met in 1979[122] and to which the British Churches of Christ belonged.[123] Of these, the World

---

[118] For a full account see P. Shepherd, *The Making of a Modern Denomination*, 114–31; Roger Hayden, 'Still at the crossroads? Revd J.H. Shakespeare and ecumenism', 31–54.

[119] J.H. Shakespeare, 'The great need', 89.

[120] See G.G. Reynolds, '75 years of the General Superintendency – what next?', 229–39.

[121] J.F.V. Nicholson, 'Towards a theology of *episcope* among Baptists', 319. The first part of this paper is in the previous issue of the journal: no. 6, April 1984.

[122] I am grateful to David M. Thompson for supplying this date.

[123] See Richard V. Pierard, ed., *Baptists Together in Christ 1905–2005*; David M. Thompson, 'Baptists and the world fellowship of the Church', 54–63. For the first 50 years see F. Townley Lord, *Baptist World Fellowship: A Short History of the Baptist World Alliance*.

Presbyterian Alliance and the International Congregational Council united in 1970 to form the World Alliance of Reformed Churches (Presbyterian and Congregational).[124]

It would be a full-scale study in itself to discuss the range of theological work undertaken by these bodies.[125] That some of it was of the highest quality can be seen from such early contributors to the World Presbyterian Alliance of J.O. Dykes and P. Carnegie Simpson; and to the International Congregational Council of R.W. Dale, A.M. Fairbairn, P.T. Forsyth and Robert Mackintosh, while the Baptist World Alliance could call upon the services of J.H. Shakespeare, Alexander Maclaren and J.H. Rushbrooke. Over the past forty decades the several Christian world communions mentioned have been engaged in international bilateral dialogues in which neuralgic theological issues, notably ministry and sacraments, have been frankly faced. I believe that through this work mutual understanding between the several traditions has been vastly improved, and that significant (and insufficiently well-known or acted upon) agreements have been reached. I shall illustrate this by reference to a selection only of conversations in which the Reformed family has been engaged, and of which I have personal experience.[126] I begin with our Free Church relatives and then move further afield.

Martin Cressey was a prominent member of the international Baptist-Reformed dialogue (1973–77). Not surprisingly, baptism was the focal point of the discussion, and the participants felt obliged to 'confront the difficult question whether Christians of Reformed and Baptists convictions who are members in good standing of their churches could recognize one another as both occupying the position of those who have received and responded to the grace of God in baptism as this grace is understood in the New Testament.' They realized that Such a mutual understanding could only arise from:

(i) an agreed understanding that a complex of elements, including baptism with water in the name of the Trinity, public profession of faith and admission to the Lord's Supper, are all parts of the reception of and response to this grace of God;

---

[124] See Marcel Pradervand, *A Century of Service: A History of the World Alliance of Reformed Churches 1875–1975*.

[125] My own study of this nature (terminus 1982) runs to 304 pages. See Alan P.F. Sell, *A Reformed, Evangelical, Catholic Theology: The Contribution of the World Alliance of Reformed Churches 1875–1982*.

[126] See further, Alan P.F. Sell, *Enlightenment, Ecumenism, Evangel*, ch. 10.

(ii) the acceptance (still problematic) that this complex of elements could find place in the life of any individual *either* contemporaneously in the act of believer's baptism, where profession of faith, water baptism and communion come together in time, *or* over a period of time, short or long, in which (infant) baptism, profession of faith (at 'confirmation' as it is often called), and admission to communion follow one another as separable stages in a process.[127]

Though not a member of the international dialogue, Morris West was among English Baptists who were open to a reconsideration of baptism within the context of a process of Christian initiation. This general approach was, as we have seen, of central importance in the steps concurrently being taken towards the union of the Churches of Christ with the United Reformed Church.

The International Reformed-Methodist dialogue called upon the services of Brian E. Beck and Geoffrey Wainwright of the Methodist Church,[128] and Colin Gunton and John Huxtable of The United Reformed Church. Here a major part of the task was to enquire how far the traditional Calvinist-Arminian points of friction should still be regarded as church-dividing issues. The conclusion was, 'we have found that the classical doctrinal issues which we were asked to review ought not to be seen as obstacles to unity between Methodists and Reformed.'[129] In the light of this, recommendations were made that steps be taken towards closer co-operation in many fields from the local to the international spheres, and that further Reformed-Methodist unions be contemplated.

The dialogue between the Reformed and the Disciples Ecumenical Consultative Council (1984–87) found Martin Cressey and myself on one side of the table and our United Reformed Colleagues from the

---

[127] *Baptists and Reformed in Dialogue*, 19–20.

[128] For papers relating to the several dialogues between his communion and others by that indefatigable Methodist ecumenist, Geoffrey Wainwright, see *Methodists in Dialog*, Nashville: Kingswood Books, 1995. For my review of this book see, *The Ecumenical Review*, LI no. 2, April 1999, 224–227.

[129] *Reformed and Methodists in Dialogue: Report of the Reformed/Methodist Conversations (1985 and 1987)*, 14. It would, of course, have been thoroughly embarrassing if any other conclusion had been reached, since Reformed and Methodists were already together in united churches in some parts of the world, and had been so since the United Church of Canada was founded in 1925.

Churches of Christ tradition, Philip Morgan and David M. Thompson, on the other. Once again, the question of baptism hove into view, on which the conciliatory statement was made that

> the difference between infant and believers' baptism becomes less sharp when it is recognized that both forms of baptism embody God's own initiative in Christ and express a personal response of faith made within a believing community. Personal confession of faith normally takes place in the presence of the congregation, either at the time of baptism in the case of the believer, or at a later time by those who are baptized as infants.[130]

As with the Methodists, the happy conclusion was reached that 'we believe there are no theological or ecclesiological issues which need to divide us as churches.'[131]

John Huxtable and Lesslie Newbigin participated in the dialogue between the Reformed family and the Anglican Consultative Council. To a greater degree than in the other dialogues noted, this one was concerned to place the neuralgic ecclesiological issues within the context of the church's mission. Areas of common ground and continuing differences were alike explored. As might be expected, the concept of *episcope* was discussed, and its location within a series of personal, collegial and communal relationships was commended. It was also pointed out that personal *episcope* is not unknown among Reformed churches,[132] but there are faint allusions only to the thorny question of *potestas*. Nevertheless, there was agreement on the potentially unifying general principle: 'Personal oversight apart from the wisdom of a corporate body is apt to become arbitrary and erratic; oversight by a corporate body without a personal pastor is apt to become bureaucratic and legalistic.'[133] Some constructive recommendations were appended to the report, among them the following:

---

[130] *Towards Closer Fellowship: Report of the Dialogue between Reformed and Disciples of Christ*, 11.

[131] Ibid., 14.

[132] Not, indeed, that such oversight has everywhere been enthusiastically received. In 1953, for example, numerous letters, both adverse and positive, were published in *The Christian World* in the wake of John G. Weller's article in that paper on 'The Place of moderators', 1–2. See also E.P.M. Wollaston, 'The first moderators: 1919', 298–301.

[133] *God's Reign and Our Unity: The Report of the Anglican-Reformed International Commission 1981–1984*, 73.

We recommend that where churches of our two communions are committed to going forward to seek visible unity, a measure of *reciprocal* communion should be made possible; for communion is not only a sign of unity achieved, but also a means by which God brings it about.[134]

It cannot be said that this recommendation has thus far universally been put into effect.

The biblical scholar George B. Caird of The United Reformed Church participated in the first phase of the international Roman Catholic-Reformed dialogue. Among the understandings reached were the following concerning the church as at once local and catholic, 'the localness and the catholicity of the Church are to be kept in perspective. It is only by participating in the local community that we share in the life of the universal Church, but the local community without universality . . . runs the risk of becoming a ghetto or of being arbitrarily dominated by individuals.'[135] No doubt the term 'local church' can, according to one's ecclesiology, mean either one particular church or a diocese; but the principle that being a Christian entails participation in the life of the Church is jointly affirmed.

In the same report the once-for-all Mediatorial work of Christ is affirmed: '[Jesus Christ's] once-for-all self-offering under Pontius Pilate is continued by him for ever in the presence of the Father in virtue of his resurrection. In this way he is our sole advocate in heaven.'[136] Unresolved questions include that concerning the way in which catholicity is experienced: 'For Roman Catholics, connection with the Bishop of Rome plays a decisive role in the experience of Catholicity. For the Reformed, catholicity is most immediately experienced through membership in the individual community.'[137] Belief in the sole Mediatorship of Christ is reaffirmed in the second phase of the dialogue, and care is taken to qualify the statement of the Second Vatican Council that the Church may be compared with 'the mystery of the Word Incarnate' because it 'is constituted from both a human aspect and a divine aspect,' with the caution: 'This analogy should not make us forget the radical difference which remains between Christ and the Church. In particular, the Church is only the spouse and the body of

---

[134] Ibid., 82.

[135] *The Presence of Christ in Church and World: Dialogue between the World Alliance of Reformed Churches and the Secretariat for Promoting Christian Unity, 1970–1977*, 19.

[136] Ibid., 23.

[137] Ibid., 32.

Christ through the gift of the Spirit.'[138] There is no attempt on the part of the participants to paper over the cracks of discord, as the following two paragraphs concerning the sacrament of the Lord's Supper demonstrate:

> The Reformed Churches take the view that, precisely because Christ himself is the host at the table, the Church must not impose any obstacles. All those who have received baptism and love the lord Jesus Christ are invited to the lord's [sic] Supper.
>
> The Roman Catholic Church, on the other hand, is convinced that the celebration of the Eucharist is of itself a profession of faith in which the whole Church recognizes and expresses itself. Sharing the Eucharist therefore presupposes agreement with the faith of the Church which celebrates the Eucharist.[139]

The examples given will suffice, I trust, to show both the kind of positive outcomes and the continuing agenda which bilateral dialogues yield.

As for multi-lateral relationships, it cannot be denied that Nonconformists played a significant part in both the predecessor bodies of the World Council of Churches (1948) and of the Council itself. In the early days A.E. Garvie was an ardent promoter of things ecumenical as well as a useful interpreter at meetings, who was not beyond exercising a translator's 'discretion' in the interests of unity and concord.[140] The Baptist Hugh Martin was another early advocate of ecumenism, and in 1941 he published a popular work entitled *Christian Reunion, A Plea for Action*.[141] To Norman Goodall, one of Congregationalism's ecumenical and missionary statesmen, we owe an account of *The Ecumenical Movement* in 1961.

---

[138] *Towards a Common Understanding of the Church: Reformed/Roman Catholic International Dialogue: Second Phase 1984–1990*, 38.

[139] Ibid., 55. However, it must be noted that on occasion Reformed churches have suspended members from communion on grounds of church discipline. It may even be that the sacrament has been used, one hopes rarely, as a stick with which to beat or threaten the recalcitrant – a sadly instrumentalist view of the sacred rite.

[140] See A.E. Garvie, *Memories and Meanings of My Life*, 185. See also, Norman Goodall, 'Some Congregational pathfinders in the ecumenical movement', 184–99.

[141] It should be noted that the English Baptists supplied a theologian, Keith Clements, to serve as General Secretary of the Conference of European churches.

The World Council's document *Baptism, Eucharist and Ministry* (1982) initiated by far the most widespread multilateral theological discussion of the twentieth century. The Council's member bodies were invited to report on 'the extent to which your church can recognize in this text the faith of the Church through the ages.'[142] Among the large number of replies received were those from the Baptist Union, the Methodist Church, The United Reformed Church, the Presbyterian Church of Wales and the Union of Welsh Independents.[143]

I now come, as promised, to my note on Unitarian ecumenism. Traditionally involved in social concerns, the Unitarians formed their Union for Social Service in 1906. They participated in the Conference on Christian Politics, Economics and Citizenship (COPEC) held in Birmingham in April 1924; and they became full members of the Life and Work strand of the World Council of Churches' pre-history. On this basis they continued as members of the British Council of Churches (1942). When the World Council of Churches was established in 1948 on a credal basis which the Unitarians could not accept, they were permitted to continue as associate members of the British Council of Churches. When the latter body was replaced by Churches Together in Britain and Ireland (1990), the Unitarians were excluded from membership largely on the question of authority. The response to their request for membership included the words:

> We found an evident want of commonly held convictions based upon a cogent understanding of the Scriptures. The freedom of the individual is not inspired, informed or controlled by any sense of a continuity of faith of the individual, either with the faith of other Unitarians, or more pertinently, with the historic faith of Christian churches in a way which would create a sufficient corporate coherence.[144]

---

[142] *Baptism, Eucharist and Ministry*, x.

[143] The replies can be found in the series of volumes edited by Max Thurian, *Churches Respond to BEM*. In order to assist the Reformed churches in their consideration of the document I, in my capacity of Theological Secretary of the World Alliance, published, *Responding to Baptism, Eucharist and Ministry: A Word to the Reformed Churches*. See also Alan P.F. Sell, 'Some Reformed responses to *Baptism, Eucharist and Ministry*', 549–65.

[144] Quoted by Alan Ruston, 'Unitarian ecumenical relations in England in the twentieth century,' 98. I am indebted to this article for the information in this paragraph. Note, however, that the Free Church Federal Council was constituted in 1940, not 1916 as stated on p. 93.

The Unitarians never belonged to the Free Church Federal Council or its predecessor bodies, the members of which coalesced under a fairly broad definition of 'evangelical'.

In the wider world, Unitarians have been supporters of the World Congress of Faiths (something else which did not endear them to narrower representatives of the evangelical cause), and, as Arthur Long has said, the International Association for Religious Freedom (1900) is 'in a sense, the international wing' of the Unitarian Movement.[145]

IV

We have now considered the Nonconformists as Protestants; we have discussed their ecclesiological self-understanding; and we have briefly surveyed the Nonconformist theological contribution to ecumenical work at home and abroad. It has become clear that an abiding issue of global significance is that of the historic episcopate. But the Nonconformists are not simply Protestants, they are Free Church people, and a number of their theologians played a part in the National Council of the Evangelical Free Churches (1896) and the Federal Council of the Evangelical Free Churches (1919), which two bodies united in 1940 to form the Free Church Federal Council.[146] In the early days these included J. Scott Lidgett, W.B. Selbie, A.E. Garvie and E. Griffith Jones. The question for us now is whether there is any theological topic distinctive of Free Churches as a whole and not of one denomination only, on which the Nonconformists of England might be expected to speak with a united voice? Living alongside the only remaining Anglican established Church as they do, the obvious candidate is the establishment question, and to this I now turn.

One may say that in the political circumstances in which they had to work out their polity, 'government by the Lord Jesus Christ alone' became for many of the Old Dissenters tantamount to a 'mark of the Church' added to the classical confessional marks of the preaching of the word, the administration of the sacraments and the exercising of church discipline. By this reckoning the Church of England was a false church – even, to some, anti-christ. If Christ were the sole head of the church, then the monarch could not be its head as well. Neither republicanism on the

---

[145] See Arthur Long, review of Marcus Braybrooke, *Pilgrimage of Hope: One Hundred Years of Global Pilgrimage*, 122.

[146] For the history see E.K.H. Jordan, *Free Church Unity: History of the Free Church Council Movement 1896–1941*.

one hand nor quietism on the other were necessary implications of this theological stance – very few members of Old Dissent adopted either position. Nor was it that Nonconformists denied the necessity of the state recognition of religion; it was, after all, the state which accorded religious toleration. They well understood the need for proper Church-state relations, but were not persuaded that the Church of England's way of prosecuting them was theologically appropriate.[147] The point was ecclesiological and, depending upon prevailing circumstances, it was articulated with varying degrees of force (and sometimes scurrility) from the sixteenth century to the first half of the twentieth century.[148] Indeed, during the first 50 years of the latter century, numerous books and articles were published on the question, and if references to the Church of England as 'anti-christ' or a 'two-headed monster' having one foot in the Bible, the other in the (unwritten) national constitution became unfashionable, so distinguished a theologian as P.T Forsyth could still pack a punch with such a sentence as this: 'What we protest against is not the abuses but the existence, the principle, of a national Church.'[149] In the declining years of the nineteenth century Forsyth had been equally pungent in his book, *The Charter of the Church* (1896), in which he defined a state church as a monopolist church so constituted as to deny the catholicity of the Church. Positively:

> However Establishment may seem to work at a given time, *the thing is wrong* . . . For my own part, any doubt of the truth of our Nonconformist principles would mean doubt of the truth of what is most distinctive in Christianity itself – free faith, free action, and free giving, as the response of men who have been moved and changed and controlled by the free gift of God and grace in Jesus Christ.[150]

---

[147] See further, Alan P.F. Sell, *Commemorations*, ch. 4. For a Baptist view see Nigel G. Wright, *Power and Discipleship: Towards a Baptist Theology of the State*.

[148] See further, Alan P.F. Sell, *Dissenting Thought and the Life of the Churches*, ch. 22; idem, *Testimony and Tradition*, ch. 11.

[149] P.T. Forsyth, 'The evangelical basis of Free Churchism', 693.

[150] Idem, *The Charter of the Church: The Spiritual Principle of Nonconformity*, 32. I have sometimes wondered whether there is any connection between the fact that this book by Forsyth was not republished when so many others were from the late 1940s to the 1960s, and a desire in the mid-century not to rock the ecumenical boat. Is it conceivable that Forsyth's style and/or content on this issue were deemed ecumenically inappropriate at a time when inter-church relations were generally improving and the World Council of Churches had recently (1948) been formed?

As the twentieth century opened J. Courtenay James published *The Philosophy of Dissent* (1900) in which he fuelled the argument not from the deeply ecclesiological side (he was a Methodist), but by invoking such considerations as liberty of conscience, the repudiation of secular control of the Church, and the way in which an established and endowed Church makes for inequality in the land.

Among more popular works of the early part of the century are J. Hirst Hollowell's *What Nonconformists Stand For* (1901), William Edwards's *A Handbook of Protestant Nonconformity* (1901), and *The Hope and Mission of the Free Churches* (n.d.) by Edward Shillito. Of these, that by Edwards, Principal of the South Wales Baptist College, was 'designed mainly for young people.' In his opinion, the establishment of religion 'is the child of the Dark Ages', and he enumerates no fewer than 50 theses against it, the last of which, beautifully circular, is that 'As the Welsh especially are a nation of Nonconformists, the presence of the Establishment is an anomaly and a grievous injustice.'[151] With the disestablishment of the Church in Wales, effective from 1920, the Welsh Nonconformists had their reward and, according to some, an identity crisis since that over against which they had defined themselves for so long had significantly changed its nature.

Much more substantial is the Congregationalist Henry W. Clark's two-volume *History of English Nonconformity* (1911, 1913). Clark's objective is to trace the development and influence of what he understands as Nonconformity's spiritual principle, namely, that life takes precedence over organization. Though it was natural that it should be so, he regrets that during the nineteenth century the forces of secular liberalism did not do more to marshal the troops against disabilities rather than directing their arrows against the 'higher ground' of the 'ultimate ideal's inspiration.'[152] Moreover,

> Nothing is more puzzling to the historian of Nonconformity than the comparative apathy with which the question of disestablishment was regarded by Nonconformists as a whole through a period when in other respects the struggle for Nonconformist rights was keen . . . [T]o a view of religion and the Church which makes the religion and the Church begin wholly in inward spiritualities and work themselves out from there, which makes the interior self-identification of the soul's life with the indwelling life of Christ the only true formative and constructive

---

[151] William Edwards, *A Handbook of Protestant Nonconformity: Designed mainly for Young People*, 200, 206.

[152] Henry W. Clark, *History of English Nonconformity*, II, 388–400.

force behind whatever religious organisation may come into being – to such a view of religion and the Church the assumption of the State by right or power to direct, control, legislate for, a Christian Church implies dishonour to religion which ought not for an instant to be brooked.[153]

We breathe a different, but still a Congregational, air in a report presented to the International Congregational Council in 1920 by a committee charged to consider 'the influence of Congregationalism in promoting Christian unity.' Among the signatories are S.M. Berry, A.E. Garvie, and W.B. Selbie – all of them committed to the cause of Christian reunion. In the course of their remarks they note that 'one element of difficulty seems to have been left out of account and will need to be reckoned with before any practical steps can be taken. We refer to the question of Establishment . . . So far, the question has been shirked but it will need to be faced in the not very distant future.'[154] Eighty-six years on, the question awaits resolution.

We reach a landmark in 1937, with the delivery by the 'Genevan' Congregationalist John Whale of the sermon commemorating the 250th anniversary of Emmanuel Congregational Church, Cambridge:

> To us a State Church is a contradiction in terms . . . There can be no such thing as territorial Christianity, as though the faith were like the English Language or English Common Law – an aspect or function of our national life. To us, State control of the deepest things by which Christendom lives would be a blasphemous betrayal of the Crown Rights of the Redeemer . . . [I]n asserting that His Church must necessarily be free from that Erastianism which is to us the supreme abomination, we are standing in a tradition of High Churchmanship which preserves and sets forth the true conception of the Church in all its spiritual nature and glory. We are asserting the Church's independence of the State and, if need be, her superiority to it; the utter inadmissibility of her being controlled and regimented by a secular power like King, Magistracy, Parliament, or Dictator; in short, her freedom, governance, and godly discipline under the sole lordship of Him whose service is perfect freedom.[155]

---

[153] Ibid., 409. For R.W. Dale's disquiet at the thought that political pressure was taking precedence over churchmanship in Nonconformist minds, see A.W.W. Dale, *The Life of R.W. Dale of Birmingham*, 378.

[154] 'The influence of Congregationalism in promoting Christian unity, and the lines upon which it should use that influence', 483.

[155] John S. Whale, 'Commemoration Sermon', 106–7.

Such points were endorsed, with characteristic wit, by that lover of the Church of England, Bernard Lord Manning, the Congregational lay historian, in his collection of papers, *Essays in Orthodox Dissent* (1939).

In 1949 the General Secretary of the Free Church Federal Council, Henry T. Wigley, wrote two sentences on the Establishment question, in the first of which he sounds what may now seem to some to have been an unduly optimistic note; and calls to mind the as yet unrealized hope of the reconciliation of memories as between the Church of England and the heirs of the Separatist martyrs and their Nonconformist partners:

> Most Anglicans now recognise that the present system of Establishment, which means the control of the Church by the State, is wrong in theory and in practice alike, and are seeking ways and means whereby, without disestablishment, supreme authority in the Church will be transferred from the King in Council to the official courts of the Church. What a lovely and gracious thing it would be if some responsible person in the Anglican Church were to acknowledge that our Free Church forefathers were right in standing, often at great cost to themselves, for the spiritual freedom of the Church of Christ, and were to pay public and ungrudging tribute to their insight and courage![156]

Wigley proceeds to quote the Joint Reply of the Free Churches to the Lambeth Conference's Appeal of 1920: 'Free Churchmen cannot be asked to consent that the civil power – which within its own sphere is called to be the servant of God – has any authority over the spiritual affairs of the Church.'[157]

In a more substantial volume entitled *The Claims of the Free Churches* (1949) Henry Townsend, Principal of Manchester Baptist College, revealed himself as being in the line of Forsyth with such a sentence as this: 'National Churches have arrested the universal ideas of the New Testament, and have thereby de-christianised the idea of God which was revealed by Jesus.'[158] He further addresses the claim, frequently advanced by members of the Church of England, not least in the Commission on Church and State of 1935, that establishment is a bulwark in society against secularism. Townsend attacks this utilitarian argument, declaring that 'the whole argument from Free Church his-

---

[156] H.T. Wigley, *The Distinctive Free Church Witness Today*, 64.

[157] Ibid.

[158] Henry Townsend, *The Claims of the Free Churches*, 200.

tory is a protest against the complacency of the principle of the utility of the Establishment.'[159] The same argument had, six years earlier, provoked even the self-effacing Congregationalist Professor George Phillips of Lancashire Independent College into one of his rare appearances in print: 'The argument, heard so often in these days even from the mouths of Free Churchmen, that the Establishment should be preserved as a barrier against the spread of secularism, belongs to a class of deliberation so low in ethical principle that even the most unscrupulous politician might blush to hear it. Surely better things are expected of us than a juggling expediency! "Fiat iustitia, ruat coelum," though pagan in origin, is a loftier standard and a safer guide.'[160]

On 14 May 1952 Ernest Payne, the General Secretary of the Baptist Union of Great Britain and Ireland, delivered a lecture to the Congregational Union Assembly entitled *The Free Churches and the State*. Holding staunchly to Free Church principles construed in an ecumenical manner, Payne nevertheless felt that the time was not ripe to press the establishment question (a) because 'We are obviously in a dangerous transitional period in regard to the theory and activity of the State'; (b) because 'The Churches are engaged in a serious and sustained conversation regarding the nature of the Church . . . A sharp Church conflict would seriously endanger the growing mutual understanding and trust, and would certainly be a grave scandal in the eyes of the world'; and (c) because 'it would be disastrous at the beginning of a new reign to embark upon a religious controversy which would inevitably be complicated, prolonged and embittered, and which would, equally inevitably, involve the status and powers of the crown.'[161] In the following year the Free Church Federal Council published the report entitled *The Free Churches and the State: The Report of the Commission on Church and State appointed by the Free Church Federal Council in March, 1950*.

---

[159] Ibid., 208.

[160] George Phillips, 'Freedom in religious thought', 60. Proponents of the utilitarian argument would do well to reflect upon the fact that the United States manages, in the absence of an established church, to be a more churchgoing nation, and perhaps a more Christian nation in some ways (some of them disturbing) than England. That this point is not lost upon some Anglicans is clear from E.L. Mascall, *Up and Down in Adria: Some considerations of Soundings*, 104.

[161] Earnest A. Payne, *The Free Churches and the State*, 28; reprinted in idem, *Free Churchmen, Repentant and Unrepentant and Other Papers*, London: Carey Kingsgate Press, 1965, ch. 5.

There the matter seems almost to have rested. The trickle of books and pamphlets by Nonconformists on the establishment question almost entirely dried up,[162] though in 1976 the Methodist historian John Munsey Turner published an article on 'Some problems of Church and state in England' in which he concluded:

> If we accept, as many do now, a style of state which is increasingly liberal and neutralist in morals and religion, it would seem proper to advocate some measure of disestablishment of the Church, though . . . we would deplore a total repudiation of the religion which has shaped our culture.[163]

In the following year John Huxtable, echoing his forebears of 1920, said that 'the Church-State relationship will have to be discussed and settled in whatever way eventually seems right.'[164]

Not even the musings of the tabloid press – and of some of the broadsheets – on the question 'Is Prince Charles fit to be the temporal head of the Church of England?' (than which no question could more completely miss the point) stimulated much by way of a Free Church response. Neither did the more serious publication by the Anglican John Habgood of his book *Church and Nation in a Secular Age* (1983), though John Munsey Turner rose to the bait,[165] as did Bernard Thorogood of The United Reformed Church, who wrote of Habgood,

> I do not think he has fully answered the theological point at issue, which is the proper ordering of the company of people who form the body of Christ. How can that company cede to another authority any

---

[162] Historians may be trusted to reflect upon why this might have been. Did the removal of almost all socio-political disabilities take the steam out of the debate? (Cf. Bernard Lord Manning, *The Protestant Dissenting Deputies*, 403). Did the growing spirit of ecumenism foster reticence on matters deemed to be 'neuralgic'? Has the increasing mobility of the population and the fact that people are less likely nowadays to find a 'church home' on grounds of traditional denominational loyalty had a stultifying effect upon the debate?

[163] J. Munsey Turner, 'Some problems of Church and state in England', 56–64.

[164] W. John F. Huxtable, *A New Hope for Christian Unity*, 78.

[165] J. Munsey Turner, 'Creative Dissent in the 1990s', 51–58, 62. See also, idem, 'Church, state and society – 2003,' 37–44.

key decision about its worship, its leaders, its theology or its forms of ministry?[166]

When addressing objections to the establishment, Habgood mentions none of the theologians of Nonconformity to whom I have here drawn attention; he appeals to the utilitarian argument which Townsend, Phillips and others trounced; and he gives the game away with his methodological statement: 'My defence of establishment . . . was based fundamentally on an assessment of the needs of the nation, and a view of the church as not confined to those whose religious commitment is most explicit and most ready to express itself in overt religious activity.'[167] Unless such pragmatism is qualified by serious consideration of those biblical and ecclesiological questions concerning the nature of the Church and the due relations of Church and state – and this with a view to honouring the crown rights of the Redeemer in his Church (and who are the Church?) – Free Church people and members of the Church of England will continue to talk past one another as they have done for so long. The martyrs cry out for something better, and the reconciliation of memories is urgently required.[168]

---

[166] Bernard Thorogood, *The Flag and the Cross: National Limits and Church Universal*, 45.

[167] John Habgood, *Church and State in a Secular Age*, 176.

[168] It must be admitted that Free Churchmen have not always been the best advocates of their cause. Too often 'Free' in 'Free Church' has been understood as 'freedom from state control,' whereas such freedom is but a corollary of the primary freedom which is that of the risen and ascended Lord to be the only Lord of the Church. Again, the emphasis has sometimes been too much upon the real or alleged privileges enjoyed by the established Church: John Habgood is thus presented with a smoke-screen which, not surprisingly, he utilizes. Yet again, it is sometimes glibly said that 'We are all established now.' But this fails to recognize the important distinction between the state recognition of religion which is necessary from the point of view of the right to freedom of worship, trust laws and the like, and establishment theology, which at its theologico-political root in the sixteenth century teaches that national cohesion, especially over against Roman Catholic Spain, is required; this is best achieved by religious conformity induced by legislation the violation of which can lead to death; to be a true English person is to be a member of the Church of England – non-members are very likely to be traitors against the nation. I do not think that a single Anglican today believes any of this. But if memories are to be reconciled, this needs to be acknowledged.

But even as I write those words concerning the martyrs – those sixteenth-century harbingers of Congregationalism – and the reconciliation of memories, I am bound to acknowledge that it is not easy for the Free Churches as a whole to speak with one mind on the establishment question. The martyrs are not within the memory of those relative youngsters the Methodists – still less so in those of the Pentecostalists and black churches. Furthermore, there have always been those among the Methodists who are but reluctant Nonconformists.[169] All power therefore to those Anglicans and Free Church people who, I understand, are currently engaged in fresh discussions of establishment. May their outlook be ecumenical and their thoughts in the first place be theological.[170]

As I emerge from the ecclesiological thickets I have been exploring, I should like to place side by side two quotations, dredged up from the nineteenth century, which between them epitomize the tightrope which must ever be walked by those who know both that they must speak of what they have seen and heard and know with equal certainty that they have not seen everything. In 1834 Thomas Binney declared:

> I am a dissenter because I am a catholic; I am a separatist, because I cannot be schismatical; I stand apart from some, because I love all; I oppose establishments because I am not sectarian; I think little of uniformity, because I long for union; I care not about subordinate

---

[169] For sociological and other factors which may perhaps conduce to the tying of Free Church tongues see David M. Thompson, 'The Free Churches in modern Britain', 99–117.

[170] Preliminary conversations took place on 30 November 1998. As one who has been urging engagement in such talks for at least a quarter of a century, I am delighted that there is some movement on this front. See reports in *The Sunday Times*, 10 January 1999 (the ST at its most tabloid-like), *The Tablet*, 16 January 1999, and *Church Times*, 22 January 1999. For end-of-the-century inner-Anglican discussion of the matter see Wesley Carr, 'A developing establishment'; Martyn Percy, 'Editorial: The big issue: is there a third way for "establishment"?'; Paul Avis, 'Establishment and the mission of a national church'. See further on Church-state relations, Alan P.F. Sell, *Commemorations*, ch. 4; idem, *Testimony and Tradition*, ch. 11. For an abbreviated version of the latter see idem, 'Establishment as a theological issue: the Dissenting witness'.

differences with my brother, for '*Christ* has received him' and so will I.[171]

In 1899 A.M. Fairbairn addressed the International Congregational Council in Boston in these terms:

[T]here is the magnanimity of Christ, – he consents to live in communities that vainly call themselves Presbyterian or Independent, Baptist or Methodist, and there is a still greater humility in his being ready to dwell in proud communities which speak of themselves as imperial, infallible or apostolic. Oh, I sometimes think that the hardest text in Scripture is, 'He that sitteth in the heavens shall laugh.' If there be divine laughter, must it not often be at the follies of men who think that they hold God in their custody and distribute him to whomsoever they will?[172]

---

[171] Thomas Binney, *Dissent Not Schism: A Discourse delivered in the Poultry Chapel, December 11, 1834, at the Monthly meeting of the Associated Ministers and Churches of the London Congregational Union*, 65.

[172] A.M. Fairbairn, 'The text and the context', 71.

Lecture 4

Rivers, Rivulets – and Encroaching Desert?

The rivers are eschatology and the Cross, both of which flow through twentieth-century Nonconformist theology; the rivulets are my attempts to notice hitherto unmentioned sources, and to reflect upon the route travelled in these lectures; the possibility that desert conditions are encroaching upon Nonconformist theology is one to be realistically assessed.

I

An inventory of twentieth-century Nonconformist works on eschatology reveals the clear preponderance of these in the first half of the century. It further reveals that Unitarians have shown a particular interest in the question of immortality. I shall return to them shortly, but first I note some eschatological flutterings in Wesleyan dovecotes as the nineteenth century gave way to its successor.

The particular question at issue was the final fate of the impenitent. Discussion of this topic had been rumbling on at least since the eighteenth century, and R.W. Dale had specified the options in 1877. There are, he said, those who cannot make up their minds on the subject: 'They cannot warn men against eternal condemnation, because they are not sure that any man will be eternally condemned.' There are those who hold that the impenitent are to be condemned to suffering, whilst hoping that 'there may be some transcendent manifestation of the Divine grace in reserve, of which as yet we have no hint.' There are those who believe that the Christ who came to seek and to save the lost will persist in this effort even though, because of the invincibility of human freedom, it cannot be affirmed that all will in fact be saved. There are those who believe that God's love cannot finally be thwarted, and hence all will finally be saved; those who hold that the impenitent will nevertheless enjoy an eternal life on a lower plane than the saved; and those who deny that the impenitent can finally be restored.[1]

It was J. Agar Beet of Richmond College who lit the touch paper among the Wesleyans by advancing yet another option into which some read 'the annihilation of the wicked.'[2] In 1897 he published *The Last Things*, a work concerning the second coming of Christ and the doom of the wicked. It was his position on the doom of the wicked which caused a stir. He argued that the Bible affirms that those who come to Christ will be saved, and that those who continue, impenitently in wickedness will suffer ruin. But, on biblical grounds, he did not feel able to affirm that the suffering of the wicked will be endless. Indeed, he argued that the idea of immortality – the endless permanence of all human souls – was a Greek importation into Christian theology, and one unsupported from Scripture. At the same time, he did not claim that annihilation of the wicked was actually taught in the Bible. His book was commended by the Methodist press; when some of the godly went after Beet's scalp the Theological Institution Committee, by a vote of thirty-one to five with two abstentions, resolved to take no action against him; and the Second London Synod unanimously supported him. Despite this, efforts were made to suppress his book, and he was removed from his post at Richmond College. In 1901 he published a follow-up work, *The Immortality of the Soul: A Protest*, in which he reiterated his position and found the celebrated Dr William Burt Pope guilty of holding to the human being's natural immortality whilst failing to prove it.[3] In 1902 he was reappointed to Richmond on condition that he would not republish his views without the consent of the Wesleyan Conference. In 1904 he sought that consent, but such was the furore that he gave twelve months' notice of his resignation with a view to republishing his book thereafter. In 1905 the revised version appeared. In the new Preface Beet urges the free discussion of theological differences over against inquisitorial attitudes; claims that no one had attempted to refute him; shows in an appendix that the respected scholar W.T. Davison, his successor at Richmond, and the Reverend George Jackson are, respectively, expressing views similar to and identical with his own; and regrets that the theme of the doom

---

[1] R.W. Dale, 'On some present aspects of theological thought', 13–15.

[2] See further, David Carter, 'Joseph Agar Beet and the eschatological crisis', 197–216.

[3] See J.A. Beet, *The Immortality of the Soul: A Protest*, 58–63. Note the non-Methodist publisher of this volume (Hodder and Stoughton).

of the lost has vanished from the pulpits because preachers no longer know what to say about it.[4]

In saying that nobody had formally responded to him, Beet overlooks his opposite number at Headingley College, J.S. Banks, who published a critique of *The Immortality of the Soul* in 1902. He charges Beet with attempting to place the onus of proof on his opponents in that Beet grants that Scripture does not positively affirm the annihilation of the wicked, and invites others to say that the Bible repudiates the doctrine. In fact, Banks claims, the biblical passages which teach eternal punishment imply unlimited immorality. In passing he repudiates the doctrine of conditional immortality on the ground that it implies that human beings have a capacity for immortality but are not actually immortal. He appreciates the motives of those who opt for annihilation, but 'If we could know sin in its nature and effects as God does, what penal consequences should we think too great?'[5] Banks further makes it clear that he deprecates caricatures of eternal punishment, and declares that 'Our main business is to preach the certainty, the freeness, the completeness of salvation in Jesus Christ – doom reversed, anger turned away, hell's curse changed into heaven's blessing.'[6]

In 1910 Sydney H. Mellone, Principal of Manchester Unitarian College, published *The Immortal Hope*. He sets out from the idea warranted, he believes, by the sciences of life and mind, as well as by general experience, 'that the Soul of Man is a living growing power.'[7] He examines a number of views dismissive of immortality and finds that they arise either from sheer dogmatism, from confused thinking, or from limited personal experience. He argues that the idea of personality entails the idea of survival and growth beyond death.

Six years later Mellone published *Eternal Life Here and Hereafter*, in which he adopts a more distinctly theological stance. He discusses the concept of eternal life in the Bible and in Christian mysticism and then critically reviews secularism which, he argues, 'leaves us, practically and theoretically, in a "blind alley",'[8] by denying us the right 'to suppose anything about the unseen part of the universe until there is distinct evidence in the way of sense-perception and experience, to

---

[4] See idem, *The Last Things*, Preface and 313–5.

[5] J.S. Banks, *Words on Immortality*, 28.

[6] Ibid., 32.

[7] S.H. Mellone, *The Immortal Hope: Present Aspects of the Problem of Immortality*, v.

[8] Idem, *Eternal Life Here and Hereafter*, 199.

warrant our hypothesis.'[9] He confronts the problem of evil, construing it as a problem both internal to the individual and external in the world: 'when good conquers in the inner conflict, it takes up into its own service an element that was in the evil, which is therefore necessary for the growth and realization of the good.'[10] Resting throughout on the conviction expressed in his Preface, that 'The sonship of every human soul to God is an eternal fact,'[11] Mellone concludes, though not glibly or sentimentally, to universalism:

> The assertion, sometimes made, that Universalism means in effect 'it does not matter what we do, for we shall be all right in the end' is unworthy of discussion. Universalism rests on the same foundation on which rests our belief in the eternity of goodness and truth in God . . . The ethical motive of belief in immortality means that compensation and retribution, to be real, must be redemptive. The religious motive means that final communion with God is the destiny of every soul, and not alone of those who know in this present by living experience what such communion is. The chief end of man is, to glorify God and enjoy him for ever.[12]

In the meantime the eschatologically irrepressible J. Agar Beet had discussed *The Last Things in a Few Words* (1913). His emphasis is upon the second coming of Christ, the doom of the lost, and the city of God. He reiterates his position, noted earlier, that while sinners may expect post-mortem retribution, and may persist in their refusal of God's love, the suffering of the lost is not endless. He is sceptical of many millennial theories. He dissents from those who predict an early return of Christ, and (which was just as well) in an appendix he stoutly repudiates the view of the Jehovah's Witnesses that Christ returned in 1874, and that the consummation would occur in 1914.

Ebenezer Griffith-Jones's book on *Faith and Immortality* appeared in 1917, and was dedicated to 'The splendid youth of Britain who, at the call of honour and duty, came forward, in the hour of their country's need, to fight, to suffer, and to die – that she may live.' He detects a decline in the influence of the Christian pulpit, and attributes this to the fact that

---

[9] Ibid.

[10] Ibid., 243.

[11] Ibid., v.

[12] Ibid., 272–273. Note the way in which, in the last, unreferenced, sentence the *Westminster Shorter Catechism* is construed in a decidedly non-Calvinistic way.

Preachers nowadays do not concern themselves so much with what happens after death, as with what happens to us here and now. The pains of hell, the bliss of heaven, the penalties and rewards which await us in the Unseen, have largely disappeared from amongst the incentives and warnings of the religious life, nor have any other taken their place. Life is dealt with as though it found its sanctions, rewards and punishments within the circle of our earthly experience, and needed no future life to round off its incompleteness and bring its tremendous issues to fruition.[13]

This state of affairs has been caused by the fact that the old beliefs have become untenable on exegetical and spiritual grounds. Accordingly, 'a fresh start may be made in the preaching of a truly evangelical and believable doctrine of the Last things.'[14]

Drawing inferences from evolutionary theory, Griffith-Jones finds that it is not irrational to posit immortality. He then turns to the biblical evidence and, finally, in a constructive section, presents his own case. He opposes theories of universal restoration (such as that expounded by Mellone):

The fatal flaw in this line of reasoning is that in order to vindicate the character and saving purpose of God, injustice is wrought to the sanctity of the moral order. In the first place, it posits a principle of veiled determinism as rigid as that of Calvinism, the difference being that in the Calvinistic scheme God's will is throughout absolute and supramoral, since men's destiny is not determined by their conduct but by the secret decrees of God . . . while in the Universalist Scheme God's will is strictly moral in that He decrees the salvation of all men. The absolute victory of God can, however, be gained only on one condition – the free consent of His creatures . . . [A]re the conditions of moral freedom such that we can confidently forecast the issue of men's final choices?[15]

Those who espouse conditional immortality equally fail to satisfy Griffith-Jones. In the first place, they deny the soul's immortality while assuming its survival of bodily death, and their theory 'emasculates and weakens the conception of personality' by relating 'man

---

[13] E. Griffith-Jones, *Faith and Immortality: A Study of the Christian Doctrine of the Life to Come*, vii–viii.

[14] Ibid., ix.

[15] Ibid., 242–3.

too organically with the brute.'[16] His own view is that we are by nature immortal; that this life is probationary, and that the probationary period continues after death either in heaven or hell; that we cannot be certain that all will be saved, and that we have no clear insight into the fate of the finally unrepentant. His vision of the heavenly state includes the idea that 'the highest energies of the redeemed community will be directed towards the salvation of the unredeemed.'[17]

The year 1918 saw the publication of P.T. Forsyth's profound meditations upon *This Life and the Next*. Among many striking sentences are the following: 'I do not see how a true believer in Christ can doubt the immortality of those who are Christ's (and He claims all), or require occult assurance of it, which means finding Him unsatisfac-tory.'[18] Again:

> The old life and the new are not parted by a bottomless pit. It is a constitutional revolution. I mean God did not create the first world of nature without reference to the second of grace. His grace is not but a new strategy to save an unforeseen reverse . . . He had the new creation in view when He issued the first . . . Though nature cannot of itself culminate in grace, at least it was not put there without regard to grace. Grace is Nature's destiny. We are born to be saved.[19]

With reference to the new life in Christ, Forsyth declares, 'The newness in the man corresponds to the new and original thing in Christ. If in Christ there was nothing essentially new, if He was but man at his spiritual best, we could not so speak. But all that makes Him the Son of God goes to differentiate the new creature He inhabits.'[20] So it is that

> To live here is to live the Christ that rules eternity. To die is more of that Kingdom . . . The foundation of our true immortality is in a redemption . . . We do not glide into heaven; we are taken, not to say plucked, into it . . . [T]he Christian idea is not happiness and it is not power, but it is perfection – which is the growth of God's image and glory as our destiny.[21]

In 1924 principal L.P. Jacks of Manchester College, Oxford, published his Hibbert Lectures, one of which was on 'Immortality in a living universe.'

---

[16] Ibid., 264.
[17] Ibid., 327.
[18] P.T. Forsyth, *This Life and the Next*, 44.
[19] Ibid., 69.
[20] Ibid., 75.
[21] Ibid., 85, 86, 87.

He is inclined to believe that if all were agreed about immortality as they are about the multiplication table, the doctrine's value would be diminished; while 'the value of life for those who deny immortality is raised by the presence in the world of people who affirm it.' Hence, the difference between those who believe in immortality and those who do not is 'one of the healthiest differences of opinion that exist among mankind. It may be that believers do not get on very well *with* deniers. But *without* the other each side would get on still worse.'[22] The New Testament teaching on the subject concerns both the individual and the cosmos, but the doctrine cannot be proved philosophically. Jacks thinks that Butler was right in holding that probability is the guide of life, and he is prepared to endorse the view that the probability of immortality is high; but he cannot affirm that immortality is our right whatever use we make of our lives. None of the New Testament writers 'represent sonship and heirship to God as a condition into which we are naturally born. The position of sons is one that we have to win, and our immortality follows from that.'[23]

Jacks's own conviction regarding immortality rests on two other doctrines: first, that the universe is essentially alive, and secondly that its life expresses a moral order, the conscious working-out of which is ongoing. Challenging his audience in a manner consistent with this idealistic view he says, 'Your purpose and business are those of a Creator of Values. You are here to add value to the world in which you find yourself. And there lies the point of contact between you and the Great Companion. There is the point where your business and purpose coincide with that of the Soul of the Living Universe.'[24]

But what does it mean to say that the world is a moral order? Jacks answers with Kant that 'A moral world is a world where *persons, individual persons, are treated as ends in themselves*, and not as means or instruments to an end beyond themselves.'[25] They would not be so treated were persons to be extinguished at death. This would go against the justice of God.[26]

---

[22] L.P. Jacks, *A Living Universe*, 101.

[23] Ibid., 105. Note the Pelagian flavour here.

[24] Ibid., 120.

[25] Ibid., 121.

[26] Although my purpose is to present the views of Nonconformists rather than to critique them, I cannot resist the temptation of saying that I do not see how this squares with Jack's stated position that immortality is not a right, and that sonship is to be won (though I should prefer to say that it is graciously given). It cannot be denied that Jacks's style is delightfully urbane.

As the Second World War was getting into its devastating stride, the Baptist F. Townley Lord published *Conquest of Death: A Christian Interpretation of Immortality*. His audience comprises two classes: those Christians who wish to know how the doctrine stands up in the light of modern thought; and those sceptics who are nevertheless 'wistful before an open grave.'[27] With the latter especially in mind he sets out from those considerations which do not turn upon distinctively Christian claims. He adverts to our consciousness of the life of the soul, and of the soul's growth, but after all that scientists, psychologists and moralists have to say, the fact is that 'The final assurance of immortality, no less than real spiritual achievement on this side of the grave, lies in the being of God.'[28] Following Kant and Plato he finds value in the idea that both justice and the non-realization of the good life in the temporal sphere demand immortality, and that 'the noblest experiences of men here below are *of such a quality* that a vista of continued life, in which the spiritual nature shall have an opportunity for continued development and in which justice shall be vindicated, is more reasonable than its denial.'[29] But this position can be held only on certain assumptions, supremely on the assumption that 'my assurance of immortality rests finally on my own spiritual reality, on the eternal value of spiritual achievement, and therefore on the reality of God.'[30] The Christian conviction (a word he prefers to use instead of 'hope' in this context) is that because of Christ's Resurrection, believers may share his victorious life. Accordingly, at death, while the body ceases to play its part in the development of an individual's personality, that personality does not cease.

This leads Lord to a consideration of heaven, which he construes qualitatively, and of the question, 'Is there hope for all?' He weighs the doctrines of eternal punishment and universal restoration, both of which assume that the human soul is by nature immortal, and finds them wanting. The notions annihilation and conditional immortality likewise fail to satisfy. Positively, he deems it reasonable to suppose that in the life to come the highest values experienced here will be perpetuated, and that the life to come will be one of progress. We should not, he thinks, eschew the idea of post-mortem probation on account of untoward Roman Catholic teachings concerning purgatory, and (following Forsyth) we should learn that it is not unacceptable to pray for our dearest dead. In conclusion, he reaffirms his basic point: 'once

---

[27] F.T. Lord, *Conquest of Death: A Christian Interpretation of Immortality*, 23.

[28] Ibid., 35.

[29] Ibid., 60.

[30] Ibid., 62.

the *fact* of [Christ's] Resurrection is accepted, the conquest of death becomes a reality . . . [I]f the Christian view of immortality is closely linked with the victory of Jesus, and if that victory is the expression of the purpose and power of God, it follows that the ultimate basis of our conviction lies in the being and nature of God.'[31]

The relation of eschatology to the doctrine of God comes to the fore in a paper by W.A. Whitehouse entitled, 'The modern discussion of eschatology.' While valuing the benefits of the exegetical work of C.H. Dodd and others, his predominant concern is 'how the Church today may grasp and reabsorb into its life the eschatological emphases which characterise the Gospel in its entirety.'[32] He is 'not persuaded that the recent exegetical developments have liberated the New Testament writings for their essential task of confronting the modern reader with the awful reality of *God*.'[33] Whitehouse recognizes that perhaps

> the scientific scholar cannot commit himself to the thesis that the logic of the eschatological theme has its source and root in the mystery of the person of the eschatological Redeemer, and that here is a thread to be followed deliberately in the exegesis of all the passages which are saturated with eschatology. It seems to me, however, that until we have found our way through that logic to that source and root, we have not taken the measure of New Testament faith in Jesus as Word and Son of God.[34]

He proceeds to argue that 'the reason why it is so necessary to discuss every problem "eschatologically" . . . is that everything in Christian theology turns on the real presence of One who is really God and really in history.'[35] Hence, 'The real presence of Jesus is His presence in the act of that "finished work" where men are brought face to face with the last things in crucial decision.'[36] As to the present state of those who have died in Christ:

> A doctrine which speaks in purely teleological terms of their having entered on a further stage of probation [cf. Jacks, Lord] appears to be

---

[31] Ibid., 179.

[32] W.A. Whitehouse, 'The modern discussion of eschatology', 64.

[33] Ibid., 67.

[34] Ibid., 69.

[35] Ibid., 72.

[36] Ibid., 75.

deficient in eschatology, as does the antithetical doctrine that they 'sleep'. The important question is not, 'What happens to me after death?', but how is my life in Christ at present enriched by communion with those dear to me on earth 'who have obtained the prize'? Here [as if in agreement with Forsyth and Lord] there is room for considerable developments in teaching and theology.[37]

Towards the end of a stimulating paper, Whitehouse suggests that 'The justification of sinners is an act which can only be wrought within a framework of eschatological magnitude, and it is perhaps true to say that the eschatological themes are not elaborated in Scripture for their own sakes so much as for the sake of this central assertion.'[38] His conclusion therefore is that

> theology should proceed from a conviction that the Bible's statement of its eschatological theme is a necessary and an adequate one, and that it should strive for an understanding where everything is integrated round the central themes of the hypostatic union of God and man in the person of Christ and the justification of man by God's grace alone which has been wrought out in Christ.[39]

Only so shall we begin to understand what we mean by 'God'.

In 1907 John Drew of Haringey Park, Middlesex, established what came to be known as the 'Drew Lecture on Immortality'. In 1979 Charles S. Duthie, formerly Principal of New College, London, published a collection of these, a number of them by Nonconformists. It would be of interest to dwell upon the paper by the Methodist New Testament scholar C.K. Barrett, in which he qualifies the distinction which Oscar Cullmann, notably though not exclusively, read out of the New Testament between the resurrection of the body and the immortality of the soul.[40] But, sticking to my systematic last, I shall briefly note two contributions in that vein.

First, Hubert Cunliffe-Jones writes on 'God's judgement of the individual after death' (1966). He is acutely aware of writing at a time of 'scepticism and indifference arising from the denial of any trans-empirical reality.' There is also 'hesitancy and uncertainty in contemporary

---

[37] Ibid., 80.

[38] Ibid., 88.

[39] Ibid., 89.

[40] See C.K. Barrett, 'Immortality and resurrection', 68–88. The reference is to Cullmann's *The Immortality of the Soul or the Resurrection of the Body?*

Christian eschatological affirmation.'[41] The latter are particularly acute concerning the judgement of God. Undaunted, Cunliffe-Jones assumes the God of Christian faith incarnate in Christ, and two corollaries of this: life after death and God's judgement on all. He points out that 'The ground for believing in life after death is not human wishes but the purpose of God. God is sovereign over the universe, and will bring [? His] purpose to fulfilment. Human life after death has its place within the fulfilment of God's purpose for the universe.'[42] The judgement relates to the whole of human history, but it is with the individual that Cunliffe-Jones is here concerned. He argues that 'God in Christ understands our life from within,' and therefore 'His judgement is not alien but intimate.'[43] But what of punishment?

The element of punishment in a true doctrine of God's judgement consists first of being confronted by the standard of God . . . In the very fact of this, we are rebuked for our falling short of it, and for our active hostility to it. Other elements are the restraint of the wicked and the self-exclusion from the presence of the Lord of those who finally refuse to respond to his judgement.[44]

The last clause here warns us that we cannot say that all will in the end be saved, for this would wrongly transform God's relation to us into one of infinite force. As it is, 'judgement, although it has an element of dread in it, is fundamentally a welcome and hopeful word. It is the gateway to God's mercy, or rather it is an instrument of his mercy.'[45] It is therefore the source of assurance, hope and joy as we contemplate post-mortem life: 'God calls us to pass through his judgement to share his serenity and blessedness.'[46]

H.F. Lovell Cocks's lecture of 1955 is entitled 'The hope of glory'. Welcoming the theological revitalization which the idea of realized eschatology has prompted, Lovell Cocks seeks still more, for 'The Last Judgement and Final Consummation of all things are not subsidiary and peripheral features of the New Testament witness. They are central to it . . . We have no assurance of final salvation from sin and death unless he who saves is Creator and Lord of all things.'[47] How, then, shall we understand the second coming and the consummation? The first 'is

---

[41] H. Cunliffe-Jones in ibid., 126.

[42] Ibid., 131.

[43] Ibid., 135.

[44] Ibid., 137.

[45] Ibid., 139.

[46] Ibid., 144.

[47] H.F. Lovell Cocks, 'The hope of glory', 146.

an event that is not an event – since it is history's consummation and not its continuation. It is a coming which is not a coming – since he who comes is already here in the plenitude of his power . . . [T]he end of the world is not the last happening in a series of happenings, but the inner meaning and ultimate significance of them all.'[48] As for ourselves, here we are sinners who come short of the glory of God: 'In the city of God we shall be complete persons.'[49] Indeed,

> We need to be radically different before we shall be ready to see God's face. And when at last we do see him, we shall also see what he sees, and shall look at our neighbours with his eyes and love them with his love . . . In heaven we shall be nearer to our friends than ever we were on earth.[50]

In 1988 the Methodist Geoffrey Wainwright contributed a paper on 'The last things' to a collection marking the centenary of the Anglican volume *Lux Mundi*. He pertinently observes that 'While universalism appears more generous [than predestinarianism], it scarcely escapes the difficulty of a totalitarian overriding of created freedom and responsibility.'[51] He further suggests that 'If there is to be further progress in the heavenly service and enjoyment of God, there is no reason why the earlier stages may not be "purgatorial",' impishly adding, 'Apart from some of us Methodists, few attain on earth even to that carefully limited perfection which Wesley preached.'[52] As the twenty-first century dawned, Paul S. Fiddes published *The Promised End. Eschatology in Theology and Literature* (2000), in which he shows the bearing of his relational-participatory understanding of the Trinity upon eschatological themes as these have been raised in literature and theology alike.

---

[48] Ibid., 148–9.

[49] Ibid., 158.

[50] Ibid., 158, 161.

[51] G. Wainwright, 'The last things', 359. The question how far it is meaningful to speak of progress in what is, presumably, a non-spatio-temporal existence is not the easiest of puzzles to solve. Hence, no doubt, Wainwright's recourse to the hypothetical form of words.

[52] Ibid., 365.

II

As I come within sight of the end of this series of lectures, I am conscious of the wealth of material to which I have not referred. Some of this can conveniently be listed under four headings as follows.

First, a selection of general compendia of doctrine: *Doctrinal Brevities* [1933] by the Baptist A. McCaig, and *Whither Theology?* (1940) by William Robinson of the Churches of Christ. Congregational authors include, Sydney Cave, *The Doctrines of the Christian Faith* (1931), A.E. Garvie, *The Christian Faith* (1936), Nathaniel Micklem, *What is the Faith?* (1936) and *The Creed of a Christian* (1940), John Whale's classic in this field, *Christian Doctrine* (1941), and John Huxtable, *The Faith that is in Us* (1953). Methodist contributions include, J.A. Beet, *A Manual of Theology* (1906), Maldwyn Hughes, *Christian Foundations: An Introduction to Christian Doctrine* (1927), Norman Snaith, *I Believe In . . .* (1949), Vincent Taylor, *Doctrine and Evangelism* (1953), and a work by the lay professional philosopher T.E. Jessop, *An Introduction to Christian Doctrine* (1960). A more substantial volume is Geoffrey Wainwright's *Doxology: The Praise of God in Worship, Doctrine and Life: A Systematic Theology* (1980). Wainwright sets theology in the context of liturgy, and shows openness both to the historical development of doctrine and to insights gleaned from ecumenical encounters. In his own words, the book 'is primarily intended as a systematic theology written from a liturgical perspective. It can also be considered as a theology of worship.'[53] He discusses God, Christ, Spirit and Church; creeds, hymns and tradition; and turns finally to ecumenism, doctrinal revision, culture, ethics and eschatology. The Welsh Presbyterian E.O. Davies's *Prolegomena to Systematic Theology* (1909) – a work which, on the author's own admission, was 'thrown into book form' from first year lecture notes is more apologetic in tone, as is John Oman's *Honest Religion* (1941); while in *Christian Theism: A Study of its Basic Principles* (1984) the Welsh Presbyterian H.P. Owen covers a wider range of doctrine than is immediately suggested by his title.

Secondly, among historical studies of Christian doctrines and critical analyses of individual theologians and trends in theology, we find the Methodist H. Watkin-Jones's *The Holy Spirit from Arminius to Wesley* (1929), and his fellow Methodist A.W. Harrison's *Arminianism* (1937). The other side of the doctrinal coin which had traditionally provoked much inner-Nonconformist pamphleteering was covered

---

[53] G. Wainwright, *Doxology*, Preface (unpaginated).

by the Baptist Arthur Dakin's *Calvinism* (1940). Mention should be made of H.D. McDonald's *Theories of Revelation: An Historical Study* (1963), of *The Grace of Law: A Study in Puritan Theology* (1964) by his fellow Baptist Ernest F. Kevan, of E.H. Robertson's brief study of *Dietrich Bonhoeffer* (1964), and of Keith Clements's thoughtful introduction to *Friedrich Schleiermacher: Pioneer of Modern Theology* (1987), and his continuing dialogue with Bonhoeffer as represented by *A Patriotism for Today* (1984) and *What Freedom?* (1990). He has also written on *The Theology of Ronald Gregor Smith* (1986). More recent Baptist contributions include, Stephen R. Holmes, *God of Grace and God of Glory: An Account of the Theology of Jonathan Edwards* (2000), and Peter K. Stevenson, *God in Our Nature: The Incarnational Theology of John McLeod Campbell* (2004). Among Congregational/United Reformed works we may note Robert Mackintosh's substantial articles – especially those on apologetics, theism and theology – in the eleventh edition of *Encyclopaedia Britannica* (1911); Sydney Cave's widely-circulated, careful, studies: *The Doctrine of the Person of Christ* (1925), *The Doctrine of the Work of Christ* (1937), *The Christian Estimate of Man* (1944) and *The Doctrines of the Christian Faith* (1931); Robert S. Franks's magisterial *A History of the Doctrine of the Work of Christ* [1918]; *The Ritschlian Theology* (1899) by A.E. Garvie and *Albrecht Ritschl and his School* (1915) by Robert Mackintosh; W.B. Selbie's *Schleiermacher* (1913); *The Atonement: Modern Theories of the Doctrine* (1949) by Thomas Hywel Hughes; *The Theology of Karl Barth: An Introduction* (1964) by Herbert Hartwell; *Christian Theology Since 1600* (1971) by Hubert Cunliffe-Jones; and four works in which John Heywood-Thomas brings the techniques of linguistic analysis to bear upon Kierkegaard, *Subjectivity and Paradox* (1957), and Tillich, *Paul Tillich: An Appraisal* (1963), *Paul Tillich* (1965), and *Tillich* (2000). The Methodist J. Arundel Chapman was among those who introduced *The Theology of Karl Barth* to English readers in 1931, while in the following year he added to the number of introductions to Schleiermacher. Benjamin Drewery reached back further than most Methodists, and published *Origen and the Doctrine of Grace* in 1960, while another Methodist, Frances M. Young, has more recently contributed *From Nicaea to Chalcedon* (1983) and *The Making of the Creeds* (1991), as well as a number of works on biblical and general theological themes.[54] The Welsh Presbyterian H.P. Owen published his lucid study of

---

[54] In the previous lecture I have noted Methodist contributions to the study of Reformation theology by E.G. Rupp, P. Stephens, P.H. Watson and A.S. Wood.

Bultmann, *Revelation and Existence*, in 1957. Last but not least – and even if the venue of the Didsbury Lectures were not the Nazarene College I would mention this – there is Herbert McGonigle's notable study of *Sufficient Saving Grace: John Wesley's Evangelical Arminianism* (2001), derived from one of the most thorough, careful and balanced doctoral theses it has been my pleasure to examine.[55]

Thirdly, Congregationalist and Unitarian theologians have been particularly productive what one might best describe as theological essayists, though we should not overlook three Baptist contributions: *The Veil of God* (1936) by H. Wheeler Robinson, *Down to Earth* (1964) by Howard Williams, and *Faith* (1981) by Keith W. Clements, or the Presbyterian/United Reformed writer, Lesslie Newbigin, to some of whose many writings I have already referred, and whose book *The Finality of Christ* (1969) is of particular interest. In labelling these writers 'essayists' I compliment them on their fluency and accessibility. Among others of this type we find two principals of Mansfield College: W.B. Selbie and Nathaniel Micklem, and Daniel Jenkins, who ministered in England and taught there and in the United States. Selbie's works include *Aspects of Christ* (1909), *Faith and Life* (1934), *Faith and Fact* [1937], *The Validity of Christian Belief* (1939), and *Freedom in the Faith: A Plea for a Liberal Theology* (1943). Micklem's contributions include *The Open Light: An Enquiry into Faith and Reality* (1919), The *Doctrine of our Redemption* (1948), *Ultimate Questions* (1955), *The Abyss of Truth* (1956), *The Place of Understanding and Other Papers* (1963) and *The Art of Thought* (1970). To Daniel Jenkins we owe *Prayer and the Service of God* (1944), *The Gift of Ministry* (1947), *Tradition and the Spirit* (1951), *The Protestant Ministry* (1958), *Equality and Excellence* (1961) and *The Christian Belief in God* (1964). Unitarian writers in this genre include two principals of Manchester College, Oxford, L.P. Jacks, *Religious Perplexities* (1923), and L.A. Garrard, *Athens or Jerusalem? A Study in Christian Comprehension* (1965).

Finally there are the shelves-full of overtly popular works by the Baptist W. Graham Scroggie, the Congregationalist G. Campbell Morgan, the Methodists Leslie D. Weatherhead and W.E. Sangster, and the erstwhile Welsh Presbyterian D. Martyn Lloyd-Jones. In this category may also be placed J.D. Jones's *Things Most Surely Believed* (1908), P.T. Forsyth's *The Soul of Prayer* (1916), John Whale's *What is a Living Church?* (1937), *Facing the Facts* (1939) and *This Christian Faith* (1940); *The Saving Work of the Holy Spirit* (1953) by Ernest F. Kevan, *The*

---

[55] Among my own contributions to historical theology are *The Great Debate: Calvinism, Arminianism and Salvation* and *Defending and Declaring the Faith*.

Reality of Heaven (1951) by Geoffrey F. Nuttall, and *Jesus, Lord and Saviour* by W. Gordon Robinson. Mention should also be made of a series published by the Baptist theologian Brian Haymes: *Looking at the Cross* (1988), *Advent* (1989), *Pentecost* (1991), and *Easter and Ascension* (1992).[56] There are, in addition, numerous volumes of sermons (though many more in the first half of the twentieth century than in the second), of which those published by H.H. Farmer in *The Healing Cross* (1938) are among the more notable. Such newspapers as *The Baptist Times, The Christian World, The Inquirer,* and *The Methodist Recorder* have played their part in the dissemination of theological ideas. By no means to be despised are those earnest attempts to face the challenge of communicating theology to the masses through such media as radio and television, in which connection the services of the following are particularly worthy of note: Congregationalist Elsie D. Chamberlain; R.T. Brooks and Vernon Sproxton of the United Reformed Church; and the Methodist Colin Morris

III

In preparing these lectures I placed myself under the self-denying ordinance of not entering into discussion with those whose views I was presenting and, difficult at times though it has been, I have, a few exceptions apart, managed to bite my tongue. Looking back on the Nonconformist theological corpus (and by way of a reward for having waded through it) I shall, in my second list, allow myself a few adjudications on what I have found, confining my attention to authors who are deceased. I marvel at the range of A.E. Garvie: biblical studies, apologetics, systematic theology, ethics – all of these fell within his purview, and he dealt with them in a most orderly fashion, though employing a somewhat cumbersome style. I enjoy the sardonic wit of Robert Mackintosh as much as I value his perceptive judgements on thinkers and movements. I applaud Oman and Farmer even more for their grasp of the realities of the Christian life than for their theoretical positions. I greatly appreciate the integrity of Drummond and Mellone, and the urbanity of Jacks and Garrard. T. Vincent Tymms would be a stimulating intellectual sparring partner, while the scholarship of C.J. Cadoux and Robert Franks is humbling. Franks's work on *The Atonement* is among the most intellectually stimulating books I

---

[56] The same author also published a philosophical study of *The Concept of the Knowledge of God.*

have reviewed, while Harold Roberts's paper of the Trinity covers much in brief compass, and would aid many Christians and enquirers who wish to improve their understanding of that doctrine. Vincent Taylor's *The Cross of Christ* remains a most helpful guide to its subject, while, nearly 60 years on from its year of publication, John Whale's *Christian Doctrine* is still the liveliest one-volume work of introduction to Christian teaching as a whole. H.F. Lovell Cocks is one of the most underrated of Nonconformist theologians, and every ecumenist should be required to read Bernard Lord Manning's *Essays in Orthodox Dissent*. Of those more recently departed, I think with gratitude of the clarity combined with learning modestly borne which characterizes the work of Huw Parri Owen, and of Colin Gunton's insistence that theological reflection be rooted in life among the gathered saints. But if I were forced to name one twentieth-century Nonconformist theologian who, more decisively than any other has driven to the heart of the gospel of God's holy love, my choice would fall upon P.T. Forsyth, in whose work there was a second revival of interest during the last decade of the twentieth century.[57]

Among the many retrospective articles prompted by the approach of the end of the twentieth century is one by Ian Markham, in which he reflects upon British theology of the previous 100 years. Admittedly his paper is short, and he concedes that there are exceptions to all his generalizations, but his work is myopic in two respects. First, apart from John Hick and Colin Gunton (and T.F. Torrance who is invoked from north of the Border, and George Newlands, who straddles the border both geographically and ecclesiastically), those discussed are almost entirely members of the Church of England – and even then we have John Milbank and Gareth Jones, but not William Temple, Leonard Hodgson and John Macquarrie. Secondly, Professor Markham writes, 'It is worth noting that lectureships in systematic theology in English universities have only developed in the past twenty years. On the whole, writing in systematic theology came from those interested in patristics.'[58] This, of course, is completely to overlook the fact that for many decades significant contributions to systematic and doctrinal theology were made to English universities, and to the University of Wales, by Nonconformist scholars whose institutions enjoyed a relationship with the universities, but who

---

[57] See Trevor Hart, ed., *Justice the True and Only Mercy*, 1995; Leslie McCurdy, *Attributes and Atonement*; Alan P.F. Sell, ed., *P.T. Forsyth*.

[58] Ian Markham, 'Looking back on the 20th century. 3. Theological reflections', 384.

were not themselves full-time employees of the universities. Some of these scholars were founder-members of university theological faculties – indeed, some were deans and secretaries of them; and it is indisputable that Forsyth, Garvie, Cave, Mackintosh, Franks, Drummond, Lofthouse, Flew, Oman, Farmer and others were theologians of note, and certainly no less deserving of mention than Lesslie Newbigin, to whom Professor Markham does briefly doff his cap. Having wellnigh exhausted myself in reading a considerable quantity of Nonconformist systematic, doctrinal and constructive theology, I trust that I may, to some extent, have redressed the balance.[59]

IV

A second self-denying ordinance I imposed upon myself was that of not mentioning my own writings in the text of these lectures (apart from one quotation already introduced and three more to come), though references to some of them will be found in the footnotes. I cannot, however, restrain myself from offering some concluding reflections on the landscape here surveyed in relation to the present position of Nonconformist doctrinal, systematic and constructive theology, or from taking up the interrogative part of this lecture's title: 'encroaching desert?'

As we saw in the first lecture of this series, in 1901 W.F. Adeney published *A Century's Progress in Religious Life and Thought*. The decline in Nonconformity's numerical strength, though already begun, was not yet dramatic; princes of the pulpit were still to be found; the positive aspects of the Social Gospel were bringing sustenance of various kinds to many; and many churches were centres of vibrant institutional life where a range of interests from Bible study

---

[59] It seems to me that William Strawson is a little less than generous to his own kind. He writes: 'Methodism has not in fact produced many outstanding scholars, and has depended upon other Churches for leadership in theological matters. One reason for this is that Methodists are never professional theologians. Methodist ministers certainly are all basically circuit men, and even those who are set aside to teach theology in colleges remain in this sense biased towards a circuit ministry; which is as it should be.' But he speaks admiringly of A.S. Peake, W.F. Lofthouse, R. Newton Flew and Vincent Taylor, among others. See 'Methodist theology 1850–1950,' in R.E. Davies, A.R. George and G. Rupp, eds., *A History of the Methodist Church in Great Britain*, III, 230.

through temperance to sporting were catered for. As far as theology was concerned, Adeney felt able to be optimistic. The more angular features of Calvinism had been filed down, to be replaced by a warmer (even in some cases, I would suggest, a cosily sentimental) view of God; the benefits of biblical criticism had been widely assimilated; and Nonconformist theologians had made peace with evolutionary thought. It could not have entered his head that one hundred years on there would be legal battles over creationism in the United States and private schools teaching it in this country; or that after more than a century of Religious Instruction in our state schools there would be such widespread ignorance of the Bible among the general – and even, in some cases, among the remaining churchgoing – population.

Which brings me to my maternal grandfather, Frederick Bushen (1880–1964), master carpenter. He was a devout Christian and a most generous man. He read his Bible and knew it; every week he read *The Christian Herald* with its sermons, articles and news,[60] *The Life of Faith* with its Keswick piety, and *The Methodist Recorder* with its news, articles and ministerial obituaries. At his piano he would play and sing tenor through *The Methodist Hymn Book* and he also knew many hymns from the Sankey and Alexander books as well. In those days there were many like him. I do not wish to suggest that the 'language of Canaan' was for ever on his lips; but he knew it and understood it. We recall that in his book of 1915 on the Holy Spirit, Thomas Rees noted that traditional Christian terminology was no longer employed in the philosophy, epistemology and ethics of the day, and this disturbed him. My concern is that so few within the Church seem to have the language today; and they do not have it, because they do not hear it. I cannot say that the language has evaporated with the same rapidity in every place, but I do not think it can be denied that many church members are not nurtured in it as once they were. This concern is not inspired by nostalgia, but by the conviction that the local church ought to be a nursery of theologians (in this connection, a class including every church member),[61] a tiny minority of whom will surface as the Church's future leaders in that field. How has this language loss among Christians occurred?

---

[60] In the week in which I write this sentence I learn that T*he Christian Herald*, founded in 1874, is to cease publication; and that at its peak in 1900 it enjoyed a sale of 250,000 copies per week, making for a sizeable readership indeed.
[61] For the idea that theology is the task of the church as a whole see Alan P.F. Sell, *Testimony and Tradition*, 10–12, 15.

First, through moral revulsion at some of the ways the language was traditionally used. It is one of the benefits of the English Enlightenment that it brought a moral critique to bear upon some unwholesome ways of speaking and thinking about God.[62] God as arbitrary will; predestination needlessly and devastatingly entangled with philosophical determinism: these were among the caricatures to be questioned.[63] Adeney, recalling the doctrinal system of his Congregational forebear, George Payne, writes:

> Dr. Payne, after beginning with the Divine sovereignty, proceeds to devote six lectures of his not very bulky volume to the doctrine of election. Can we imagine any influential theological writer proceeding on these lines to-day? In point of fact, we have ceased to be interested in the doctrine of election at all.[64]

Out goes the baby with the bath water! This from a theologian whose Congregational church polity turned upon the truth of Paul's claim that the Church comprises those who are 'saints by calling' (Romans 1:8), gathered by grace. We need not exchange God the oriental despot for a God whose call we cannot, and do not need to, hear.

Another way of losing the language is to keep talking about other things. The pulpit becomes a place from which calls for peace and justice are issued, the rights of homosexuals occupy the agenda of church assemblies, and many theologians betake themselves to the science and religion, or the world religions debate. I see nothing wrong, indeed, much that is commendable in all of these discussions, but they can become ways of avoiding the one thing needful; and perhaps in the case of some theologians, they have.[65]

Yet again, as we have seen, the decade of the 1960s was a shaky time for theology with secularization, the death of God, and *Honest to God*, to be contended with. The foundations of the theological house seemed to be shaking, and it is not surprising that in that decade a number of ministers of religion wondered what they could preach, and even whether they could continue to preach at all. Some of these found their way into social work, teaching and other useful pursuits (I do not imply that they had no sense of vocation in making their

---

[62] See further, Alan P.F. Sell, *Enlightenment, Ecumenism, Evangel*, ch. 3.

[63] Ibid., 325–38.

[64] W.F. Adeney, *A Century's Progress in Religious Thought and Life*, 120.

[65] See further on churchly ethical pronouncements, Alan P.F. Sell, *Aspects of Christian Integrity*, 68–71.

moves), and some of those who remained felt that they would do best to avoid unsettling theological topics and elevate humanistic values.

At the same time there were those educational theories which were popularly construed as maintaining that until children were 'ready' – that is to say, until they were old enough to grasp particular concepts – many topics should not be broached in their presence. This found expression across many disciplines, especially those which had traditionally relied a good deal upon rote learning, which was now taboo in 'advanced' educational circles. I well remember an academic colleague from a department of mathematics who, when he saw certain experts in primary education approaching, would say loudly to those around him in the Senior Common Room, 'Of course, I don't hold with all this concepts nonsense; I believe in teaching children their tables by rote so that one day they will be able to handle themselves down at the bookies.' I also remember attending two public lectures during that period. One was given by a professor of primary education, who began by saying, 'I am sick and tired of hearing of infant teachers who sit around all day doing their knitting, waiting for readiness to descend upon their children.' The other was given by the philosopher H.D. Lewis who was roused to Welsh fervour in denouncing what he called 'the dead hand of Piaget which rests across British education.' In Sunday school and junior church circles the suspect theory ran out at its extreme into lessons which amounted to little more than 'God loves you – draw a picture.'[66] At a time when there was, rightly, great concern for physically and emotionally deprived children, there was not always an equal concern for the deprivation of language and memory which resulted from the readiness theory narrowly construed and applied. By contrast, in some Reformed churches to this day, the preparation of young people for reception as church members entails a two-year course on the *Heidelberg Catechism*. If we think that such a catechism is too out of touch (and by no means all of it is), on what should we invite the young theologians who remain in our churches to cut their theological teeth? There must surely be something more nourishing than the hard rusks of five-point Calvinism on the one hand and the blancmange of the Sea of Faith on the other? Or do we continue to think, in my view mistakenly, that catechetics is a rightly discarded practice? It is not unkind to place people within earshot of concepts which will sustain them through life.

---

[66] For some devotees of the theory, the 'bible' was *Readiness for Religion* by Ronald Goldman who (tell it not in Gath) was an alumnus of my own theological college.

Sometimes language can be lost through what might be termed ecumenical politeness. We suppress and we trim, in order not to offend Christians of other persuasions, or people of other faiths – in the latter case notably in connection with the scandal of particularity. This is clearly counter-productive, for if any participant in an inter-Christian or inter-faith dialogue feels, or is made to feel, that he or she cannot honestly express sincerely held convictions, however unacceptable they may sometimes be to others present, the integrity of the dialogue is lost. Along this route we may reach a variety of unfortunate destinations, anodyne dialogue reports and amorphous spirituality among them.[67]

Then there is the current intellectual climate which many label, problematically, 'postmodern'. The thought which claims this label frequently seems to run out into relativism – a grand narrative if ever there was one – and the consequence is that some Christians cannot readily conceive of anything as definite as a universally true proposition. This is a splendid way to get off the hook of witnessing, because if your language is good enough for you, you do not need even to hear mine. This situation is in no way helped by those more popular Christian writers whose books enjoy a relatively wide circulation, who lambast the Enlightenment on every possible occasion in a quite unscholarly and undiscriminating way, whilst at the same time employing against their intellectual foes those very canons of rationality which the several Enlightenments did so much to uphold.[68]

Language can also be lost as a result of the application of politically correct policy. It would be foolish to utter blanket condemnations against something so fluid as political correctness, or to take extreme examples ('personhole' for 'manhole') as representative of the whole. On the contrary, the politically correct have wisely and rightly made us take care over the way in which we use language so that when speaking or writing we do not appear to exclude women from the human race, or veer towards racism, or insult the sincere beliefs of others. But there is a shadow side to political correctness as it is advocated in Christian circles. It is not too much to say that Christians are being deprived of some of their language by those bent on pressing particular agendas. When this is done by those who edit our hymn books the word 'imperialism' (an attitude which, paradoxically most

---

[67] For another approach to spirituality see Alan P.F. Sell, *Enlightenment, Ecumenism, Evangel*, ch. 8.

[68] See further on postmodernism, idem, *Confessing and Commending the Faith*, 132–48 and *passim*.

of the politically correct eschew) comes to mind. Some do not like us to sing about God the *Father*;[69] some do not like masculine pronouns being used even of Jesus of Nazareth; and concepts such as 'Lord' are banned on the ground that they are unwholesomely hierarchical. Note that none of this is a matter of removing archaisms with a view to making older hymns singable today. It is a matter of the removal on ideological grounds of language deemed inappropriate by those charged with facilitating for *the peoples'* praise. One or two examples will suffice. I refer to *The New Century Hymnal* of the United Church of Christ, which was used in a service I recently attended in Philadelphia. The hymn was 'All hail the power of Jesus' name.' The last line of each stanza known to most of us is, 'Crown him Lord of all.' This is altered to, 'Crown Christ servant of all.' The fact that the line no longer scans is a secondary consideration. More important is the reason for the change: 'Lord' is deemed to be an hierarchical term, and as such it has only limited place in this hymnal.[70] But the slightest acquaintance with the New Testament would reveal that the Lordship of Christ is the Lordship of one who takes a towel and does a slave's work by washing his disciples' feet; the Christological hymn in Philippians 2 makes it strikingly plain that he humbles himself and makes himself as nothing for our salvation. All of this is the very reverse of hierarchical: it is what real Lordship means. My point is that if we deprive ourselves and our people of this language, it will not be available for our use when, as counter-cultural agents, we wish to tell 'the world' that it has not understood what true Lordship is. In the same hymnal, and for similar reasons, 'Rejoice, the Lord is King' (two allegedly hierarchical-*cum*-patriarchal 'sins' there) becomes 'Rejoice, give thanks and sing', which is not so much an amendment to the original as a new hymn altogether. So one could go on.[71] Nonconformists, of whom it has been said that they learned their

---

[69] See further idem, *Enlightenment, Ecumenism, Evangel*, 365–75.

[70] Some sought to excise the term altogether, but the 1993 Synod of the United Church of Christ overruled this by 420 to 250 votes, whereupon 'Lord' was restored to the book, but not to all of the hymns from which it had been proposed to remove it.

[71] For many further examples see Richard L. Christensen, ed., *How Shall We Sing the Lord's Song? An Assessment of The New Century Hymnal*. There are parallels in other fields, as witness the Local Education Authority whose officers did not wish children in inner-city areas to hear Beatrix Potter's story about Peter Rabbit because Peter Rabbit was middle class and used middle class language.

theology from their hymns, would do well to ponder these matters carefully.

It may even be that in some quarters the language is lost for the practical reason that ministers and church members live at such a pace and, in the case of church members, frequently work away from home, or at various periods during a 24 -hour day, that opportunities for consistent, consecutive Christian teaching are few and far between. Certainly it is very difficult to accommodate the edification of the saints, the evangelization of the uncommitted, the observance of the sacraments, all the parts of prayer, and four or five hymns within the one hour per week which is the most that many seem able to devote to their corporate religious duties. Moreover, since it is desirable that language acquisition (which is not the same as 'indoctrination') begin early, the impact of the dramatic increase in family mobility during the past 50 years as a result of the wider availability of cars and caravans makes the consistent nurture of the young difficult to achieve if confined to Sundays; and recourse to weekday evenings is more difficult than once it was owing to the ever-increasing load of homework, sports, musical other activities that many children nowadays carry on weekdays.

I fear that the most serious issue concerning the loss of language is the possibility that we shall lose touch with the realities which prompted the forging of the language in the first place.[72] To come straight to the point: have we lost the gospel which engendered the language traditionally used by the Church? At the mid-way point in the twentieth century Hubert Cunliffe-Jones felt impelled to declare, 'It is only as the Church throughout its membership attains a new sense of the Gospel and of the meaning of its distinctive life that it can speak the word of power.'[73] Elsewhere, when pondering the cause of the Church's loss of power he asked, 'Is it possible that one reason for our failure to commend the Gospel of the saving grace of God is that we have not believed in its utter necessity? That we have taken the primary fact of human nature that man needs a Saviour at less than its full valuation.'[74]

It is my deepest conviction that that 'word of power' is centred in the Cross of Christ.[75] In saying this I believe that I am in accord with

---

[72] We recall Thomas Rees's fear, expressed as early as 1915, that language pertaining to the doctrine of the Holy Spirit was in danger of being lost, and with it the experience which the language had hitherto been employed to articulate.

[73] H.Cunliffe-Jones, 'Christian theology for the twentieth century', 128.

[74] H. Cunliffe-Jones, 'The historic Gospel', 1943.

[75] See further, Alan P.F. Sell, *Confessing and Commending the Faith*, ch. 2.

the predominant witness of the New Testament and in the line of the majority of Nonconformist theologians of the twentieth century. As to the latter point, it is interesting to note that in T. Hywel Hughes's survey of writings by English or England-domiciled theologians on the atonement in the first half of the twentieth century, 16 writers out of the 29 authors discussed were Nonconformists.[76] But if speaking the 'word of power' is the task of the whole Church, reflecting upon it is the primary duty of the theologian. With reference to the path travelled in these lectures, I shall hope to suggest (and I can do no more here than suggest)[77] that it is from the Cross that we may most satisfactorily adjust our theological sights both in respect of every other Christian doctrine, and with reference to the Church's apologetic task.

It is, even at this late stage, still necessary to enter a number of caveats when speaking of the Cross. It will not do to say with the old-time evangelist (or even the modern television one) that 'Jesus came to die' – as if nothing else that he did was of any importance. Calvin and others insisted that we take due account of the whole course of Christ's obedience, and Forsyth declared that 'You cannot sever the death of Christ from the life of Christ.'[78] At the same time, he would have us understand that while

> The Cross was not central to Christ's teaching as the kingdom was . . . it was central to what is more than His teaching – to His healing, to His person, work and victory. It is more original than His teaching, and more universal . . . Christianity spread not as a religion of truth, but of power, help, healing, resurrection, redemption.[79]

Embedded in the final words here is one of Forsyth's many unfortunate disjunctions. Christianity does claim to be a religion of truth.

---

[76] See T. Hywel Hughes, *The Atonement*.

[77] But see Alan P.F. Sell, *Christ Our Saviour; Confessing and Commending the Faith*, ch. 2; *Testimony and Tradition*, 348–52; *Enlightenment, Ecumenism, Evangel*, ch. 13.

[78] P.T. Forsyth, *The Work of Christ*, 153. Though his younger colleague, A.E. Garvie, thought that Forsyth downplayed the life. See his *The Christian Certainty amid the Modern Perplexity: Essays, Constructive and Critical towards the Solution of some Current Theological Problems*, 460–3; idem, 'Placarding the Cross: the theology of P.T. Forsyth', 352. A.S. Peake was of a similar mind, See his *Recollections and Appreciations*, 193. Garvie himself was not above giving one of his books the ambitious title, *Studies in the Inner Life of Jesus*.

[79] P.T. Forsyth, *Missions in State and Church: Sermons and Addresses*, 11.

What Forsyth means is that it is not simply one more collection of religious teachings: it is founded upon a divine act of cosmic significance. On the main point, however, I believe that he is right, for we do not have the gospel in (as much as we can assimilate of) its fullness until after the resurrection, when the realization dawns upon the apostles that the victory is secure, sin and death are vanquished, and the Last Supper becomes the Lord's Supper. Then the life and teaching of Jesus up to Calvary begin to be seen in their true significance, and the future of the Church – always a challenging, and frequently a forbidding one – can be viewed with hope.[80]

Further, it is necessary to repudiate the grotesque view that the Father could not be merciful until his Son had died. Against this disastrous doctrine, which quite unwarrantably drives a wedge between the Father and the Son, Forsyth uttered what I have sometimes called the most important single sentence in the whole of twentieth-century theology: 'The atonement did not procure grace, it flowed from grace.'[81] The view of a minority of feminists that they will have nothing to do with a God who is a 'child batterer' is, for the same reason, unacceptable to the point of blasphemous.[82] Paul held matters in their true balance, I believe, when he announced that 'God was in Christ reconciling the world to himself' (2 Corinthians 5:19).

Next, it is essential that we grasp the fact that atonement (no matter what theories about it take our fancy) is not something achieved only for humanity; it is the vindication of God's holy love, and the Cross is the site of the triumph of that holy love, that sovereign grace, the consequence, confirmation and manifestation of which victory is the Easter gospel, 'He is risen.' (Incidentally, how important it is in theology to associate adjectives and nouns appropriately; for love without holiness sooner or later becomes sentiment, sovereignty apart from grace can become despotism.) It is important, however, that there be no misunderstanding here. As Robert Mackintosh wrote, it is 'Not that "Man is saved and *yet* God's honour stands fast." Rather, God is supremely glorified in the fact that man is redeemed.'[83]

---

[80] I am encouraged to find that this general approach is endorsed by the New Testament scholar I. Howard Marshall, who advises that Jesus's teaching 'is to be understood in the light of the continuing revelation in the post-Easter period.' See his *Beyond the Bible: Moving from Scripture to Theology*, 69.

[81] P.T. Forsyth, *The Cruciality of the Cross*, 41; cf. his *The Work of Christ*, 180.

[82] See Alan P.F. Sell, *Enlightenment, Ecumenism, Evangel*, 288–9, 381–2.

[83] R. Mackintosh, *Historic Theories of Atonement*, 306.

In all of this I am insisting upon the Cross as the place where the decisive act is done to defeat sin and death; it is not simply the place where God shows us something about his love or our need. This motif can be obscured by those theologians who elevate the incarnation above, and at the expense of, the Cross. I do not find that the twentieth century's Nonconformist theologians have been particularly guilty of this, though in a rather atypical way Geoffrey Wainwright occasionally steers close to the wind when his sacramentalism, which he construes as underscoring God's relationship to the world and humanity, is treated too much as a datum, with insufficient place being given to the disruptive tragedy of sin. Thus he can write, 'faith, sacraments and ecclesiology engage human life at a more fundamental and decisive level than the social, cultural, psychological, economic and political.'[84] I am not concerned with his comparison, but with the omission from his list of factors which engage life fundamentally and decisively of the word – the word of the Cross, the word proclaimed.[85]

More traditionally, a stream of Anglican theology flowing down from the Romanticism of Coleridge and F.D. Maurice, fertilized by the revival of patristics at Oxford in the middle decades of the nineteenth century, and stimulated by post-Hegelian immanentism and evolutionary thought in its teleological aspect which, when divorced from counter-balancing transcendence and unmoved by historical particularities can yield pantheism,[86] has likewise elevated the theme of incarnation of Christ. Among recent examples we find Gareth Jones's *Critical Theology: Questions of Truth and Method* (1995), of which Terrence Tilley has complained that according to Jones 'the Incarnation is, at best, a representation of the relationship of time and eternity',[87] a tendency which Forsyth was not slow to denounce: 'Any theology that places us in a spiritual *process*, or native movement between the finite and the infinite, depreciates the value of spiritual

---

[84] Geoffrey Wainwright, *Worship with One Accord: Where Liturgy and Ecumenism Embrace*, vii.

[85] Cf. Dietrich Ritschl, 'Praising God as interpreter and critic of history', 71: 'I must admit . . . that in Wainwright's theology I miss an emphasis on proclamation.'

[86] For a discussion of transcendence, immanence and history see Alan P.F. Sell, *Confessing and Commending the Faith*, ch. 5, and *Philosophical Idealism and Christian Belief*, *passim*; for some reflections on pantheism see idem, *Enlightenment, Ecumenism, Evangel*, ch. 7.

[87] Terrence Tilley, review in *Modern Theology*, 468.

act, and thus makes us independent of the grace of God.'[88] Another Anglican, Brian Hebblethwaite, confidently assures us that 'What is necessary . . . for our salvation is not so much the death of Christ as the incarnation.' While not unaware of the reality of sin and the need of forgiveness, he denies that 'it is the death as such that effects salvation for the world.'[89] Yet Paul proclaimed that 'we proclaim Christ nailed to the cross . . . the power of God and the wisdom of God' (1 Corinthians 1:23,24); and much later the Methodist W.F. Lofthouse noted that 'To the Christian . . . the death of Christ was but the beginning, as St Luke finely put it, of what he did and taught; the new religion was born at the moment of the discovery that Christ's death was not the end, but the commencement, of the kingdom which he preached.'[90] By contrast, F.D. Maurice, according to Robert Mackintosh, 'with his Alexandrian preoccupations, hardly knows what to say about the death on Calvary.'[91]

It is only proper to point out that a number of Anglican writers have taken the point I am concerned to urge. For example, the philosopher H.A. Hodges observed that

> We have known a kind of Catholicism which had talked as if this were the heart of the gospel; we have been told that Christianity and in particular Catholicism is the religion of the Incarnation. By the mere fact of living among us, God has sanctified our race. By wearing a human body He has declared once and for all the sanctity of matter and put an end to the dreams of the Platonist and the Manichee. He sanctified human labour by participation in it, and on the fact of Christ the carpenter a Christian sociology has been built. All this is true, but this is not yet the full gospel. These are the beginnings of His ways. The Catholic faith is more than this.
>
> The Apostles did not preach a religion of the Incarnation. They preached the Resurrection . . . but there can be no resurrection unless there has been a death. . . . In the death . . . the Christian mind has come more and more to see the heart of the mystery. The Cross after all has become the symbol of the faith.[92]

---

[88] P.T. Forsyth, *Positive Preaching and the Modern Mind*, 146.

[89] Brian Hebblethwaite, 'The doctrine of the atonement. (5) Does it make moral sense?', 73.

[90] W.F. Lofthouse, *Ethics and Atonement*, 189.

[91] R. Mackintosh, *Historic Theories of Atonement*, 203. See further, Alan P.F. Sell, *Aspects of Christian Integrity*, 39–40.

[92] H.A. Hodges, *The Pattern of Atonement*, 26–27.

Again, A.M. Ramsey regretted that J.R. Illingworth, one of the *Lux Mundi* contributors, had, in his eagerness to elevate the incarnation to the central principle of theology, written 'in depreciation of those who gave centrality to the Atonement . . . this was incautious, inasmuch as the formulation of the doctrine of the Incarnation had sprung, alike in the apostolic age and in the patristic period, from out of the experience of Redemption; the saving act had been the key to the Church's faith in the divine Christ.'[93] Forsyth would have agreed. The doctrine of the incarnation 'has no such centrality as the principle of atoning forgiveness. The doctrine of the Incarnation did not create the Church; it grew up (very quickly) in the Church out of the doctrine of the cross which did create it – in so far as that can be said of any doctrine, and not rather of the act and power which the doctrine tries to state.'[94]

This leads me directly to my next point: I believe that the most appropriate path towards Christology is via soteriology,[95] and I concur with Sydney Cave: 'It is through our experience of Christ's work that we learn the meaning of His person.'[96] It cannot have gone unnoticed that the first Christians did not sit around the markets discussing the two nature theory of Christ's person. Rather, the crucified had been raised; they had found forgiveness, salvation and new life in him; but since these are gifts of God alone, who must he be? Among the criticisms which Robert Mackintosh levelled against John McLeod Campbell was one to the effect that 'Campbell too much assumes the incarnation of the Son of God as a datum, and says what such a fact once given must imply; we ought rather to infer what Christ is from our own and the Church's experience of what he does. Christology must affirm what is implied concerning Christ's person in His work, or else be silent.'[97] Of course the incarnation is temporally prior to the Cross; of course it is logically prior also, for Christ can do what he does only because he is who he is. But in the order of our approaching the matter, we do so on the basis of what he has done, and done once-for-all at the Cross;[98] and we do it as enabled and guided by God the Holy Spirit, by whom I understand

---

[93] A.M. Ramsey, *From Gore to Temple*, 40. This is a running theme of Alan P.F. Sell, *Philosophical Idealism and Christian Belief*, in which the thought of Illingworth and others is critically examined; see especially ch. 5. See also idem, *Confessing and Commending the Faith*, 29–35.

[94] P.T. Forsyth, *The Cruciality of the Cross*, 50 n. 1.

[95] See further Alan P.F. Sell, *Aspects of Christian Integrity*, ch. 2.

[96] S. Cave, *The Doctrines of the Christian Faith*, 194.

[97] R. Mackintosh, *Christianity and Sin*, 130.

[98] This dictated the method of my book, *Christ Our Saviour*.

the fatherly God of holy love whom we know in the victorious Christ of the Bible, as generously active in the world; as life-givingly active in us; as drawing out and enabling our response of faith, love, and service; as uniting us to Christ and therefore to each other in his Church; as ever renewing and refining our life in this world; and as holding us in fellowship with himself eternally.'[99]

But already I have slipped into Trinitarian language and, as we have seen, there was a revival of interest in the Trinity on the part of Nonconformist theologians (and not they only) during the last three decades of the twentieth century. In my opinion this was a welcome revival, though, once again, I deem it important that the Cross, in the sense in which I have expounded it, be clearly related to this doctrine which, though it may justifiably be designated the rock on which systematic theology is built, is not the first to have been formulated by the Church. This is not surprising given the dramatic revision of ideas previously held dear by the early Christians which was required as they came to terms with the Good Friday-Easter-Pentecost events. Their questions were 'Who alone can *save* us?' Answer: God alone. 'Who alone can save *us*?' Answer: A perfect representative of humanity only. So, on the basis of their experience of salvation and new life in the Spirit and, which is crucial, in relation to the word received in fellowship and the encounter in a missionary situation with alternative world views, they gradually formulated their positions on the person of Christ as truly divine and truly human, and on the Trinity.

When we review recent writings on the Trinity, we find that a bifurcation of views found in the wider world of theology is found within Nonconformist contributions too. This becomes apparent if we place Robert Franks and Colin Gunton side by side. Franks, we recall, opposes the social Trinity on the grounds that it does not yield an intelligible conception of God, and that Christians do not experience three divine personalities, but one.[100] In this he shows himself to be more inclined towards Augustine and Aquinas than towards the Cappadocians. Gunton, on the other hand, is impressed by the

---

[99] Alan P.F. Sell, *The Spirit Our Life*, 1. The rest of the book consists in the unpacking of this, 'the longest and clumsiest sentence in this book' (p. 1).

[100] Against the Anglicans F.R. Tennant and C.C.J. Webb, H. Wheeler Robinson urged the same point: 'The conception of a "social" Trinity does not really help us to conceive the unity of divine personality, and really leads us, with Tennant, to replace theism by pluralism.' See his *The Christian Experience of the Holy Spirit*, 230–231.

Cappadocians, notably because they hold that 'the first thing to be said about the being of God is that it consists in personal communion.'[101] He is aware of the danger of drawing logical inferences from the inner relations of the Trinity, because we do not have 'detailed knowledge of the inner constitution of the Godhead.'[102] He is also, of course, fully aware of the perils of tritheism. Nevertheless at times he seems to forget his cautionary word regarding our imperfect knowledge of the inner-Trinitarian relationships of the divine persons, as when he declares that 'The Church is called to be the kind of reality at a finite level that God is in eternity.'[103] This kind of language may serve as a stimulating homiletic flight, but as an analogy it must be said that its divine pole is, given our epistemic limitations, not very secure, for we do not know a great deal about how the Godhead is in eternity. Those intensely practical exhortations regarding personal relationships within the empirical Church with which the New Testament is peppered, are more than sufficient to challenge and reprove.

Gunton is not the only theologian to veer at times towards the kind of statement analogous to the statements of some older Calvinist theologians who seemed to know a good deal about God's *inscrutable* will where elections and predestination were concerned, or some Catholic theologians, ancient and modern, who, notwithstanding their insistence upon the mystery at the heart of faith seem to have an uncannily precise insight into what happens when the prayer of consecration is said at the Mass. The problem is exacerbated when the several persons of the Trinity are assigned particular functions – as if the Godhead were a celestial committee with each member having specific roles. This threatens the unity of God, and also overlooks Calvin's proper point that 'In each hypostatis the whole divine nature is understood, with this qualification – that to each belongs his own peculiar quality.'[104]

It has always seemed to me that the most responsible theology is that which sets out from what God has been pleased to make known to us, and not from what he has not, and that it is salutary for theologians ever to remember that competence in Trinitarian exposition has never been a condition of entry to the kingdom of heaven. I am more

---

[101] Colin E. Gunton in *On Being the Church: Essays on the Christian Community*, 66. See also my review of this book.

[102] Ibid., 69.

[103] Ibid., 78.

[104] J. Calvin, *Institutes of the Christian Religion*, I.13.19.

than content to stand with Sydney Cave in affirming that 'As he has revealed Himself, so we may believe Him to be: God, the Father, Son and Holy Spirit, unindividualized by time and space, perfectly one in character, purpose and in interpenetrating love.'[105]

It is no less important to have the Cross within view when we turn to the doctrine of humanity. Sydney Cave put the point in a nutshell: 'It is because of Calvary, not because of Eden, that we are compelled to judge gravely of human sin.'[106] In other words, we learn what sin means when we see what it cost God to deal with it. In my opinion this learning is not as likely to occur in the context of those sermons which belabour sin for fifty-five minutes and then open the gospel escape hatch in the closing five,[107] as when the gospel of God's sovereign grace, supremely active at the Cross, is proclaimed. Then we glimpse something of who God is in his awesome holy majesty, who we are in our sin and guilt, how great is the gulf between us, and how rich is God's loving supply to meet out need.

It would seem that the doctrine of humanity has not received the degree of attention from Nonconformist theologians that might have been expected. H. Wheeler Robinson contributed a largely biblical and historical study, *The Christian Doctrine of Man* (1911), Robert Mackintosh wrote on *Christianity and Sin* (1913), Sydney Cave published *The Christian Estimate of Man* (1944), and H.H. Farmer contributed *God and Men* (1948). But there is a crying need of fresh work on this topic which will not only treat of sin and grace, but will harvest insights from feminist theologians, and will also recover for us that constellation of terms, including adoption, assurance,[108] forgiveness, sanctification – that is to say, those terms bearing upon the life of the new person in Christ which were so prominent a part of the discourse of apostles, Reformers and Puritans alike, but which are now, for many Christians, part of the lost language to which I earlier referred.[109] Although I have not strayed into the field of pastoral

---

[105] S. Cave, *The Doctrines of the Christian Faith*, ch. 8.

[106] S. Cave, *The Christian Estimate of Man*, 228.

[107] In the opinion of W.F. Adeney, 'It is to [F.D.] Maurice more than to any other teacher that we owe the change from the popular conception of Christianity as chiefly a contrivance for escaping the penalties of sin, to the higher, more spiritual conception of a redemption of life and character, personal and social.' See his *A Century's Progress in Religious Life and Thought*, 24.

[108] Though the Methodist Arthur S. Yates published a historical study of *The Doctrine of Assurance with Special Reference to John Wesley*.

[109] For some reflections on the doctrine of humanity see Alan P.F. Sell, *Christ Our Saviour*, ch. 7.

theology in these lectures,[110] I cannot forbear to quote what now appears to have been a prophetic word uttered by Albert Peel in 1927:

> If the ministry can recover the true pastoral instinct, and with sympathy and skill effect 'the cure of souls,' a revival of religion may not be far distant. Otherwise the growth of psycho-analysis may mean that the therapeutist will trespass still further on the province of the preacher.[111]

The slightest acquaintance with counselling literature, much of which has found its way into what are announced as courses in pastoral theology, will reveal that it is innocent of the language of the 'cure of souls', and that the doctrine of humanity underlying these tomes is seldom articulated and still less frequently exposed to criticism. Christians, having swept their house clean of their native vocabulary, should not be unduly surprised if seven Carl Rogerses rush in to take its place. I fervently hope that that last remark did not sound implicitly judgmental.[112]

One of the under-expounded terms, adoption, is of crucial importance in ecclesiology. On the ground of Christ's saving work at the Cross, the Father calls out by the Spirit one people for his praise and service. Whereas Jesus Christ is Son of God by right, the saints are God's adopted sons and daughter – adopted by grace. If this is so, two principles of Nonconformity at its best are at once established: first, over against sectarianism whether sacerdotal or biblicist, the Church is one, comprising all those in heaven and on earth who own Christ as Lord and Saviour; secondly and more parochially, over against Church-state establishments the Church confesses Christ as the only head of the Church. Let me unpack each of these points a little more.

Contrary to the impression given by some evangelists, Forsyth was right to insist that 'Salvation is personal, but it is not individual. . . . It is personal in its appropriation but collective in its nature.'[113] In other words, the Church comprises those who are saints by calling, but these saints are not isolated atoms; they are branches united to Christ

---

[110] Though see idem, *Aspects of Christian Integrity*, ch. 6.

[111] Albert Peel, *The Free Churches 1903–1926*, being an additional chapter to a reprint of C. Silvester Horne's *A Popular History of the Free Churches*, 447–8.

[112] For some suggestions towards an antidote see Melvin D. Hugen, 'The shaping influence of the Heidelberg Catechism on the pastoral care of the Church', 133–138.

[113] P.T. Forsyth, *The Work of Christ*, 119.

the Vine, and therefore to one another. The Church catholic comprises all such, in heaven and on earth.[114] The saints' unmerited status is the gift of God's free, adoptive grace. On the ground of Christ's finished work at the Cross, the Father calls out one people by his Spirit. Furthermore, as A.E. Garvie pointed out, 'If it is Christ's presence in and with believers which constitutes His Church, then wherever He is present, His Church, not in parts but as a whole, is present.'[115] P.T. Forsyth drew the ecclesiological conclusion: 'the unity of the Church is founded in the creative act of our moral redemption which creates our faith to-day and which created the Church at first; it is not in the traditional polity, creed, or cultus we inherit. If unity is in polity, Christ died in vain.'[116]

As we have already seen, and as I can readily confirm from personal experience of engagement in bilateral dialogues at the international level, the supremely important stumbling-block to the manifestation of the unity God has given all Christians in Christ is that constellation of doctrines which surrounds the historic episcopate. It is this which causes those who embrace it to cast doubt on the validity, or at least the regularity, of ministries and sacraments other than their own. It is this which divides Christ's people at the table of the Lord; and it is a thoroughly sectarian stance: sectarian in the sense that it turns upon a policy which says, sometimes implicitly, sometimes explicitly, 'Unless and until you agree with our interpretations and our practices, we will unchurch you, or at least regard you as second-class churches.'[117] In a threatened and divided world, this is doubly intolerable. But above all it is blasphemous. It is knowing better than God when he made us one. It is elevating the small print of polity above the gracious call of the gospel. It is an illegitimate anthropocentric stance which is more concerned with how we interpret things than with what God in Christ has done. Listen to the following three assertions:

1. 'Sharing the Eucharist . . . presupposes agreement with the faith of the Church which celebrates the Eucharist.'[118]

---

[114] See further, Alan P.F. Sell, 'Reformed identity: a non-issue of catholic significance', 17–27.

[115] A.E. Garvie, 'The Free Churches in England', 132.

[116] P.T. Forsyth, *Congregationalism and Reunion*, 21.

[117] Cf. Norman H. Snaith, 'Comments and Criticisms', in *Conversations between the Church of England and the Methodist Church*, 199.

[118] *Towards a Common Understanding of the Church*, 55.

2. Those 'are not "one", nor in a state of unity, who disagree about fundamental questions.'[119]
3. 'The New Testament teaches that unity is always unity in truth and faithfulness to the apostolic witness.'[120]

Here, in unaccustomed concord, are the Roman Catholics of the second phase of Roman Catholic-Reformed international dialogue, Martyn Lloyd-Jones, and the Orthodox Bishop Arias. Of course, unity is in the truth, but although God gives us to know enough, we see only puzzling reflections in a mirror (1 Corinthians 13:13). That is to say, we are all interpreters of the truth, and it may be that some of us are more adept at it than others. But we have no right to place our interpretations, any more than our polity, above the fact that in Christ by the Spirit, God has made us one.

So it is that, having so often heard the argument, 'We cannot do x until we agree about y', I have begun to plead for some lateral thinking.[121] It seems to me that it is a forlorn hope that we shall ever agree on all points of polity; and I do not think that we need to. Rather, we should be asking, 'What has God in Christ done by the Spirit?' I believe the answer is that he has called out one Church, and that the first thing his saints, confessing the Lordship and Saviourhood of Christ, should do is to obey his call to the one table. I have been pleased to note measures of agreement attained in some of the bilateral dialogues. But how much more able we might be to come closer on neuralgic points if we were first obedient to our true, not to sectarian, catholicity – a contradiction in terms indeed. What at first sounds like cheeky one-upmanship on the part of Sydney Cave can equally well be construed as a remark prompted by despair: '"Catholics", whether Roman or Anglican, are "Evangelical", for they, too, profess the Gospel; "Evangelicals" are "Catholic", for they also belong to the one Catholic Church of Christ, and are, indeed, more catholic than the "Catholics", for they do not unchurch even those who unchurch them.'[122]

Lovell Cocks was even blunter: 'it is not the bishop we repudiate, but the theory which makes him essential to the being of the Church. It is Catholicism – let it be said with the utmost plainness – which is

---

[119] M. Lloyd-Jones, quoted by John Brencher, *Martyn Lloyd-Jones*, 139.

[120] Bishop Arias, quoted by Alan P.F. Sell, *Enlightenment, Ecumenism, Evangel*, 286.

[121] See further, *Enlightenment, Ecumenism, Evangel*, ch. 11.

[122] S. Cave, *The Doctrines of the Christian Faith*, 250 n. 1.

standing in the way of the catholicity of the gospel.'[123] And tied into the theory that episcopacy is of the *esse* of the Church (which is not, I gather, formal Anglican teaching, though many Anglicans seem committed to it)[124] is the understanding of a special grace conveyed through episcopal ordination which creates a sacerdotal caste within the priesthood of believers. Hence, as John Huxtable remarked,

> When Anglicans talk of the Church they almost always give the impression of meaning the hierarchy and the priesthood, almost as if the laity were little more than a necessary background to the labours of bishop, priest and deacon. This is particularly striking to a Congregationalist, for whom the local Church is a whole after a fashion in which, apparently, the parish church is not. A Congregational minister and his people are so closely knit that he cannot function without them; and this is an indication of the belief that Church acts are indeed acts of the Church and not simply of Church officials: the Church, *not the minister*, celebrates the Eucharist.[125]

Small wonder that to Nonconformists, 're-ordination' is what the philosophers would call a non-instantiated concept.

One of the saddest utterances I have come across in preparing these lectures is that of A.E. Garvie, loyal Free Churchman and pioneer ecumenist. Towards the end of his life he wrote, 'Much as I have pondered this matter I must admit that I have not yet got even a glimpse of the synthesis in which the Catholic thesis and the Protestant antithesis can be harmonized . . . I have tried to understand the Catholic position so as to rise, if I could, above the opposition, but I have failed.[126]

Can it be – I ask the question in all seriousness – that he was trying to understand what, on the basis of the gospel, is strictly unintelligible? However that may be, I am convinced that because of God's saving work at the Cross, and his resultant calling out of one Church there is a most important Free Church witness to be made against ecclesiastical sectarianism in whatsoever guise it presents itself.

---

[123] H.F. Lovell Cocks, *The Faith of a Protestant Christian*, 46.

[124] See further, Alan P.F. Sell, *Aspects of Christian Integrity*, ch. 4.

[125] W. John F. Huxtable, 'Introduction' to *John Owen, The True Nature of a Gospel Church and its Government*, 15. Cf. A.E. Garvie, 'The Free Churches in England', 130.

[126] Quoted by Norman Goodall, 'Some Congregational pathfinders in the ecumenical movement', 198.

I turn to the more parochial question of the Free Churches *vis-à-vis* the world's only established Anglican Church. Here I can be brief.[127] Cutting through extraneous arguments concerning privilege and the ideologically and religiously diverse composition of Parliament, we come to the three important theological questions: 'Who comprise the Church?' – to which the Free Churches have traditionally replied 'The regenerate', that is, one is not a Christian simply by being born in England (as many of other faiths will cheerfully testify); 'Can the Church be national when it is catholic?' – to which Free Churchpeople have generally returned a negative answer; and, most important of all, 'How may we best honour the sole Lordship of Christ in his Church?' The traditional answer to this last question has been that while it is well that religions be recognized by the state, the Church may not place itself under state authority as regards the conduct of its worship and witness, and the appointment of its officers. In a word, the Church is to be spiritually free: 'The Church's *one* foundation Is Jesus Christ, her Lord.' In this country, a continuing witness on these matters is necessary in the interests of Christ's sole Lordship over his Church, and it needs to be accompanied by a reconciliation of memories with the Church of England – something which I hoped might have happened as the third millennium dawned; but the time was evidently not ripe. (It goes without saying that I am not advocating breast-beating, morality-and-liturgy-confusing acts of contrition and confession which imply the objective moral responsibility of us who were unborn in the sixteenth century.)[128]

Much might be gained if at all foci of churchly life, Free Churchpeople and Anglicans together discussed the following questions posed in the report of the international Anglican-Reformed dialogue:

7. For good and for ill, in what ways is your church bound to and moulded by your culture, or by an alien culture?
8. How is your church conditioned by a sense of national identity?
9. In what ways is your church related to the state?
10. What are the implications of your answers to questions 7, 8 and 9 for your understanding of:

---

[127] For a fuller treatment of the matter see Alan P.F. Sell, *Testimony and Tradition*, ch. 11.

[128] See further on this point, idem, *Aspects of Christian Integrity*, 65–68.

  (i)   the nature of the Church;
  (ii) the Lordship of Christ in his Church;
  (iii) the prophetic role of the Church vis-à-vis the State?
  (iv) the mission of the Church?[129]

Underlying any Free Church answers to those questions must surely be that freedom under the gospel which Forsyth (twice) designated 'founded freedom'. He further explains that

> Not freedom alone is our genius; for freedom alone is but caprice, atomism, and anarchy in the end. But it is freedom created and founded and reared by an authority which cannot be either evaded or shaken; and which created our emancipation, in the very depth and crisis of our soul, by the eternal redemption at the heart of all history in Christ's cross.[130]

Here we come full circle to the Cross, the fount of grace and the seat of authority, for the Cross is that to which the Bible witnesses, and to which the Church at large and our consciences witness when they are being faithful; and it is God's action at the Cross which sets all our polities and interpretations in perspective.[131] For it is on the ground of what was done at Calvary that new life is given, forgiveness is experienced, fellowship is engendered, and the command to mission and service is delivered. It is possible to agree with the Methodist John T. Wilkinson who writes, 'I hold that the fundamental ground of religion is neither in the authority of the church nor in the authority of an infallible book but in the verdict of man's own inward personal experience,'[132] provided that we insist that it is an experience *of* something, and that the verdict is enabled by God the Holy Spirit. It was in order to maintain this position that Hubert Cunliffe-Jones opposed C.J. Cadoux's exaltation of the individual's inner light as the final authority: 'I have no intention of belittling, or limiting, or thwarting the Inner Light of man at all. . . . My denial of the *ultimacy* of the inner Light does not imply any limitation; it only refuses to ascribe to the Inner Light something that does not belong to it. . . . [We] acknowledge

---

[129] *God's Reign and Our Unity*, 84.

[130] P.T. Forsyth, *Faith, Freedom and the Future*, 347; cf. 336.

[131] See further, Alan P.F. Sell, *Commemorations*, ch. 1.

[132] Quoted by J. Munsey Turner, 'Preaching, theology, and spirituality in twentieth-century Methodism', 113.

beyond the inner Light the authority of Christ under which we stand.'[133]

But what of the End? When we review the contributions to eschatology by twentieth-century Nonconformist theologians we find that whereas at the beginning of the century their interests centred to a considerable extent in personal immortality, at the beginning of the twenty-first century eschatological discussion begins to be set within the context of the creation and re-creation of all things – the *oikoumene* – by God the Holy Trinity. Thus, for example, in his posthumous work, *Father, Son and Holy Spirit*, Colin Gunton writes, 'In relation to the created order, and particularly in relation to the human creature . . . it is the Spirit's function, through God the Son, to enable the creation to become that which it was created to be.'[134] More specifically, 'through his Son and Spirit, his two hands, the Father both prevents the creation from slipping back into the nothingness from which it came and restores its teleology, its movement to perfection.[135]

Others will, no doubt, offer further expositions along this line, and it will be interesting to see how much of the traditional language of 'the last things', some of it all but lost in many Christian circles, will be dusted off and recycled. But once again, in so far as I understand the matter, it is the victory of the Cross which gives us the assurance that the kingdom, or kingly rule, of God, inaugurated already, will, in God's good time, be consummated in that new heaven and new earth, the re-creation of all things, the unity of the 'whole inhabited earth.' For the present, while the saints may, and should, properly contemplate the bliss of heaven, none should presume upon God's mercy. While there is ground for hope that God's undefeatable love will at last win over the hardest rebel, that love is holy love. There are sufficient warnings in the gospels to preclude universalism; sufficient indications that the 'religious' would do well not to gloat over the presumed fate of others for, come the judgement, there will be surprises all round; and sufficient encouragements to be for Christ rather than against him.

---

[133] Hubert Cunliffe-Jones, 'Christian theology for the twentieth century', 129–30. Cf. R. Newton Flew and R.E. Davies, eds., *The Catholicity of Protestantism*, 126. For a Unitarian view of authority see Fred Kenworthy, *Freedom, Authority and Liberal Christianity*. For the findings on authority of the international Roman Catholic-Reformed dialogue (first phase) see *The Presence of Christ in Church and World*, 10–14.

[134] Colin E. Gunton, *Father, Son and Holy Spirit*, 157.

[135] Ibid., 117. For similar thoughts in devotional vein see Alan P.F. Sell, *God Our Father*, 67–69.

As I have elsewhere put it,

> There was an eternal purpose of the eternal God expressed in the creation and redemption of the world. Eternity has broken into time, and love's victory, already won, will be fully worked out. But this victory is the victory of holy love, which cannot both be true to itself and fail to pass adverse judgment on sin. All of this we affirm when, as the people of God, we take the bread and wine at the Lord's Supper 'till he come' (2 Corinthians 11:26).[136]

In the meantime, we do well to remember that

> It is an awesome biblical principle that from those to whom much has been given much will be expected. We should rejoice in our security, but not idly bask in it. The hope of glory to come should make us more, not less, earnest: 'Therefore, my beloved brothers, stand firm and immovable, and work for the Lord always, work without limit, since you know that in the Lord your labour cannot be lost' (2 Corinthians 15:58).[137]

Enough has been said to show how language, other than archaic language, may be lost, to suggest that the rounded enculturation of the saints is a pressing need, and to propose that a theology which finds its centre in the Cross is the most hopeful line of advance. There is much work to be done in all of these connections. But there is one thing more to be said. It is perfectly legitimate for theologians to speak from faith to faith. It is, therefore, quite in order for Geoffrey Wainwright, for example, to deny in the Preface to his *Doxology* that he is concerned with philosophy and apologetics. But speaking from faith to faith does not exhaust the theologian's calling, for the challenge of commending the faith to others remains. In this connection we may be concerned not so much with the loss of a language, as with attempting to acquaint our interlocutors with a language with which they are unfamiliar if, indeed, they have heard it at all, or which they repudiate. It is most unfortunate in my opinion that some of the twentieth century's most notable theologians have proceeded as if, or at least have enabled themselves to be construed as if, it will suffice to utter the word and trust the Spirit to apply it. Those Free Church theologians who were adversely critical of Karl

---

[136] Alan P.F. Sell, *The Spirit Our Life*, 83.

[137] Ibid., 95.

Barth's repudiation of natural theology were not altogether without excuse.[138]

But this is a wide-ranging issue, and here I simply note the need for the Church as a whole to be a body which confesses and commends the faith, and one which understands that an important aspect of that commending is the addressing of intellectual challenges to, or misunderstandings of, the faith by those whose calling such work is, and whose analytical skills are finely honed.[139] As I said, theologians ought not to speak only from faith to faith.[140] The implications for the Church's mission are clear; and if they are not, Forsyth will remind us of them:

> It is a curious thing, but it is possible for a movement or a church to be very evangelical on the extensive scale but not at all on the intensive. That is to say it is Low Church. It spreads its gospel over the face of the earth but not into the thought and temper of the age. It covers, but it does not leaven. . . . That is why missions, which owe so much to Low Church, are losing their staying power. They spread the Word rapidly – but so thin that it cracks.[141]

As Scott Lidgett more succinctly put it, 'God has given us length and breadth; may he give us depth and height.'[142]

At the end of his paper on *Current Trends in British Unitarianism* Arthur Long quoted the former Archbishop Runcie thus: 'A church which listens only to its own tradition will end up speaking only to itself. A Church

---

[138] See further idem, *Confessing and Commending the Faith*, 267–76.

[139] I have myself sought to examine the presuppositions of undertaking this task in my trilogy published by the University of Wales Press: *Philosophical Idealism and Christian Belief, John Locke and the Eighteenth-Century Divines, and Confessing and Commending the Faith.*

[140] It might go some way towards revitalizing theology if there were a more incisive and better-informed class of atheist to contend with. It would be a bonus if they had the wit of the best of the late nineteenth-century secularists. Universities in particular should be lively centres of debate between world views of all kinds; and some Departments of Religious Studies will have come of age when they employ theologians of the several religions studied, and not simply exegetes, phenomenologists, sociologists and the like.

[141] P.T. Forsyth, *Faith, Freedom and the Future*, 93–94.

[142] Quoted by E. Gordon Rupp, *Protestant Catholicity*, 54. See further on mission, Alan P.F. Sell, *Aspects of Christian Integrity*, ch. 5.

which listens only to what is happening in the world, will end up becoming only a dull echo of the latest liberal [or, we might nowadays add, neo-conservative] fashion.'[143] But, say I, a Church which lives by and proclaims the gospel of God's redeeming grace will be anchored in the tradition, open to fresh interpretations of it, and impelled into the world with both Good News and relevant, costly service.

V

The question presses, 'Who from the ranks of Nonconformity will rise to the theological challenges before us?' Or, to advert to the somewhat alarmist question in this lecture's title, 'Are desert conditions encroaching upon us?' Undeniably, the bulk of Nonconformist theological writings appeared during the first half of the twentieth century. Since then the denominations have declined significantly in numerical strength. News of rising educational standards notwithstanding, the remaining readers of Nonconformist newspapers are treated to less substantial theological articles than were their grandparents, while the readership for sermons has all but evaporated. Many Nonconformist theological colleges have been closed, or have amalgamated, and the universities have undertaken and paid for much teaching that was previously a charge upon denominational funds.[144] In many cases the university teachers are church members, and increasingly – more perhaps in biblical studies, ecclesiastical history and philosophy of religion than in theology as such – they are not ordained. When at one and the same time Norman Snaith (Old Testament), Vincent Taylor (New Testament), H. Watkin-Jones (Church History) and Harold Roberts (Theology) were on the staff of Headingly Methodist College that was a vintage period indeed in terms of theological scholarship; and other Nonconformist theological colleges were similarly blessed. By contrast, Paul Fiddes of Regent's Park Baptist College is one of a declining number of Nonconformists who at the end of the twentieth century were publishing significant works in systematic, doctrinal or constructive theology from a base in a Nonconformist theological college.

But it is not simply that more Nonconformists are teaching theology in universities than taught in the theological colleges 50 years ago – if,

---

[143] Arthur Long quoting Robert Runcie, in *Current Trends in British Unitarianism*, 32.

[144] Cf. the terminus date of Alan P.F. Sell, *Philosophy, Dissent and Nonconformity 1689–1920*.

indeed, that is the case – it is that as far as ministers are concerned some at least of the denominations do not have the 'critical mass' of scholarship that they once had. To take one example, which assumes that the earned English and Welsh DD is indicative of world-class scholarship:[145] from figures published in 1950 we learn that the Congregationalists had 1968 ministers (including 407 retired ministers) of whom seven then in employment held the earned (as distinct from the honorary) degree of DD. Of these, six were working under the auspices of the denomination, one (C.H. Dodd) under that of a university. At the same period there were two ministers of the Presbyterian Church of England in employment who held the earned DD. In 1999, out of 1825 United Reformed Church ministers (including 759 retired and 193 non-stipendiary ministers), one only[146] below the age of retirement had an earned DD (Colin Gunton), and he was not employed by the denomination.[147] This difference is explained partly by the decline in the number of ministers in general and of the pool of church members from which they might be drawn, and partly by the demographic fact that more and more ministers are now second career people. However valuable these latter may be as preachers and pastors, it is unlikely that many of them will have the time or the inclination to become the Church's scholars. Here I state a fact; I do not intend to diminish anyone's vocation, and I have more than once testified that of the three ministers who influenced me most when I was growing up, none had a university degree and one was trained not in a college but through an external denominational course. In any case, I firmly believe that theologizing is the task of the Church as a whole;[148] but in the discharging of this task a leaven of deeply learned theologians – by which I mean theologians deeply learned in the things of God as well as technically competent – is a gift not to be despised. The Nonconformists have much smaller pools of younger ministerial candidates in which to fish for these than once they had.

---

[145] For the benefit of readers unfamiliar with English and Welsh higher education I ought to explain that nowadays such senior doctorates, when earned (they may also be granted *honoris causa*), are awarded upon the positive assessment of submitted or published works which are deemed to have made a substantial and original contribution to scholarship.

[146] The present writer, though of Congregational/United Reformed Church origins, and now returned to the fold, was working under the auspices of the Presbyterian Church of Wales in 1999.

[147] See the Congregational and Presbyterian year books for 1950; *The United Reformed Church Year Book*, 1999.

[148] See, for example, Alan P.F. Sell, *Testimony and Tradition*, ch. 1.

Theological education passed through considerable changes during the twentieth century, and these have had implications for theological scholarship. While by no means all Nonconformist ministerial candidates received six years of training leading to the BA and BD degrees, a significant number did between the years 1900 and (roughly) 1975. But partly in response to financial difficulties; partly owing to calls for the increasing 'professionalization' of ministerial education which have led here to time-consuming internship methods of training, there to a smorgasbord of modules which encourage tasting rather than digesting or, to change the metaphor, courses which, by prescribing such small doses, threaten to inoculate students against particular disciplines for life; and, most recently, partly as a result of 'customer resistance' – students now being fee-payers, courses have been curtailed in length or otherwise modified, so that theological students are in many cases plunged into philosophy of religion (if, indeed, they are plunged into it at all) without a background in philosophy and logic, into ecclesiastical history without a background in history, and into biblical studies without a strong linguistic background. The foundations for theological study have thus to some extent (some would say to a considerable extent) been eroded.[149] I am not arguing that all ministerial

---

[149] It is not, of course, suggested either that theology is the only discipline to have undergone such changes, or that problems emerge only at the level of higher education. A professor of Modern Languages has told me that when his career began mastery of the language was assumed on entry to university, whereas nowadays the language is still being taught in the third year of the degree course. An academic engineer once ruefully (if with some exaggeration) told me that he needed a year added to the BSc course because in the first term of the first year he had to teach basic English, in the second term, basic mathematics, and in the third term, how to close his door quietly! Only then could he proceed with engineering science. I cannot say how reliable such anecdotal evidence is, but it is conceivable that what one might call 'seed-corn' disciplines are at risk in more than one quarter. As these lectures go to press a report of the views of university admissions tutors is leaked. It makes for depressing reading both as regards the competence (or lack of it) of many undergraduates on arriving at university, and the implications of this for the content of university courses. As an example of the latter, the following remark is recorded: 'No civil engineering is done in the first semester and second-year material has now been moved to the third year.' One wonders whether third year civil engineering students will be under excessive pressure, or whether some third-year material will not be covered. See *The Times Higher Education Supplement*, 10 February 2006, 1, 9.

candidates require exactly the same programme of training; I am simply urging that the churches take steps to ensure that their younger candidates at least receive a full and rigorous academic course. If this means fewer visits to hospitals and prisons during a candidate's college years, so be it; required in-service training for licensed probationers prior to ordination is not impossible to provide, and it is never more readily received than by those at the pastoral 'coal face'.[150]

In terms of the disciplines with which I have been especially concerned in these lectures – doctrinal, systematic and constructive theology – I see no viable substitute for practitioners' having a solid grounding in the Bible, a thorough acquaintance with the history of Christian thought (which is broader than historical theology, but includes both it and the linguistic competence to read salient texts), and sufficient philosophical-analytical skills to probe presuppositions, analyse arguments and avoid the writing of incoherent gobbledegook. None of this is achieved without real time and effort; and the churches would do well to encourage in all possible ways those ministerial candidates whose gifts take them in these directions, and whose academic lungs can withstand prolonged immersion in extensive and sometimes choppy waters.

I have heard the challenge, 'What is the point of ordinands undertaking advanced theological studies given the decline in the number

---

[150] I am here concerned with academic study (which can, and ought, to be formative), but I by no means doubt the importance of other aspects of ministerial formation. See further Alan P.F. Sell, *Testimony and Tradition*, ch. 1. What was possible in the quasi-monastic life I led in theological college for six years, during which time students (certainly those from a distance) seldom went home, were not permitted to marry, engaged twice-daily in chapel worship (but not in carpet slippers!), were sent out far and wide to conduct worship on Sundays, and were treated to a number of college courses and regular Bible examinations additional to the full-time university degree courses, is impossible to achieve when married students (understandably enough) live at home, so many commute to college for one or two days only per week, and an increasing number have to take paid employment to maintain themselves. The Bible examinations, which were held on the first and last Saturdays of every term (yes, on Saturdays) had been instituted by Principal A.J. Grieve. Those students whose education for ministry extended over six years had, by the time they left, been examined on every book of the English Bible. Something of a burden at the time, I now look back on that requirement to be familiar with the whole text of Scripture (and not just with the university set texts in Hebrew and Greek) with gratitude.

of academic posts supported by the Nonconformist denominations?' As already mentioned, the fact of the decline cannot be denied. To take one example: in 1950 *The Congregational Year Book* listed ten theological colleges in England and Wales in which its ministers might be educated. Today *The United Reformed Year Book* lists four, of which one is the former Presbyterian college, Westminster, Cambridge, and another is the ecumenical Queens Foundation in Birmingham. But from the fact that the denominations support fewer academic posts we ought not to conclude that a leaven of highly-trained ministers is not required. There are positions on doctrinal and ecumenical commissions to be filled; those able to contribute to the in-service education of ministers are needed; and the ministry of the scholar-pastor is by no means to be despised. Apart from such utilitarian considerations, there is the challenge laid upon the individual to be the best possible steward of gifts which have been given. You see how the urgency of the situation tempts me to wax homiletic. It does not, however, prompt me to don the mantle of a prophet of doom, for I recall that within a decade of D.W. Simon's lament of 1891 regarding the dismal state of systematic theology in Congregationalism there was ushered in something of a golden age of that discipline within Nonconformity at large.

It is impossible to predict what form theological education will take in 50 years' time. It is even more difficult to predict whether there will be any Nonconformist theology at the turn of the twenty-first century. Unless the End come, theology will surely be written, but by whom and under whose auspices? Will Nonconformity *as we have known it*[151] dwindle away to nothing? Or will the Church of England? Or will the latter become disestablished? Or will the monarchy fall? Who can say? These would be the conditions for the demise of Nonconformist theology. Under whatsoever auspices they travel, I hope that the theologians of the future will hold high the Cross,[152] declare the gospel of the triune God of all grace, and combat those sectarianisms which deny the unity which in Christ by the Spirit the Father has already given his Church. As theologians of the future, as well as those of today, set about their task, they and we should do

---

[151] There may, of course, be significant contributions from such groups as the Brethren, the Pentecostals, the black churches, and from the several networks of independent evangelical churches.

[152] See further, Alan P.F. Sell, *Enlightenment, Ecumenism, Evangel*, ch. 13, where one of my points is that to glory in the Cross is by no means the same as legitimating a triumphalist Church – an abomination indeed.

well to ponder some words of Eustace Conder which have lost none of their pertinence during the 132 years since he uttered them:

> The Theology of the future, as I venture to forecast it in my own mind, will not be the fruit either of the destruction of the past, or of a reproduction of the past, or of the fusing all doctrines into one featureless mass, where faith is replaced by feeling; although these three seem the prevailing theological tendencies of the present. It will be the fruit of deeper study of God's truth. Despising no ray of light from the past, it will fill its own lamp with fresh oil and kindle it with altar-fire. Its great instrument will be neither Controversy, which poisons, nor Criticism, which freezes all it handles (indispensable though these are in their place); but Interpretation, which, because it has to deal with the spirit as well as the letter, is impossible without faith, love, and reverence.[153]

---

[153] E.R. Conder, 'The decay of theology', 79–80.

Biographical References

This list, which is restricted to theologians who died during the twentieth century, includes some, like P.T. Forsyth, whose stimulus continues; some, like W.F. Adeney, who contributed to more than one theological discipline; some, like J.A. Beet, who were more than ordinarily intellectually adventurous in their own time; some, like R.S. Franks, who were eminent scholars; and some, like J. Drummond and T.V. Tymms, who deserve to be better remembered than they are. In the estimation of the author, those listed here comprise the most notable of twentieth-century Nonconformist doctrinal, systematic and constructive theologians.

Abbreviations

BH   *The Baptist Handbook*
CYB   *The Congregational Year Book*
DHT   *The Dictionary of Historical Theology*, ed. Trevor A. Hart, Carlisle: Paternoster, 2000
DMBI   *A Dictionary of Methodism in Britain and Ireland*, ed. John A. Vickers, Peterborough: Epworth Press, 2000
DNCBP   *Dictionary of Nineteenth-Century British Philosophers*, ed. W.J. Mander and A.P. F. Sell, Bristol: Thoemmes Press, 2002
DSCHT   *Dictionary of Scottish Church History and Theology*, ed. N.M. deS. Cameron, Edinburgh: T. & T. Clark, 1993
DTCBP   *Dictionary of Twentieth-Century British Philosophers*, ed. Stuart Brown, Bristol: Thoemmes Press, 2005
ERF   *Encyclopedia of the Reformed Faith*, ed. D.K. McKim, Louisville: Westminster/John Knox, 1992
MMC   *Minutes of the Methodist Conference*
ODCC   *The Oxford Dictionary of the Christian Church*, 3rd edn. ed. E.A. Livingstone, Oxford: OUP, 1997
ODNB   *The Oxford Dictionary of National Biography*
URCYB   *Year Book of The United Reformed Church*
WWW   *Who Was Who*

Adeney, Walter Frederic (1849–1920).
Congregationalist.
Hon.DD (St And.).
CYB, 1921; WWW, 1916–28.

Beet, Joseph Agar (1840–1924).
Wesleyan.
Hon.DD (Glas.).
DMBI; WWW, 1916–28.
Carter, D., 'Joseph Agar Beet and the eschatological crisis', in *Proceedings of the Wesley Historical Society*, LI pt. 6 (October 1998), 197–216.

Cave, Sydney (1883–1953).
Congregationalist.
DD (Lond.) Hon.DD (Glas.)
CYB, 1954; DHT; ODNB; WWW, 1951–60.
Bocking, Ronald, 'Syndey Cave (1883–1953) – Missionary, Principal, Theologian,' *The Journal of the United Reformed Church, History Society*, VII no 1, October 2002, 36–44.

Cocks, Harry Francis Lovell (1894–1983).
Congregationalist/United Reformed.
DD (Lond.).
URCYB, 1984; ODNB.
Sell, Alan P.F., *Commemorations: Studies in Christian Thought and History* (1993; repr. Eugene, OR: Wipf & Stock, 1998), ch. 13.

Cunliffe-Jones, Hubert (1905–91).
Congregationalist/United Reformed.
Hon.DD (Edin.).
URCYB, 1991/2; WWW 1991–95.
Kaye, Elaine, *For the Work of Ministry: A History of Northern College and its Predecessors* (Edinburgh: T. & T. Clark, 1999), 200–201, 203–4, and *passim*.

Davison, W. Theophilus (1846–1935).
Wesleyan/Methodist.
Hon.DD (Lond.).
DMBI; DNCBP; MMC, 1936; WWW, 1929–40.
Sell, Alan P.F., *Philosophy, Dissent and Nonconformity* 1689–1920 (Cambridge: James Clarke, 2004), 164–66, 201–2.

Drummond, James (1835–1918).
Unitarian.
LLD (TCD), Hon.LittD (TCD).
ODCC; ODNB; WWW, 1916–28; *The Inquirer*, 22 June 1918.
Davis, V.D., *A History of Manchester College from its Foundation in Manchester to its Establishment in Oxford* (London: Allen & Unwin, 1932), 179–80.

Farmer, Herbert Henry (1892–1981).
Presbyterian/United Reformed.
Hon.DD (Glas.).
DHT; DTCBP; ODNB; WWW, 1981–90.
Donovan, P., 'Phenomenology as apologetics', in *The Scottish Journal of Theology*, XXVII, (1974), 402–7.
Haymes, B., 'The supernatural is personal', in *The Baptist Quarterly*, XXVI, (1979), 2–13.
Healey, F.G., ed., *Prospect for Theology: Essays in Honour of H.H. Farmer* (Welwyn: Nisbet, 1966).
Langford, T.A., 'The theological methodology of John Oman and H.H. Farmer', in *Religious Studies*, I, (1966), 229–40.
Partridge, C.H., *H.H. Farmer's Theological Interpretation of Religions* (Lampeter: Edwin Mellen Press, 1998).

Flew, Robert Newton (1886–1962).
Wesleyan/Methodist.
DD (Oxon), Hon.DD (Aber.).
DMBI; ODNB; WWW, 1961–70.
Tice, Frank, *The History of Methodism in Cambridge* (London: Epworth Press, 1966).
Wakefield, G.S., *Robert Newton Flew, 1886–1962* (London: Epworth Press, 1971).

Forsyth, Peter Taylor (1848–1921).
Congregationalist.
Hon.DD (Aber.).
CYB, 1922; DHT; DSCHT; ERF; ODCC; ODNB; WWW 1916–28.
Mozley, J.K., *The Heart of the Gospel* (London: SPCK, 1925).
Griffith, Gwilym O., *The Theology of P.T. Forsyth* (London: Lutterworth, 1948).
Bradley, W.L., *P.T. Forsyth: The Man and His Work* (London: Independent Press, 1952).

Brown, R.M., *P.T. Forsyth: Prophet for Today* (Philadelphia: Westminster, 1952).

Rodgers, John H., *The Theology of P.T. Forsyth: The Cross of Christ and the Revelation of God* (London: Independent Press, 1965).

Hunter, A.M., *P.T. Forsyth: Per Crucem ad Lucem* (London: SCM Press, 1974).

Huxtable, W.J.F., 'P.T. Forsyth: 1848–1921', in *The Journal of the United Reformed Church History Society*, IV no. 1 (October 1987), 72–78.

Hart, Trevor, ed., *Justice the True and Only Mercy* (Edinburgh: T. & T. Clark, 1995).

McCurdy, Leslie, *Attributes and Atonement: The Holy love of God in the Theology of P.T. Forsyth* (Carlisle: Paternoster, 1999). Includes a substantial bibliography.

Sell, Alan P.F., ed., *P.T. Forsyth: Theologian for a New Millennium* (London: The United Reformed Church, 2000).

Sell, Alan P.F., *Testimony and Tradition: Studies in Reformed and Dissenting Thought* (Aldershot: Ashgate, 2005), chs. 7, 8.

Franks, Robert Sleightholme (1872–1964).

Congregationalist.

DLitt (Oxon), Hon.LLD (Bristol).

CYB 1964–65; DHT; ODNB; WWW, 1961–70.

Hughes, T.H., *The Atonement: Modern Theories of the Doctrine* (London: Allen & Unwin, 1949).

Garvie, Alfred Ernest (1861–1945).

Congregationalist.

Hon.DD (Glas), Hon.DD (Lond.), Hon. DTh. (Berlin).

CYB, 1946; DHT; DSCHT; ODNB; WWW, 1941–50.

Garvie, A.E., *Memories and Meanings of My Life* (London: Allen & Unwin, 1938).

Lidgett, John Scott (1854–1953).

Wesleyan/Methodist.

Hon.DD (Aber.), Hon.LLD (Lond.).

DHT; DMBI; DNCBP; MMC, 1953; ODNB; WWW, 1951–60.

Lidgett, J.S., *Reminiscences* (London: Epworth Press, 1928).

Lidgett, J.S., *My Guided Life* (London: Methuen, 1936).

Davies, R.E., ed., *Scott Lidgett: A Symposium* (London: Epworth Press, 1957).

Beasley, J.D., *The Bitter Cry Heard and Heeded* (London: South London Mission, 1989).

Turberfield, Alan F., *John Scott Lidgett: Archbishop of Methodism?* (London: Epworth Press, 2003).

Lofthouse, William Francis (1871–1965).
Wesleyan/Methodist.
Hon.DD (Aber.).
DMBI; WWW, 1961–70.
Strawson, W.F., 'W.F. Lofthouse 1871–1965', in *The Epworth Review*, XIII no. 3 (1986), 21–27.

Mackintosh, Robert (1858–1933).
Presbyterian/Congregationalist.
DD (Glas.).
CYB, 1934; DNCBP; DSCHT; DTCBP; ODNB; WWW, 1929–40.
Phillips, G., 'Dr. Mackintosh', in *The Congregational Monthly* (March 1933).
Sell, Alan P.F., *Robert Mackintosh: Theologian of Integrity* (Bern: Peter Lang, 1977).

Mellone, Sydney Herbert (1859–1956).
Unitarian.
DSc. (Edin).
DTCBP; WWW, 1951–60.
The Inquirer, 28 July 1956.
Andrew M. Hill, 'Too soon forgotten: Sydney Herbert Mellone 1869–1956', in Leonard Smith, ed., *Unitarian to the Core: Unitarian College Manchester, 1854–2004* (Manchester: Unitarian College, 2004), 105–20.

Oman, John (1860–1939).
Presbyterian.
Hon.DD (Glas.), Hon.DD (Oxon).
DHT; DSCHT; DTCBP; ERF; ODCC; ODNB; WWW, 1929–40.
Farmer, H.H., 'Theologians of our time: John Wood Oman (1860–1939)', in *The Expository Times*, LXXIV, (February 1963), 132–5.
Healey, F.G., *Religion and Reality: The Theology of John Oman* (Edinburgh: Oliver & Boyd, 1965).
Morris, J.S., 'Oman's conception of the personal God in The Natural and the Supernatural', in *Journal of Theological Studies*, XXIII, April 1972, 82–94.
Bevans, S., *John Oman and his Doctrine of God* (Cambridge: CUP, 1992).

Hood, Adam, Baillie, *Oman and Macmurray: Experience and Religious Belief* (Aldershot: Ashgate, 2003).

Townsend, Henry (1879–1955).
Baptist.
DD (Lond.).
BH, 1956; WWW, 1951–60.

Tymms, Thomas Vincent (1842–1921).
Baptist.
Hon.DD (St And.).
BH, 1922; DNCBP; WWW, 1916–28.
Sell, Alan P.F., *Philosophy, Dissent and Nonconformity 1689–1920* (Cambridge: James Clarke, 2004), 193–6.

Whale, John Seldon (1896–1997).
Congregationalist/United Reformed.
Hon.DD (Glas.).
CYB, DHT; ODNB; WWW, 1996–2000.
Binfield, C., 'A learned and gifted Protestant minister: John Seldon Whale, 19 December 1896 – 17 September 1997', in *The Journal of the United Reformed Church History Society*, VI no. 2 (May 1998), 97–131.

Bibliography

Note: The Bibliography is confined to works referred to in the text and notes. See also the Biographical References.

Abbott, E.S., et al., *Catholicity: A Study in the Conflict of Christian Traditions in the West, Being a Report to the Archbishop of Canterbury* (Westminster: Dacre Press, 1947).

Adeney, Walter F., 'The Trinity', in *Studies in Christian Evidences, Series I* (London: Charles H. Kelly, n.d.), 120–37.

—, 'The atonement in modern religious thought', in *The Atonement in Modern Religious Thought: A Theological Symposium* (London: James Clarke, 1900), 141–56.

—, *A Century's Progress in Religious Life and Thought* (London: James Clarke, 1901).

—, *The Christian Conception of God* (London: Thomas Law, 1909).

—, *Faith Today* (London: James Clarke, 1915).

Anon., *Drummond, Eminent Unitarian Teachers*, 15 (London: The Lindsey Press, n.d.).

—, *The Atonement in Modern Religious Thought: A Theological Symposium* (London: James Clarke, 1900).

—, 'The influence of Congregationalism in promoting Christian unity, and the lines upon which it should use that influence', in *Proceedings of the Fourth International Congregational Council* (New York: National Council of the Congregational Churches of the United States, 1921), 478–85.

—, *The Nature of the Christian Church according to the Teaching of the Methodists* (London: The Methodist Publishing House, 1937).

—, *A Free Religious Faith* (London: The Lindsey Press, 1945).

—, *The Baptist Doctrine of the Church* (London: The Carey Kingsgate Press, 1948).

—, pamphlets published by the Congregational Union of England and Wales: *Church Membership* (1947), *50 Questions About Congregationalism* (1951), *The Church Meeting* (1952), *Worship* (1952), *The Meaning of the Communion Service* (n.d.), and *Our Heritage of Free Prayer* [by W. Gordon Robinson], (n.d.).

—, *The Free Churches and the State: The Report of the Commission on Church and State appointed by the Free Church Federal Council in March 1950* (London: Free Church Federal Council, 1953).

—, *Eschatology: Four papers read to The Society for the Study of Theology* (Edinburgh: Oliver and Boyd, 1953).

—, *Relations between Anglican and Presbyterian Churches: A Joint Report* (London: SPCK, 1957).

—, A Short Affirmation of Faith', in *World Congregationalism*, III no. 8 (May 1961), 22–23.

—, *Conversations between the Church of England and the Methodist Church: A Report to the Archbishops of Canterbury and York and the Conference of the Methodist Church* (London: Church Information Office, 1963).

—, *The Book of Order: Being the Rules and Forms of Procedure of the Presbyterian Church of England*, 7th ed. (London: Presbyterian Church of England, 1964).

—, *Unity Begins at Home: A Report from the First British Conference of Faith and Order Nottingham 1964* (London: SCM Press, 1964).

—, *A Declaration of Faith* (London: Congregational Church in England and Wales, 1967); reprinted in David M. Thompson, *Stating the Gospel: Formulations and Declarations of Faith from the Heritage of the United Reformed Church* (Edinburgh: T. & T. Clark, 1990).

—, *Anglican-Methodist Unity: Report of the Anglican-Methodist Unity Commission, Part 2: The Scheme* (London: SPCK and Epworth Press, 1968).

—, *The Manual of The United Reformed Church* (London: United Reformed Church in England and Wales, 1972).

—, *The Presence of Christ in Church and World: Dialogue between the World Alliance of Reformed Churches and the Secretariat for Promoting Christian Unity, 1970–1977* (Geneva: World Alliance of Reformed Churches; and Rome: The Vatican, 1977).

—, *Unity in the Spirit: Quakers and the Ecumenical Pilgrimage* (London: Quaker Home Service, 1979).

—, *Negotiations between The United Reformed Church and the Re-formed Association of Churches of Christ: Revised Proposals for Unification* (London: The United Reformed Church, 1980).

—, *Baptism, Eucharist and Ministry* (Geneva: World Council of Churches, 1982).

—, *The Failure of the English Covenant: An Assessment of the Experience of the Churches' Council for Covenanting* (London: British Council of Churches, n.d.).

—, *Baptists and Reformed in Dialogue* (Geneva: World Alliance of Reformed Churches, 1984).

—, *God's Reign and Our Unity: The Report of the Anglican-Reformed International Commission 1981–1984* (London: SPCK; and Edinburgh: The Saint Andrew Press, 1984).

—, *Baptist Basics* (a series of leaflets published by the Baptist Union, London).

—, *Reformed and Methodists in Dialogue: Report of the Reformed/Methodist Conversations (1985 and 1987)* (Geneva: World Alliance of Reformed Churches, 1988).

—, *Towards Closer Fellowship: Report of the Dialogue between Reformed and Disciples of Christ* (Geneva: World Alliance of Reformed Churches, 1988).

—, *Towards a Common Understanding of the Church: Reformed/Roman Catholic International Dialogue: Second Phase 1984–1990* (Geneva: World Alliance of Reformed Churches, 1991).

Armstrong, Richard A., *The Trinity and the Incarnation* (London: Philip Green, 1904).

Avis, Paul, 'Establishment and the mission of a national church', in *Theology*, CIII, (January–February 2000), 3–12.

Badham, Paul, ed., *Religion, State and Society in Modern Britain* (Lampeter: The Edwin Mellen Press, 1989).

Banks, J.S., *Words on Immortality* (London: Charles H. Kelly, 1902).

Barber, B. Aquila, *A Methodist Pageant: A Souvenir of the Primitive Methodist Church* (London: The Holborn Publishing House, 1932).

Barrett, C.K., 'Immortality and resurrection', in C.S. Duthie, ed., *Resurrection and Immortality*, q.v., 68–88.

Bartlet, J.V. 'Congregationalism', in *The Encyclopaedia Britannica*, VI, (1910).

Bartram, Richard, ed., *Religion and Life: Eight Essays, and an Essay on Modern Religious Developments* (London: British and Foreign Unitarian Association, 1891).

Bebbington, David W., *Holiness in Nineteenth-Century England* (Carlisle: Paternoster, 2000).

Beet, J. Agar, *The Immortality of the Soul: A Protest* (London: Hodder and Stoughton, 1901).

—, *The Last Things*, rev. ed. (London: Hodder and Stoughton, 1905).

—, *A Manual of Theology* (London: Hodder and Stoughton, 1906).

—, *The Last Things in a Few Words* (London: Hodder and Stoughton, 1913).

Berry, Charles A., 'The Churches of Christ and the Kingdom of God', in D. Macfadyen ed., *Constructive Congregational Ideals*, q.v., 177–202.

Bett, Henry, *The Spirit of Methodism* (London: Epworth Press, 1937).

—, *What Methodists Believe and Preach* (London: Epworth Press, 1938).

Bevans, Stephen, *John Oman and his Doctrine of God* (Cambridge: CUP, 1992).

Binfield, Clyde, 'A learned and gifted Protestant minister: John Seldon Whale, 19 December 1896 – 17 September 1997', in *The Journal of the United Reformed Church History Society*, VI no. 2 (May 1998), 97–131.

—, ed., *Reformed and Renewed 1972–1997: Eight Essays, a supplement to The Journal of the United Reformed Church History Society*, V Supp. 2 (September 1997).

Binney, Thomas, *Dissent Not Schism. A Discourse delivered in the Poultry Chapel, December 11, 1834, at the Monthly meeting of the Associated Ministers and Churches of the London Congregational Union* (London: Joseph Ogle Robinson, 1835).

Bocking, Ronald, 'The United Reformed Church: background, formation, and after', in C. Binfield, ed., *Reformed and Renewed*, 7–17.

Bolam, C.G., 'Theological liberalism: a vindication', in Kenneth Twinn, ed., *Essays in Unitarian Theology*, q.v., 126–36.

Brash, W. Bardsley, *Methodism* (London: Methuen, 1928).

Brencher, John, *Martyn Lloyd-Jones (1899–1981) and Twentieth-Century Evangelicalism* (Carlisle: Paternoster, 2002).

Briggs, J.H.Y., 'Double affirmations: Baptists since 1945', in *Faith, Heritage and Witness*, q.v., 60–64.

—, ed., *Faith, Heritage and Witness. A Supplement to The Baptist Quarterly Published in Honour of Dr W.M.S. West* (London: Baptist Historical Society, 1987).

—, ed., *Bible, Church and World: A Supplement to The Baptist Quarterly published in Honour of Dr. D.S. Russell* (London: Baptist Historical Society, 1989).

Brunner, Emil and Karl Barth, *Natural Theology* (London: Geoffrey Bles, 1946).

Bunyan, John, *The Pilgrim's Progress*, numerous editions.

Cadoux, C.J., *Christianity and Catholicism: A Vindication of Progressive Protestantism* (London: Allen & Unwin, 1928).

—, *Roman Catholicism and Freedom* (London: Independent Press, 1936).

—, *The Case for Evangelical Modernism* (London: Hodder and Stoughton, 1938).

—, *The Message about the Cross: A Fresh Study of the Doctrine of the Atonement* (London: Allen & Unwin, 1924).

—, *Christian Pacifism Re-examined* (Oxford: Basil Blackwell, 1940).

—, *The Congregational Way* (Oxford: Blackwell, 1945).

—, 'Scripture and theology', in *The Congregational Quarterly*, XXV no. 1 (April 1947), 21–26.

Calvin, J., *Institutes of the Christian Religion*, ed. John T. McNeil, trans. Ford Lewis Battles, 2 vols. (Philadelphia: Westminster Press, 1960).

Campbell, R.J., *A Faith for To-day: Suggestions towards a System of Christian Belief* (London: James Clarke, 1901).

—, *The New Theology* (London: Chapman and Hall, 1907).

—, *New Theology Sermons* (London: Williams and Norgate, 1907).

—, *Christian Faith in Modern Light* (London: Ernest Benn, 1932).

Carpenter, J. Estlin, ed., *Ethical and Religious Problems of the War* (London: The Lindsey Press, 1916).

—, ed., *Freedom and Truth: Modern Views of Unitarian Christianity* (London: The Lindsey Press, 1925).

Carr, Wesley, 'A developing establishment', in *Theology*, CII (January–February 1999), 2–10. Also ibid., (May–June 1999), 230–31.

Carter, David, 'Joseph Agar Beet and the eschatological crisis', in *Proceedings of the Wesley Historical Society*, LI pt. 6 (October 1998), 197–216.

—, 'The context and content of mid-Victorian Wesleyan Ecclesiology' *Proceedings of the Wesley Historical Society*, LII pt. 6 (October 2000), 219–35.

—, *Love Bade Me Welcome: A British Methodist Perspective on the Church* (London: Epworth Press, 2002).

Cave, Sydney, *Redemption, Hindu and Christian* (London: OUP, 1919).

—, *The Doctrine of the Person of Christ* (London: Duckworth, 1925).

—, *Christianity and some Living Religions of the East* (London: Duckworth, 1929).

—, *The Doctrines of the Christian Faith* (London: Hodder and Stoughton, 1931).

—, *What Shall We Say of Christ?* (London: Hodder and Stoughton, 1932).

—, *The Doctrine of the Work of Christ* (London: Duckworth, 1937).

—, *The Christian Estimate of Man* (London: Duckworth, 1944).

Chapman, J. Arundel, *The Theology of Karl Barth: A Short Introduction* (London: Epworth Press, 1931).

—, *An Introduction to Schleiermacher* (London: Epworth Press, 1932).

—, *Modern Issues in Religious Thought* (London: Epworth Press, 1937).

Chesterton, W. Ridley, and P.W. Evans, *The Authority of Christ in a Lawless Age* (London: Morgan & Scott, 1920).

Christensen, Richard L., ed., *How Shall We Sing the Lord's Song? An Assessment of The New Century Hymnal* (Centerville, Massachusetts: Confessing Christ, 1997).

Chryssides, George, *The Elements of Unitarianism* (Shaftesbury: Element, 1998).

—, ed., *Unitarian Perspectives on Contemporary Religious Thought* (London: Lindsey Press, 1999).

Clark, Henry W., *History of English Nonconformity*, 2 vols. (London: Chapman and Hall, 1911, 1913).

—, *The Cross and the Eternal Order* (London: Lutterworth, 1943).

Clements, Keith W., *Faith* (London: SCM Press, 1981).

—, *A Patriotism for Today* (Bristol: Bristol Baptist College, 1984).

—, *The Theology of Ronald Gregor Smith* (Leiden: E.J. Brill, 1986).

—, *Friedrich Schleiermacher: Pioneer of Modern Theology* (London: Collins, 1987).

—, *Lovers of Discord* (London: SPCK, 1988).

—, *What Freedom? The Persistent Challenge of Dietrich Bonhoeffer* (Bristol: Bristol Baptist College, 1990).

—, ed., *Baptists in the Twentieth Century: Papers Presented to a Summer School, July 1982* (London: Baptist Historical Society, 1983).

Cocks, H.F. Lovell, *The Faith of a Protestant Christian* (London: Independent Press, 1931).

—, *By Faith Alone* (London: James Clarke, 1943).

—, *A Church Reborn: Address from the Chair of the Congregational Union of England and Wales delivered in Westminster Chapel, London, on May 15th 1950* (London: Independent Press, 1950).

—, *The Wondrous Cross* (London: Independent Press, 1957).

—, 'The hope of glory', in C.S. Duthie, ed., *Resurrection and Immortality*, q.v., 145–62.

Conder, E.R., 'The decay of theology', in *The Congregational Year Book* (1874), 64–80.

Condon, H.E.A., et al, 'A re-statement of Christian thought', in *The Christian World* (9 February 1933), 7.

Cook, Henry, *What Baptists Stand For* (London: Kingsgate Press, 1947).

Cooke, Leslie E., 'Upon this Rock,' *Congregationalism, Its Heritage and Task* (London: Independent Press, 1939).

Copestake, R.H., *The Methodist Way* (London: Epworth Press, 1951).

Cox, Harvey, *The Secular City* (London: SCM Press, 1966).

Crabtree, Herbert, *The Doctrine of the Trinity* (London: The Lindsey Press, 1946).

Crawford, R.G., *The Saga of God Incarnate* (Pretoria: University of South Africa, 1987).

Creasey, Maurice A., *Bearings, or Friends and the New Reformation* (London: Friends Home Service Committee, 1969).

Cressey, M.H., 'Notes on the theology of union: theological aspects of the formation and process of The United Reformed Church before and after 1972', in C. Binfield, ed., *Reformed and Renewed*, q.v., 22.

Cross, Anthony R., 'Service to the ecumenical movement: The contribution of British Baptists', in *The Baptist Quarterly*, XXXVIII no. 3 (July 1999), 107–22.

—, *Baptism and the Baptists: Theology and Practice in the Twentieth Century* (Carlisle: Paternoster, 2000).

—, 'Baptists and baptism – a British perspective', in *Baptist History and Heritage*, XXXV no. 1 (Winter 2000), 104–21.

—, and Philip E. Thompson, eds., *Baptist Sacramentalism* (Carlisle: Paternoster, 2003).

Cullmann, Oscar, *The Immortality of the Soul or the Resurrection of the Body?* (London: SCM Press, 1958).

Cunliffe-Jones, Hubert, 'The historic Gospel', in J. Marsh, ed., *Congregationalism Today*, q.v., 16–29.

—, *The Holy Spirit* (London: Independent Press, 1943).

—, *The Authority of Biblical Revelation* (London: James Clarke, 1945).

—, 'Christian theology for the twentieth century', in *The Congregational Quarterly*, XXV (April 1947), 127–32.

—, 'God's judgement of the individual after death', in C.S. Duthie, ed., *Resurrection and Immortality*, q.v., 124–44.

—, 'The meaning of the atonement today', in *Theology*, LXXIV (March 1971), 119–23.

—, *Christian Theology since 1600* (London: Duckworth, 1971).

Cunningham, David S., Ralph del Colle and Lucas Lamadrid, *Ecumenical Theology in Worship, Doctrine and Life: Essays Presented to Geoffrey Wainwright on his Sixtieth Birthday* (New York: OUP, 1999).

Dakin, Arthur, *Calvinism* (London: Duckworth, 1940).

—, *The Baptist View of Church and Ministry* (London: Baptist Union, 1944).

Dale, A.W.W., *The Life of R.W. Dale of Birmingham* (London: Hodder and Stoughton, 1899).

Dale, R.W., 'On some present aspects of theological thought among Congregationalists', in *The Congregationalist*, VI (1877), 1–15.

Davie, Martin, *British Quaker Theology since 1895* (Lampeter: The Edwin Mellen Press, 1997).

Davies, E.O., *Prolegomena to Systematic Theology* (London: Hodder and Stoughton, 1909).

Davies, Horton, review of J.S. Whale, *The Protestant Tradition*, in *The Congregational Quarterly*, XXXIV no. 2 (April 1956), 175–6.

Davies, Rupert E., *Methodists and Unity* (London: Mowbray, 1962).

—, *Methodism* (London: Epworth Press, 1963).

—, A.R. George and G. Rupp, eds., *A History of the Methodist Church in Great Britain*, III (London: Epworth Press, 1983).

Davison, W.T., *The Christian Conscience: A Contribution to Christian Ethics* (London: T. Woolmer, 1888).

—, *The Indwelling Spirit* (London: Hodder and Stoughton, 1911).

—, The Holy Spirit and divine immanence', in *London Theological Studies by Members of the Faculty of Theology in the University of London* (London: University of London Press, 1911), 247–83.

—, *The Historic Episcopate* (London: Epworth Press, 1919).

Dillistone, F.W., *C.H. Dodd, Interpreter of the New Testament* (Grand Rapids, MI: Eerdmans, 1977).

Dix, Kenneth, *Strict and Particular: English Strict and Particular Baptists in the Nineteenth Century* (Didcot: The Baptist Historical Society for the Strict Baptist Historical Society, 2001).

Drake, Philip, 'Joining the dots: Methodist membership and connectedness', in Clive Marsh, et al., eds., q.v., 131–41.

Drewery, Benjamin, *Origen and the Doctrine of Grace* (London: Epworth Press, 1960).

Drummond, James, *The Christian Revelation of God: A Sermon preached on October 27th 1889, at the First Religious Service held in connection with the establishment of Manchester New College at Oxford* (London: Williams & Norgate, 1889).

—, 'Religion and theology', in Richard Bartram, ed., *Religion and Life*, q.v., 1–40.

—, *Sermons on Christian Faith and Life* (London: Longmans, Green, 1879).

—, *Via, Veritas, Vita: Lectures on 'Christianity in its most simple and intelligible form'* (London: Williams and Norgate, 1894).

—, *The Pauline Benediction* (London: Philip Green, 1897).

—, *Some Thoughts on Christology* (London: Philip Green, 1902).

—, *Studies in Christian Doctrine* (London: Philip Green, 1908).

Drummond, James S., *Charles A. Berry, D.D., A Memoir* (London: Cassell, 1899).

Duthie, Charles S., *God in His World* (London: Independent Press, 1954).

—, *Outline of Christian Belief* (London: Lutterworth, 1968).

—, 'Ultimate triumph', in *Resurrection and Immortality*, q.v., 192–210.

—, ed., *Resurrection and Immortality* (London: Bagster, 1979).

Dykes, J.O., *The Divine Worker in Creation and Providence* (Edinburgh: T. & T. Clark, 1909).

Edwards, D. Miall, *Crist a Gwareiddiad* (Dolgellau: Hughes, 1921).

—, *Crefydd a Diwylliant* (Wrexham: Hughes, 1934).

Edwards, William, *A Handbook of Protestant Nonconformity, Designed mainly for Young People* (Bristol: W. Crofton Hemmons, 1901).

Evans, J. Young, 'The New Theology in Wales', in T. Stephens, ed., *Wales: To-day and To-morrow*, q.v., 28–31.

Evans, Percy W., 'Christ's intellectual authority', in W. Ridley Chesterton and P.W. Evans, *The Authority of Christ in a Lawless Age*, q.v., 19–30.

—, et al., *Infant Baptist To-day* (London: Carey Kingsgate Press, 1951).

Fairbairn, A.M., 'The text and the context', in *Proceedings of the Second International Congregational Council* (Boston: Samuel Usher, 1900), 64–75.

Farmer, H.H., *The World and God* (London: Nisbet, 1935).

—, *The Healing Cross* (London: Nisbet, 1938).

—, *Towards Belief in God* (London: SCM Press, 1942).

—, *God and Men* (London: Nisbet, 1948).

—, *Revelation and Religion* (London: Nisbet, 1954).

—, *The Word of Reconciliation* (London: Nisbet, 1966).

Fiddes, Paul S., *The Creative Suffering of God* (Oxford: Clarendon Press, 1988).

—, *Past Event and Present Salvation* (London: Darton, Longman & Todd, 1989).

—, *Participating in God: A Pastoral Doctrine of the Trinity* (London: Darton, Longman & Todd, 2000).

—, *Tracks and Traces: Baptist Identity in Church and Theology* (Carlisle: Paternoster, 2003).

Fitzgerald, W.B., *The Roots of Methodism* (London: Charles H. Kelly, 1903).

Flew, R. Newton, *The Idea of Perfection in Christian Theology: An Historical Study of the Christian Ideal for the Present Life* (London: OUP, 1934).

—, *Jesus and His Church* (London: Epworth Press, 1938).

—, and Rupert E. Davies, eds., *The Catholicity of Protestantism, being a report presented to His Grace the Archbishop of Canterbury by a group of Free Churchmen* (London: Lutterworth, 1951).

Forsyth, P.T., *The Charter of the Church: The Spiritual Principle of Nonconformity* (London: Alexander and Shepheard, 1896).

—, The Holy Father (1897), reprinted in *God the Holy Father* (London: Independent Press, 1957).

—, *Rome, Reform and Reaction* (London: Hodder and Stoughton, 1899).

—, 'The atonement in modern religious thought', in *The Atonement in Modern Religious Thought: A Theological Symposium* (London: James Clarke, 1900), 61–88.

—, 'The evangelical basis of Free Churchism', in *The Contemporary Review*, LXXXI, (January–June 1902), 680–95.

—, *Positive Preaching and the Modern Mind* (1907; repr. London: Independent Press, 1964).

—, 'Immanence and Incarnation', in C.H. Vine, ed., *The Old Faith and the New Theology*, q.v., 47–61.

—, *Missions in State and Church: Sermons and Addresses* (London: Hodder and Stoughton, 1908).

—, *The Cruciality of the Cross* (1909; repr. London: Independent Press, 1948).

—, *The Person and Place of Jesus Christ* (1909; repr. London: Independent Press, 1946).

—, *The Work of Christ* (1910; repr. London: Independent Press, 1938).

—, *Faith, Freedom and the Future* (1912; repr. London: Independent Press, 1955).

—, 'Faith, metaphysic, and incarnation', in *Methodist Review*, XCVII (September 1915), 696–719.

—, *The Christian Ethic of War* (London: Longmans, Green, 1916).

—, *The Soul of Prayer* (1916; repr. London: Independent Press, 1949).

—, *The Church and the Sacraments* (1917; repr. London: Independent Press, 1947).

—, *The Justification of God* (1917; repr. London: Independent Press, 1948).

—, *This Life and the Next* (1918; repr. London: Independent Press, 1946).

—, *Congregationalism and Reunion* (London: Independent Press, 1952).

Franks, R.S., *A History of the Doctrine of the Work of Christ in its Ecclesiastical Development*, 2 vols. (London: Hodder and Stoughton, [1918]).

—, review of F.C.N. Hicks, *The Fullness of Sacrifice*, in *The Congregational Quarterly* (October 1930), 505–8.

—, *The Atonement* (London: OUP, 1934).

—, 'Trends in recent theology', in *The Congregational Quarterly*, XXIII no. 1 (January 1945), 19–29.

—, review of D. Jenkins, *The Gift of the Ministry*, in *The Congregational Quarterly*, XXV no. 4 (September 1947), 366–7.

—, *The Doctrine of the Trinity* (London: Duckworth, 1953).

Garrard, L.A., *Athens or Jerusalem? A Study in Christian Comprehension* (London: Allen & Unwin, 1965).

Garvie, A.E., *The Ritschlian Theology* (Edinburgh: T. and T. Clark, 1899).

—, *Studies in the Inner Life of Jesus* (London: Hodder and Stoughton, 1907).

—, *The Christian Certainty amid the Modern Perplexity: Essays Constructive and Critical towards the Solution of some Current Theological Problems* (London: Hodder and Stoughton, 1910).

—, *The Christian Doctrine of the Godhead, or, The Apostolic Benediction as the Christian Creed* (London: Hodder and Stoughton, 1925).

—, 'Fifty years' retrospect', in *The Congregational Quarterly*, VII no. 1 (January 1929), 18–25.

—, 'The Free Churches in England', in James Marchant, ed., *The Reunion of Christendom*, q.v., 129–48.

—, *The Christian Belief in God in Relation to Religion and Philosophy* (London: Hodder and Stoughton, 1932).

—, *The Fatherly Rule of God* (London: Hodder and Stoughton, 1934).

—, *Revelation Through History and Experience: A Study of the Historical Basis of the Revelation of the Godhead* (London: Ivor Nicholson and Watson, 1934).

—, *The Christian Faith* (London: Duckworth, 1936).

—, *Memories and Meanings of My Life* (London: Allen & Unwin, 1938).

—, 'Freedom of the Church in Christ', in *The Congregational Quarterly*, XX no. 2 (April 1942), 108–14.

—, 'Placarding the Cross: the theology of P.T. Forsyth', in *The Congregational Quarterly*, XXI no. 4 (October 1943), 343–52.

Gilmore, A., Neville Clark and W.M.S. West, *The Pattern of the Church: A Baptist View* (London: Lutterworth, 1963).

Glanville, Norman, *Why We Still Say No* (London: The Voice of Methodism, 1964).

Glover, Willis B., *Evangelical Nonconformists and Higher Criticism in the Nineteenth Century* (London: Independent Press, 1954).

Goldman, Ronald, *Readiness for Religion: A Basis for Developmental Religious Education* (London: Routledge and Kegan Paul, 1965).

Goodall, Norman, 'Some Congregational pathfinders in the ecumenical movement', in *Transactions of the Congregational Historical Society*, XX no. 6 (October 1967), 184–99.

Goodrich, Albert, *A Primer of Congregationalism* (1894; repr. London: Congregational Union of England and Wales, 1902).

Gore, Charles, *The Old Religion and the New Theology* (London: John Murray, 1907).

Goulder, Michael, ed., *Incarnation and Myth: The Debate Continued* (London: SCM Press, 1979).

Grieve, A.J., 'Congregationalism's contribution to theology. Some materials for a bibliography', in Albert Peel, ed., *Essays Congregational and Catholic*, q.v., 357–81.

Griffith-Jones, Ebenezer, *The Challenge of Christianity to a World at War* (London: Duckworth, 1915).

—, *Faith and Immortality: A Study of the Christian Doctrine of the Life to Come* (London: Duckworth, 1917).

—, *Providence – Divine and Human: A Study of the World-Order in the Light of Modern Thought* (London: Hodder and Stoughton, 1925).

—, *The Dominion of Man* (London: Hodder and Stoughton, 1926).

Gunton, Colin E., *Becoming and Being: The Doctrine of God in Charles Hartshorne and Karl Barth* (Oxford: OUP, 1978).

—, *Yesterday and Today: A Study of Continuities in Christology* (London: Darton, Longman & Todd, 1983).

—, *Enlightenment and Alienation: An Essay towards a Trinitarian Theology* (Basingstoke: Marshall, Morgan & Scott, 1985).

—, *The Actuality of Atonement: A Study of Metaphor, Rationality and the Christian Tradition* (Edinburgh: T. & T. Clark, 1988).

—, 'Trinity, ontology and anthropology: towards a renewal of the doctrine of the *imago dei*', in Christoph Schwöbel and Colin E. Gunton, eds., *Persons, Divine and Human*, q.v., 47–61.

—, *Christ and Creation* (London: Paternoster, 1992).

—, *The Promise of Trinitarian Theology* (Edinburgh: T. & T. Clark, 2nd edn, 1997).

—, *Father, Son and Holy Spirit: Toward a Fully Trinitarian Theology* (London: T. & T. Clark, 2003).

—, and Daniel Hardy, eds., *On Being the Church: Essays on the Christian Community* (Edinburgh: T. & T. Clark, 1989).

Habgood, John, *Church and State in a Secular Age* (London: Darton, Longman and Todd, 1983).

Hall, Alfred, *Beliefs of a Unitarian* (London: The Lindsey Press, [1910]).

Hamilton, Kenneth, *The Protestant Way* (London: Epworth Press, 1956).

Harrison, A.W., *Arminianism* (London: Duckworth, 1937).

—, B. Aquila Barber, G.G. Hornby and E. Tegla Davies, *The Methodist Church: Its Origin, Divisions, and Reunion* (London: Methodist Publishing House; Holborn Publishing House; and Henry Hooks, 1932).

Hart, Trevor, ed., *Justice the True and Only Mercy: Essays on the Life and Theology of Peter Taylor Forsyth* (Edinburgh: T. & T. Clark, 1994).

Hartwell, Herbert, *The Theology of Karl Barth: An Introduction* (London: Duckworth, 1965).

Hayden, Roger, 'Still at the crossroads? Revd. J.H. Shakespeare and ecumenism', in K.W. Clements, ed., *Baptists in the Twentieth Century*, q.v., 31–54.

Haymes, Brian, *A Question of Identity: Reflections on Baptist Principles and Practice* (Leeds: Yorkshire Baptist Association, 1986).

—, *The Concept of the Knowledge of God* (London: Macmillan, 1988).

—, *Looking at the Cross* (Redhill: International Bible Reading Association,1988).

—, *Looking at Advent* (Redhill: International Bible Reading Association, 1989).

—, *Looking at Pentecost* (Redhill: International Bible Reading Association, 1991).

—, *Looking at Easter and Ascension* (Redhill: International Bible Reading Association, 1992).

Healey, F.G., *Religion and Reality: The Theology of John Oman* (Edinburgh: Oliver & Boyd, 1965).

—, ed., *Prospect for Theology: Essays in Honour of H.H. Farmer* (Welwyn: Nisbet, 1966).

Hebblethwaite, Brian, 'The doctrine of the atonement. (5) Does it make moral sense?' *The Epworth Review*, XIX no. 3 (September 1992), 63–74.

Hewgill, W., 'The confession of a County Union secretary', in D. Macfadyen, ed., *Constructive Congregational Ideals*, q.v., 203–6.

Heywood-Thomas, John, *Subjectivity and Paradox: A Study of Kierkegaard's Contribution to the Philosophy of Religion* (Oxford: Blackwell, 1957).

—, *Paul Tillich: An Appraisal* (London: SCM Press, 1963).

—, *Paul Tillich* (London: Carey Kingsgate Press, 1965).

—, *Tillich* (London: Continuum, 2000).

Hick, John H., *God and the Universe of Faiths* (London: Macmillan, 1974).

—, *God has Many Names* (London: Macmillan, 1982).

—, *Problems of Religious Pluralism* (London: Macmillan, 1985).

—, *An Interpretation of Religion* (Basingstoke: Macmillan, 1989).

—, ed., *The Myth of God Incarnate* (London: SCM Press, 1977).

Hodges, H.A., *The Pattern of Atonement* (London: SCM Press, 1955).

Hodgkins, Harold, *The Congregational Way: Apostolic Legacy, Ministry, Unity, Freedom* (Nottingham: The Congregational Federation, 1982).

Hollowell, J. Hirst, *What Nonconformists Stand For* (London: The Free Church Library, 1901).

Holmes, Stephen R., *God of Grace and God of Glory: An Account of the Theology of Jonathan Edwards* (Edinburgh: T. & T. Clark, 2000).

Hostler, John, *Unitarianism* (London: Hibbert Trust, 1981).

Hugen, Melvin D., 'The shaping influence of the Heidelberg Catechism on the pastoral care of the Church', in *Reformed Review*, LV no. 2 (Winter 2001–2002), 133–8.

Hughes, H. Maldwyn, *The Theology of Experience* (London: Charles H. Kelly, 1915).

—, *What is the Atonement? A Study of the Passion of God in Christ* (London: James Clarke, 1924).

—, *Christian Foundations: An Introduction to Christian Doctrine* (London: Epworth Press, 1927).

Hughes, T. Hywel, 'A Barthian before Barth?' *The Congregational Quarterly*, XII no. 3 (July 1934), 308–15.

—, *The Atonement: Modern Theories of the Doctrine* (London: Allen & Unwin, 1949).

Humphries, A.L. *The Holy Spirit in Faith and Experience* (London: W.A. Hammond, Primitive Methodist Publishing House, 1911).

Huxtable, W. John F., 'Introduction' to John Owen, *The True Nature of a Gospel Church and its Government* (London: James Clarke, 1947).

—, *The Faith that is in Us* (London: Independent Press, 1953).

—, *Christian Unity: Some of the Issues* (London: Independent Press, 1967).

—, 'The United Reformed Church', in *The Expository Times*, LXXXIV no. 1 (October 1972), 4–6.

—, *A New Hope for Christian Unity* (London: Fount Paperbacks, 1977).

—, *As it Seemed to Me* (London: The United Reformed Church, 1990).

Jacks, L.P., *Religious Perplexities* (London: Hodder and Stoughton, 1923).

—, *A Living Universe* (London: Hodder and Stoughton, 1924).

James, J. Courtenay, *The Philosophy of Dissent: Analytical Outlines of some Free Church Principles* (London: James Clarke, 1900).

[James, John Gwyn], obituary of E. Griffith-Jones, *The Congregational Year Book* (1943), 428.

James, T.T., *The Work and Administration of a Congregational Church* (London: Congregational Union of England and Wales, 1925).

Jenkins, Daniel T., *The Nature of Catholicity* (London: Faber & Faber, 1942).

—, *Prayer and the Service of God* (London: Faber & Faber, 1944).

—, *The Church Meeting and Democracy* (London: Independent Press, 1944).

—, *The Gift of Ministry* (London: Faber & Faber, 1947).

—, *Tradition and the Spirit* (London: Faber & Faber, 1951).

—, *Congregationalism: A Restatement* (London: Faber & Faber, 1954).

—, *The Strangeness of the Church* (Garden City, NY: Doubleday, 1955).

—, *The Protestant Ministry* (London: Faber & Faber, 1958).

—, *Equality and Excellence* (London: SCM Press, 1961).

—, *The Christian Belief in God* (London: Faber & Faber, 1964).

—, *Beyond Religion* (London: SCM Press, 1966).

Jessop, T.E., *An Introduction to Christian Doctrine* (London: Nelson, 1960).

Jones, Bernard E., 'Society and church in Wesleyan Methodism, 1878–93', in *Proceedings of the Wesley Historical Society*, XXXVI pt. 5 (June 1968), 134–8.

Jones, J.D., *Reasons Why for Congregationalists* (Bournemouth: Bright's Stores, 1904).

—, *Things Most Surely Believed* (London: James Clarke, 1908).

—, *Congregational High Churchmanship: Three Discourses delivered during his Visit to Australasia, issued by the Congregational Union of New South Wales* (n.d.).

Jones, Keith G., 'Rethinking Baptist ecclesiology', in *Journal of European Baptist Studies*, I no. 1 (September 2000), 4–18.

Jones, R. Tudur, *Congregationalism in Wales*, edited by Robert Pope (Cardiff: University of Wales Press, 2004).

Jordan, E.K.H., *Free Church Unity: History of the Free Church Council Movement 1896–1941* (London: Lutterworth, 1956).

Kaye, Elaine, 'Cecil John Cadoux', in *The Oxford Dictionary of National Biography* (Oxford: OUP, 2004).

Kenworthy, Fred, *Freedom, Authority and Liberal Christianity* (London: The Lindsey Press, 1954).

—, 'A Unitarian comment' [on the Anglican-Methodist conversations], *The London Quarterly and Holborn Review* (October 1963), 298–9.

Kevan, Ernest F., *The Saving Work of the Holy Spirit* (London: Pickering and Inglis, 1953).

—, *The Grace of Law: A Study in Puritan Theology* (London: Carey Kingsgate Press, 1964).

Kielty, J., *British Unitarianism, Past, Present and Future* (London: The Lindsey Press, 1960).

Kingston, A. Richard, *God in One Person* (London: Routledge, 1993).

Lewis, Thomas, 'Higher Criticism and Welsh preaching', in T. Stephens, ed., *Wales: To-day and To-morrow*, q.v., 24–27.

Lidgett, J.S., *The Spiritual Principle of the Atonement* (London: Charles H. Kelly, 1897).

—, *The Fatherhood of God* (Edinburgh: T. & T. Clark, 1902).

—, *Apostolic Ministry: Sermons and Addresses* (London: Charles H. Kelly, 1909).

—, *God and the World: Essays in Christian Theism* (London: Epworth Press, 1943).

Lofthouse, W.F., *Ethics and Atonement* (London: Epworth Press, 1906).

Long, Arthur, review of Marcus Braybrooke, *Pilgrimage of Hope*, in *Faith and Freedom*, XLV pt. 3 (Autumn 1992), 121–3.

—, *Current Trends in British Unitarianism* (Belfast: Ulster Unitarian Christian Association, 1997).

—, 'Unitarian Thought in the twentieth century – A preliminary survey', in Part I: *Transactions of the Unitarian Historical Society*, XXII no. 3 (April 2001), 247–60; Part II: ibid., XXIII no. 1 (April 2003), 445–64.

Lord, F. Townley, *Conquest of Death: A Christian Interpretation of Immortality* (London: SCM Press, 1940).

—, *Baptist World Fellowship: A Short History of the Baptist World Alliance* (London: Carey Kingsgate Press, 1955).

Macarthur, Arthur L., 'The background to the formation of The United Reformed Church (Presbyterian and Congregational) in England and Wales in 1972', in *The Journal of the United Reformed Church*, IV no. 1 (October 1987), 3–22.

—, 'The Presbyterian road to 1972', in C. Binfield, ed., *Reformed and Renewed*, q.v., 4–7.

McCaig, Archibald, *Doctrinal Brevities* (London: Marshall, Morgan & Scott, 1933).

McCurdy, Leslie, *Attributes and Atonement: The Holy Love of God in the Theology of P.T. Forsyth* (Carlisle: Paternoster, 1999).

McDonald, H.D., *Theories of Revelation: An Historical Study* (London: Allen & Unwin, 1963).

Macfadyen, Dugald, ed., *Constructive Congregational Ideals: A Series of Addresses and Essays illustrating the Growth of Corporate Life and Feeling in the Congregational Churches during Forty Years, and the Significance of this Movement as a True Modern Development of Early Free Church Ideals* (London: H.R. Allenson, 1902).

McGonigle, Herbert, *Sufficient Saving Grace: John Wesley's Evangelical Arminianism* (Carlisle: Paternoster, 2001).

Mackintosh, Robert, 'Apologetics', 'Theism' and 'Theology', in *Encyclopaedia Britannica* (1911).

—, *Christianity and Sin* (London: Duckworth, 1913).

—, *Albrecht Ritschol and His School* (London: Chapman and Hall, 1915).

—, *Historic Theories of Atonement* (Glasgow: Maclehose, 1920).

—, 'The genius of Congregationalism', in A. Peel, ed., *Essays Congregational and Catholic*, q.v., 103–25.

Maltby, W.R., *Christ and His Cross* (London: Epworth Press, 1935).

Manning, Bernard Lord, *Essays in Orthodox Dissent* (1939; repr. London: Independent Press, 1952).

—, *The Protestant Dissenting Deputies* (Cambridge: CUP, 1952).

Manson, T.W., *The Church's Ministry* (London: Hodder and Stoughton, 1948).

—, *Ministry and Priesthood: Christ's and Ours: Two Lectures* (London: Epworth Press, 1958).

Marchant, James, ed., *The Coming Renaissance* (London: Kegan Paul, Trench and Trubner, 1923).

—, *The Reunion of Christendom* (London: Cassell, 1929).

Markham, Ian, 'Looking back on the 20th century: 3. Theological reflections', in *The Expository Times*, CX no. 12 (September 1999), 384–8.

Marsh, Clive, 'Appealing to "experience": what does it mean?', in *Unmasking Methodist Theology*, q.v., 118–30.

—, B. Beck, A. Shier-Jones and H. Wareing, eds., *Unmasking Methodist Theology* (London: Continuum, 2004).

Marsh, John, 'Obedience to the Gospel in terms of churchmanship and church order', in J. Marsh, ed., *Congregationalism To-day*, q.v., 45–61.

—, *For the Church Member* (London: Independent Press, 1946).

—, ed., *Congregationalism To-day* (London: Independent Press, 1943).

Marshall, I. Howard, 'Strange prospects for reconciliation', in *The Christian and Christianity Today* (11 August 1967), 16–17.

—, *Beyond the Bible: Moving from Scripture to Theology* (Carlisle: Paternoster, 2004).

Martin, A.D., *The Principle of the Congregational Churches* (London: Congregational Union of England and Wales, 1927).

Martin, Paul, and David Tennant, 'Believer' baptism, the fellowship of believers and faith development', in *The Baptist Quarterly*, XXXIX nos 2 and 3 (April and July 2001), 96–104, 121–31.

Martineau, James, *The Seat of Authority in Religion* (London: Longmans, 1890).

Mascall, E.L., *Up and Down in Adria: Some considerations of Soundings* (London: Faith Press, 1963).

Mayor, Stephen, 'Congregationalism and the Reformed tradition', in *The Reformed World*, XXXIII no. 5 (March 1975), 196–208.

Mellone, S.H., *Converging Lines of Religious Thought* (London: Philip Green, 1903).

—, *The Immortal Hope: Present Aspects of the Problem of immortality* (London: The Lindsey Press, 1910).

—, *Eternal Life Here and Hereafter* (London: The Lindsey Press, 1916).

—, 'The moral equivalent of war', in J. Estlin Carpenter, ed., *Ethical and Religious Problems of the War*, q.v., 163–75.

—, *The Religion of Authority and the Religion of Reason* (London: The Lindsey Press, 1924).

—, 'Unitarian Christianity in the 20th Century' in J. Estlin Carpenter, ed., *Freedom and Truth: Modern Views of Unitarian Christianity*, q.v.

Micklem, Nathaniel, *The Open Light: An Enquiry into Faith and Reality* (London: Headley, 1919).

—, *What is the Faith?* (London: Hodder and Stoughton, 1936).

—, *Congregationalism To-day* (London: Hodder and Stoughton, 1937).

—, *The Creed of a Christian* (London: SCM Press, 1940).

—, *Congregationalism and the Church Catholic* (London: Independent Press, 1943).

—, *The Doctrine of our Redemption* (London: Eyre and Spottiswoode, 1948).

—, *Ultimate Questions* (London: Geoffrey Bles, 1955).

—, *The Abyss of Truth* (London: Geoffrey Bles, 1956).

—, *The Place of Understanding and Other Papers* (London: Geoffrey Bles, 1963).

—, *The Art of Thought* (London: Epworth, 1970).

Mitton, C.L., 'Honest to God', in *The Expository Times*, LXXIV (June 1963, 276–9).

Moore, A.E. Clucas, *What is the Voice of Methodism?* (Camborne, n.d.).

Morgan, D. Densil, 'The early reception of Karl Barth's theology in Britain: A supplementary view', in *Scottish Journal of Theology*, LIV no. 4 (2001), 504–27.

Morgan, Philip, '1972 and the Churches of Christ', in C. Binfield, ed., *Reformed and Renewed*, q.v., 23–29.

Murray, A. Victor, *Personal Experience and the Historic Faith* (London: Epworth Press, 1939).

Newbigin, J.E. Lesslie, *The Household of God* (London: SCM Press, 1953).

—, *Honest Religion for Secular Man* (London: SCM Press, 1966).

—, *The Finality of Christ* (London: SCM Press, 1969).

—, *The Reunion of the Church* (London: SCM Press, 1948).

—, *The Open Secret* (London: SPCK, 1978).

Newton, John A., 'Protestant Nonconformists and ecumenism', in Alan P.F. Sell and Anthony R. Cross, eds., *Protestant Nonconformity in the Twentieth Century*, q.v., ch. 12.

Nicholson, J.F.V., 'Towards a theology of episcope among Baptists', in *The Baptist Quarterly*, XXX nos 6 and 7 (April and July 1984), 265–81, 319–31.

Nightingale, Benjamin, *Congregationalism Reexamined* (London: Congregational Union of England and Wales, 1918).

Nuttall, Geoffrey F., *The Holy Spirit in Puritan Faith and Experience* (Oxford: Blackwell, 1946).

—, *The Reality of Heaven* (London: Independent Press, 1953).

—, review of J.S. Whale, *The Protestant Tradition*, in *The Congregational Quarterly*, XXXIV no. 1 (January 1956), 74–75.

—, 'Relations between Presbyterians and Congregationalists in England', in *Studies in the Puritan Tradition, a Joint Supplement of the Congregational Historical Society Transactions and the Presbyterian Historical Society Journal* (December 1964), 1–7.

—, *The Holy Spirit and Ourselves* (London: Epworth Press, 1966).

Oman, John, *Vision and Authority* (London: Hodder and Stoughton, 1902).

—, *The Church and the Divine Order* (London: Hodder and Stoughton, 1911).

—, *Grace and Personality* (Cambridge: CUP, 1917).

—, *The Natural and the Supernatural* (Cambridge: CUP, 1931).

—, *Honest Religion* (Cambridge: CUP, 1941).

Owen, H.P., *Revelation and Existence: A Study in the Theology of Rudolf Bultmann* (Cardiff: University of Wales Press, 1957).

—, *Concepts of Deity* (London: Macmillan, 1971).

—, *Christian Theism: A Study of its Basic Principles* (Edinburgh: T. & T. Clark, 1984).

Owen, John, *The Works of John Owen*, edited by William H. Goold, (Johnstone and Hunter, 1850–53, repr. London: The Banner of Truth Trust, 1996).

Packer, J.I., ed., *The Church of England and the Methodist Church* (Marcham: Marcham Manor Press, 1963).

Pailin, David A., *A New Theology?* (London: Epworth Press, 1964).

—, *God and the Processes of Reality: Foundations of a Credible Theism* (London: Routledge, 1989).

—, *Probing the Foundations: A Study in Theistic Reconstruction* (Kampen: Kok Pharos, 1994).

Partridge, Christopher H., *H.H. Farmer's Theological Interpretation of Religion: Towards a Personalist Theory of Religions* (Lampeter: The Edwin Mellen Press, 1998).

Paul, Robert S., 'Congregationalism and Presbyterianism: X. Theological trends', in *The Christian World* (15 April 1954), 2.

—, *The Atonement and the Sacraments* (London: Hodder and Stoughton, 1961).

Paul, S.F., *Historical Sketch of the Gospel Standard Baptists* (London: Gospel Standard Publications, 1961).

Payne, Ernest A., *The Fellowship of Believers: Baptist Thought and Practice Yesterday and Today* (London: Kingsgate Press, 1944).

—, *The Free Churches and the State* (London: Independent Press, 1952).

—, 'Baptist-Congregational relationships', in *The Congregational Quarterly*, XXXIII no. 3 (July 1955), 216–26.

—, *The Baptist Union: A Short History* (London: The Carey Kingsgate Press, 1959).

—, *Free Churchmen, Repentant and Unrepentant and Other Papers* (London: Carey Kingsgate Press, 1965), ch. 5.

—, 'Baptists and Christian initiation', in *The Baptist Quarterly*, XXIV no. 4 (October 1975), 147–57.

Peake, A.S., *Recollections and Appreciations*, edited by W.F. Howard (London: Epworth Press, 1938).

Peel, Albert, *The Congregational Principle* (London: James Clarke, 1917).

—, *The Free Churches 1903–1926*, being an additional chapter to a reprint of C. Silvester Horne's *A Popular History of the Free Churches* (London: Congregational Union of England and Wales, 1927).

—, *Inevitable Congregationalism* (London: Independent Press, 1937).

—, *Robert Forman Horton* (London: Allen & Unwin, 1937).

—, *Christian Freedom: The Contribution of Congregationalism to the Church and to the World* (London: Independent Press, 1939).

—, 'Progress', (a set of nine book reviews) in *The Congregational Quarterly*, I no. 2 (April 1923), 229–33.

—, ed., *Essays Congregational and Catholic issued in Commemoration of the Centenary of the Congregational Union of England and Wales* (London: CUEW, [1931]).

Peel, David R., *Reforming Theology* (London: The United Reformed Church, 2002).

Percy, Martyn, 'Editorial: The big issue: is there a third way for "establishment"?', in *Modern Believing*, XLII no. 2 (1999), 2–5.

Perkins, H.W., *The Doctrine of Christian or Evangelical Perfection* (London: Epworth Press, 1927).

Pierard, Richard V., *Baptists Together in Christ 1905–2005* (Birmingham, Alabama: Samford University Press, 2005).

Phillips, George, 'Freedom in Religious Thought', in *The Fourth Freedom* (London: Independent Press, 1943).

Plant, Michael and Alan Tovey, eds., *Telling Another Generation* (Beverley: An Evangelical Fellowship of Congregational Churches, 1994).

Platt, Frederick W., *Immanence and Christian Thought: Implications and Questions* (London: Charles H. Kelly, 1915).

Poole-Connor, E.J., *Evangelicalism in England* (Worthing: Henry E. Walter, rev. ed., 1966).

Powicke, F.J., 'Historic Congregationalism in Britain', in *Proceedings of the Third International Congregational Council* (London: Congregational Union of England and Wales, 1908), 260–9.

—, *David Worthington Simon* (London: Hodder & Stoughton, 1912).

Pradervand, Marcel, *A Century of Service: A History of the World Alliance of Reformed Churches 1875–1975* (Edinburgh: The Saint Andrew Press, 1975).

Price, E.J., *A Handbook of Congregationalism* (1924; repr. London: Independent Press, 1957).

—, *Baptists, Congregationalists and Presbyterians* (1933; repr. London: Independent Press, 1945).

Pryce, R. Vaughan, 'The redemptive work of the Lord Jesus Christ', in *The Ancient Faith in Modern Light* (Edinburgh: T. & T. Clark, 1897), 193–226.

Punshon, John, *Letter to a Universalist* (Walingford: Pendle Hill Publications, 1989).

—, 'The significance of tradition. Reflections on the writing of Quaker history', in *Journal of the Friends Historical Society*, LX no. 2 (2004, issued 2005), 77–96.

Rack, Henry D., 'Wesleyanism and "the world" in the later nineteenth century', in *Proceedings of the Wesley Historical Society*, XLII pt. 2 (September 1979), 35–54.

Ramsey, A.M., *From Gore to Temple* (London: Longmans, 1960).

Randall, Ian M., *Evangelical Experiences: A Study in the Spirituality of English Evangelicalism 1918–1939* (Carlisle: Paternoster, 1999).

—, *Educating Evangelicalism: The Origins, Development and Impact of London Bible College* (Carlisle: Paternoster, 2000).

Rashdall, Hastings, *The Idea of Atonement in Christian Theology* (London: Macmillan, 1919).

Rees, Thomas, *The Holy Spirit in Thought and Experience* (London: Duckworth, 1915).

Reynolds, G.G., '75 years of the General Superintendency – what next?' *The Baptist Quarterly*, XXXIV no. 5 (January 1992), 229–39.

Ritschl, Dietrich, 'Praising God as interpreter and critic of history', in David S. Cunningham, et al, eds., *Ecumenical Worship, Doctrine and Life*, q.v., 69–77.

Roberts, Harold, 'The Holy Spirit and the Trinity' in *The Doctrine of the Holy Spirit* (London: Epworth, 1937), 105–28.

Robertson, E.H., *Dietrich Bonhoeffer* (London: Carey Kingsgate Press, 1964).

Robinson, H. Wheeler, *Baptist Principles* (London: Kingsgate Press, 1925).

—, *The Life and Faith of the Baptists* (London: Methuen, 1927).

—, *The Christian Experience of the Holy Spirit* (1928; repr. London: Collins Fontana, 1962).

—, *The Veil of God* (London: Nisbet, 1936).

Robinson, J.A.T., *Honest to God* (London: SCM Press, 1963).

Robinson, William, *Everyday Chemistry* (London: Methuen, 1919).

—, *Essays on Christian Unity* (London: James Clarke, 1923).

—, *What the Churches of Christ Stand For* (Birmingham: Churches of Christ Publishing Company, 1926).

—, *Whither Theology? Some Essential Biblical Patterns* (London: Lutterworth, 1940).

Robinson, W. Gordon, 'A Congregationalist comment' [on the Anglican-Methodist conversations], *The London Quarterly and Holborn Review* (October 1963), 294–6.

—, *Jesus, Lord and Saviour* (Nutfield, Surrey: Denholme House Press, 1975).

Ross, J.M., *Presbyterian Bishops?* (London: Presbyterian Publishing Committee, [1952]).

Routley, Erik, review of J.A.T. Robinson, *Honest to God*, in *The British Weekly* (21 March 1963) and further comment in ibid. (16 May 1963).

Rupp, E. Gordon, *The Righteousness of God* (London: Hodder and Stoughton, 1953).

—, *Methodism in Relation to the Protestant Tradition* (London: Epworth Press, 1954).

—, *Protestant Catholicity* (London: Epworth Press, 1960).

—, 'A dissentient view of the dissentient view concerning Scripture and Tradition', in *The London Quarterly and Holborn Review* (July 1963), 187–92.

—, *Consideration Reconsidered* (London: Epworth Press, 1964).

—, *Luther's Progress to the Diet of Worms* (New York: Harper and Row, 1964).

—, 'Meadley's Medley', in *The London Quarterly and Holborn Review*, (April 1964), 154–6.

—, *The Old Reformation and the New* (London: Epworth Press, 1967).

Ruston, Alan, 'Unitarian ecumenical relations in England in the twentieth century', in *Faith and Freedom*, LIV pt. 2 (Autumn–Winter 2001), 92–103.

—, 'Protestant Nonconformist attitudes towards the First World War', in Alan P.F. Sell and Anthony R. Cross, eds., *Protestant Nonconformity in the Twentieth Century*, q.v., ch. 9.

Sangster, W.E., *Methodism can be Born Again* (London: Hodder and Stoughton, 1938).

Sansbury, C. Kenneth, 'Episcope in the Anglican communion', in *Friends of Reunion Bulletin*, no. 48 (January 1954), 24–30.

Schwöbel, Christoph, and Colin E. Gunton, eds, *Persons, Divine and Human* (Edinburgh: T. & T. Clark, 1999).

Selbie, W.B., *Aspects of Christ* (London: Hodder and Stoughton, 1909).

—, *Schleiermacher: A Critical and Historical Study* (London: Chapman and Hall, 1913).

—, *Congregationalism* (London: Methuen, 1927).

—, *Faith and Life* (London: Hodder and Stoughton, 1934).

—, *The Fatherhood of God* (London: Duckworth, 1936).

—, *Faith and Fact* (London: James Clarke, [1937]).

—, *The Validity of Christian Belief* (London: Nicholson and Watson, 1939).

—, *Freedom in the Faith: A Plea for a Liberal Theology* (London: Independent Press, 1943).

Sell, Alan P.F., 'Friends and philosophy', in *The Friends Quarterly*, XVIII nos. 1 and 2 (April and July 1973), 72–82, 111–22.

—, *Robert Mackintosh: Theologian of Integrity* (Bern: Peter Lang, 1977).

—, *God Our Father* (1980; repr. Shippensburg, PA: Ragged Edge Press, 2000).

—, *The Great Debate: Calvinism, Arminianism and Salvation* (1982; repr. Eugene, OR: Wipf & Stock, 1998).

—, *Responding to Baptism, Eucharist and Ministry: A Word to the Reformed Churches* (Geneva: World Alliance of Reformed Churches, 1984).

—, *Saints: Visible, Orderly and Catholic: The Congregational Idea of the Church* (Geneva: World Alliance of Reformed Churches and Allison park, PA: Pickwick Publications, 1986).

—, 'Some Reformed responses to Baptism, Eucharist and Ministry', in *The Reformed World*, XXXIX no. 3 (September 1986), 549–65.

—, *Theology in Turmoil: The Roots, Course and Significance of the Conservative-Liberal Debate in Modern Theology* (1986; repr. Eugene, OR: Wipf & Stock, 1998).

—, *Defending and Declaring the Faith: Some Scottish Examples 1860–1920* (Exeter: Paternoster and Colorado Springs: Helmers & Howard, 1987).

—, *The Philosophy of Religion 1875–1980* (1988; repr. Bristol: Thoemmes Press, 1996).

—, review of C.E. Gunton and D.W. Hardy, eds., *On Being the Church*, q.v., *The Ecumenical Review*, XLI no. 4 (October 1989), 626–9.

—, *Aspects of Christian Integrity* (1990; repr. Eugene, OR: Wipf & Stock, 1998).

—, *Dissenting Thought and the Life of the Churches: Studies in an English Tradition* (Lewiston, NY: The Edwin Mellen Press, 1990).

—, *A Reformed, Evangelical, Catholic Theology: The Contribution of the World Alliance of Reformed Churches 1875–1982* (1990; repr. Eugene, OR: Wipf & Stock, 1998).

—, review of C. Gunton, *The Actuality of Atonement*, in *The Irish Theological Quarterly*, LVII no. 1 (1991), 82–84.

—, *Commemorations: Studies in Christian Thought and History* (1993; repr. Eugene, OR: Wipf & Stock, 1998).

—, *Philosophical Idealism and Christian Belief* (Cardiff: University of Wales Press and New York: St Martin's Press, 1995).

—, *John Locke and the Eighteenth-Century Divines* (Cardiff: University of Wales Press, 1997).

—, review of D.A. Pailin, *Probing the Foundations*, in *Calvin Theological Journal*, XXXIII no. 1 (April 1998), 215–6.

—, review of G. Wainwright, *Methodists in Dialog*, in *The Ecumenical Review*, LI no. 2 (April 1999), 224–7.

—, *Christ Our Saviour* (Shippensburg, PA: Ragged Edge Press, 2000).

—, *God Our Father* (1980; repr. Shippensburg, PA: Ragged Edge Press, 2000), 67–69.

—, *The Spirit Our Life* (Shippensburg, PA: Ragged Edge Press, 2000).

—, 'Reformed identity: a non-issue of catholic significance', in *Reformed Review*, LVI no. 1 (Autumn 2000), 17–27.

—, *Confessing and Commending the Faith: Historic Witness and Apologetic Method* (Cardiff: University of Wales Press, 2002).

—, 'Establishment as a theological issue: the Dissenting witness', in *Theology*, CVI (July/August 2003), 237–49.

—, *Philosophy, Dissent and Nonconformity 1698–1920* (Cambridge: James Clarke, 2004).

—, *Enlightenment, Ecumenism, Evangel: Theological Themes and Thinkers 1550–2000* (Carlisle: Paternoster, 2005).

—, *Testimony and Tradition: Studies in Reformed and Dissenting Thought* (Aldershot: Ashgate, 2005).

—, ed., *P.T. Forsyth: Theologian for a New Millennium* (London: The United Reformed Church, 2000).

—, and Anthony R. Cross, eds., *Protestant Nonconformity in the Twentieth Century* (Carlisle: Paternoster, 2003).

Shakespeare, J.H., *The Churches at the Crossroads: A Study in Church Unity* (London: Williams and Norgate, 1918).

—, 'The great need', in J.H. Marchant, ed., *The Coming Renaissance*, q.v., 79–92.

Shepherd, Peter, *The Making of a Modern Denomination: John Howard Shakespeare and the English Baptists, 1898–1924* (Carlisle: Paternoster, 2002).

—, *The Making of a Northern Baptist College* (Manchester: Northern Baptist College, 2004).

Shillito, Edward, *The Hope and Mission of the Free Churches* (Edinburgh: T.C. and E.C. Jack, n.d.).

Simon, D.W., *The Redemption of Man: Discussions Bearing on the Atonement* (Edinburgh: T. & T. Clark, 1889).

—, 'The present direction of theological thought in the Congregational churches of Great Britain', in *Proceedings of the International Congregational Council* (London: James Clarke, 1891), 77–85.

—, *Reconciliation by Incarnation* (Edinburgh: T. & T. Clark, 1898).

Simpson, P. Carnegie, *The Evangelical Church Catholic* (London: Hodder and Stoughton, 1934).

Smith, C. Ryder, *The Christian Experience: A Study in the Theology of Fellowship* (London: Epworth Press, 1926).

Smith, Henry, John E. Swallow and William Treffry, eds, *The Story of the United Methodist Church* (London: Henry Hooks, [1932]).

Snaith, Norman, *I Believe In . . .* (London: SCM Press, 1949).

—, 'Conversations between the Church of England and the Methodist Church: A Report. Comments and Criticisms, V', in *The London Quarterly and Holborn Review* (July 1963), 196–99.

Stanley, Howard S., *The Next Ten Years* (London: Independent Press, 1959).

Stephens, T., ed., *Wales To-day and To-morrow* (Cardiff: Western Mail, 1907).

Stephens, W. Peter, *The Holy Spirit in the Theology of Martin Bucer* (Cambridge: CUP, 1970).

—, *The Theology of Huldrych Zwingli* (Oxford: Clarendon Press, 1992).

—, *Zwingli: An Introduction to his Thought* (Oxford: Clarendon Press, 1992).

Stevenson, Peter K., *God in Our Nature: The Incarnational Theology of John McLeod Campbell* (Carlisle: Paternoster, 2004).

Strawson, William, 'Methodist theology 1850–1950', in R.E. Davies, et al, eds., *A History of the Methodist Church in Great Britain*, q.v., III, 182–321.

Tarrant, W.G., *Unitarianism* (London: Constable, 1912).

Tayler, J. Lionel, *Unitarianism: Essays and Addresses* (London: J.L. Tayler Trustees, 1939).

Taylor, Vincent, *Jesus and His Sacrifice* (London: Macmillan, 1937).

—, *The Atonement in New Testament Teaching* (London: Epworth Press, 1940).

—, *Forgiveness and Reconciliation* (London: Macmillan, 1941).

—, *Doctrine and Evangelism* (London: Epworth Press, 1953).

—, *The Cross of Christ* (London: Macmillan, 1956).

Thomas, Roger, 'When is a Unitarian not a Unitarian?' *Transactions of the Unitarian Historical Society*, XIV no. 3 (October 1969), 107–18.

Thompson, David M., *Let Sects and Parties Fall: A Short History of the Association of Churches of Christ in Great Britain and Ireland* (Birmingham: Berean Press, 1980).

—, 'Baptists and the world fellowship of the Church', in J.H.Y. Briggs, ed., *Bible, Church and World*, q.v., 54–63.

—, 'The Free Churches in modern Britain', in Paul Badham, ed., *Religion, State and Society in Modern Britain*, q.v., 99–117.

—, *Stating the Gospel: Formulatons and Declarations of Faith from the Heritage of the United Reformed Church* (Edinburgh: T. & T. Clark, 1990).

Thompson, John, 'Was Forsyth really a Barthian before Barth?' in T. Hart, ed., *Justice the True and Only Mercy*, q.v., 237–55.

Thompson, Philip E. and Anthony R. Cross, eds, *Recycling the Past or Researching History? Studies in Baptist Historiography and Myths* (Carlisle: Paternoster, 2005).

Thorogood, Bernard, *The Flag and the Cross: National Limits and Church Universal* (London: SCM Press, 1988).

Thurian, Max, *Churches Respond to BEM, Geneva: World Council of Churches*, 6 vols. (1986–88).

Tilley, Terrence, review of Gareth Jones, *Critical Theology: Questions of Truth and Method*, in *Modern Theology*, XIV no. 3 (July 1998), 467–8.

Tomes, Roger, ed., *Christian Confidence: Essays on A Declaration of Faith of the Congregational Church in England and Wales* (London: SPCK, 1970).

Townsend, Henry, *The Claims of the Free Churches* (London: Hodder and Stoughton, 1949).

Townsend, W.J., H.B. Workman and George Eayrs, eds, *A New History of Methodism*, 2 vols. (London: Hodder and Stoughton, 1919).

Travell, John, *Doctor of Souls: A Biography of Dr. Leslie Dixon Weatherhead* (Cambridge: Lutterworth, 1999).

Turner, B.S., 'Discord in modern Methodism', in *Proceedings of the Wesley Historical Society*, XXXVII pt. 5 (June 1970), 154–9.

Turner, J. Munsey, 'Some problems of Church and state in England', in *The Epworth Review*, III no. 1 (January 1976), 56–64.

—, *Conflict and Reconciliation: Studies in Methodism and Ecumenism in England 1840–1982* (London: Epworth Press, 1985).

—, 'Victorian values – or whatever happened to John Wesley's scriptural holiness?' *Proceedings of the Wesley Historical Society*, XLVI pt. 6 (October 1988), 165–84.

—, 'Creative Dissent in the 1990s', in T*he Epworth Review*, XIX no. 3 (September 1992), 51–58.

—, 'Preaching, theology, and spirituality in twentieth-century Methodism', in *The Expository Times*, CXI no. 4 (January 2000), 112–7.

—, 'Church, state and society – 2003', in *The Expository Times*, XXXI no. 1 (January 2004), 37–44.

Twinn, Kenneth, ed., *Essays in Unitarian Theology: A Symposium* (London: The Lindsey Press, 1959).

Tymms, T.V., *The Mystery of God: Some Intellectual Hindrances to Faith* (London: Eliot Stock, 4th ed., 1890).

—, *The Christian Idea of Atonement* (London: Macmillan, 1904).

Vine, Aubrey, *An Approach to Christology* (London: Independent Press, 1948).

Vine, C.H., ed., *The Old Faith and the New Theology: A Series of Sermons and Essays on some of the Truths held by Evangelical Christians, and the Difficulties of Accepting much of what is called the 'New Theology'* (London: Sampson, Low, Marston, 1907).

Wainwright, Geoffrey, *Doxology: The Praise of God in Worship, Doctrine and Life* (London: Epworth Press, 1980).

—, 'The last things', in G. Wainwright, ed., *Keeping the Faith*, q.v., 341–70.

—, *Methodists in Dialogue* (Nashville: Kingswood Books, 1995).

—, *Worship with One Accord: Where Liturgy and Ecumenism Embrace* (Oxford: OUP, 1997).

—, ed., *Keeping the Faith: Essays to Mark the Centenary of* Lux Mundi (Philadelphia: Fortress Press and Allison park: Pickwick Publications, 1988).

Walton, Robert C., *The Gathered Community* (London: Carey Press, 1946).

Waterhouse, Eric S., *The Philosophy of Religious Experience* (London: Epworth Press, 1923).

Watkin-Jones, H., *The Holy Spirit from Arminius to Wesley* (London: Epworth Press, 1921).

—, *Methodist Churchmanship and its Implications* (London: Epworth Press, 1946).

Watson, Philip S., *Let God be God: An Interpretation of the Theology of Martin Luther* (London: Epworth Press, 1947).

Watts, Trevor, 'History in reverse: reflections on the events of 1972', in *The Congregational History Circle Magazine*, II no. 4 (June 1988), 20–26.

Weatherhead, Leslie D., *The Transforming Friendship* (London: Epworth Press, 1928).

Weller, John G., 'The place of moderators', in *The Christian World* (23 July 1953), 1–2.

West, W. Morris S., *Baptist Principles* (London: Baptist Union, 1969).

Whale, John S., 'Commemoration sermon', in *Congregationalism Through the Centuries: Four Lectures and a Commemoration Sermon delivered on the occasion of the 250th Anniversary of Emmanuel Congregational Church, Cambridge, May, 1937* (London: Independent Press, 1937).

—, *What is a Living Church?* (London: Edinburgh House Press, 1937).

—, *Facing the Facts* (London: Hodder and Stoughton, 1939).

—, *This Christian Faith* (London: SCM Press, 1940).

—, *Christian Doctrine* (Cambridge: CUP, 1941).

—, *The Protestant Tradition: An Essay in Interpretation* (Cambridge: CUP, 1955).

—, *Victor and Victim* (Cambridge: CUP, 1960).

—, *Christian Reunion: Historic Divisions Reconsidered* (London: Lutterworth, 1971).

Whitehouse, W.A., 'The modern discussion of eschatology', in *Eschatology: Four papers read to The Society for the Study of Theology* (Edinburgh: Oliver and Boyd, 1953), 63–90.

—, *Order, Goodness, Glory* (London: OUP, 1960).

—, 'What does Christian believing mean today?' in *World Congregationalism*, VII, no. 19 (January 1965), 6–7.

—, 'Making the Declaration of Faith', in Roger Tomes, ed., *Christian Confidence*, q.v., 13–25.

Wigley, H.T., *The Distinctive Free Church Witness Today* (Wallington, Surrey: The Religious Education Press, 1949).

Wigmore-Beddoes, D.G., ed., *Concerning Jesus* (London: The Linsdey Press, 1975).

Wilkinson, Wilfred R., *Religious Experience: The Methodist Fundamental* (London: Holborn Publishing House, 1928).

Williams, H. Howard, *Down to Earth: An Interpretation of Christ* (London: SCM Press, 1964).

Williams, T.C., 'The influence of higher criticism on Welsh preaching', in T. Stephens, ed., *Wales To-day and To-morrow*, q.v., 21.

Williams, T. Rhondda, *The Working Faith of a Liberal Theologian* (London: Williams & Norgate, 1914).

Wollaston, E.P.M., 'The first moderators: 1919', in *The Journal of the United Reformed History Society*, V no. 5 (November 1994), 298–301.

Wood, A. Skevington, *Captive to the Word: Martin Luther, Doctor of Sacred Scripture* (Exeter: Paternoster, 1969).

Woods, G.F., 'Revised reviews: VI: John Oman's The Natural and the Supernatural', in *Theology*, LXV (June 1961), 233–7.

Workman, H.B., *The Letters of John Hus* (London: Hodder and Stoughton, 1904).

—, *The Dawn of the Reformation* (London: Charles Kelly, 3rd ed., 1911).

—, *Methodism* (London: Cambridge: CUP, 1912).

—, *John Wyclif: A Study of the English Medieval Church* (Cambridge: CUP, 1926).

Wotherspoon, H.J., and J.M. Kirkpatrick, *A Manual of Church Doctrine* (London: Hodder and Stoughton, 1919).

Wright, Charles J., *The Meaning and Message of the Fourth Gospel: A Study in the Application of Johannine Christianity to the Present Theological Situation* (London: Hodder and Stoughton, 1933).

Wright, Nigel G., *Power and Discipleship: Towards a Baptist Theology of the State* (Oxford: Whitley Publications, 1996).

—, 'Covenant and covenanting', in *The Baptist Quarterly*, XXXIX no. 6 (April 2002), 287–90.

Wycherley, R. Newman, *The Pageantry of Methodist Union* (London: Epworth Press, 1936).

Yates, Arthur S., *The Doctrine of Assurance with special reference to John Wesley* (London: Epworth Press, 1952).

Young, Frances M., *From Nicaea to Chalcedon* (London: SCM Press, 1983).

—, *The Making of the Creeds* (London: SCM Press, 1991).

Index of Persons

Index of Subjects